Class Ideology
and
Ancient Political Theory

ELLEN MEIKSINS WOOD
And NEAL WOOD

Class Ideology
and
Ancient Political Theory
Socrates, Plato, and Aristotle in Social Context

OXFORD UNIVERSITY PRESS
NEW YORK

First published in the United Kingdom by Basil Blackwell, Oxford.

Published in the U.S.A. by Oxford University Press, New York.

Library of Congress Cataloging in Publication Data

Wood, Ellen Meiksins.
Class ideology and ancient political theory.

Includes bibliographical references and index.
1. Political science--Greece--History.
2. Socrates--Political science. 3. Plato--
Political science. 4. Aristoteles--Political
science. 5. Greece--Politics and government--To
146 BC. I. Wood, Neal, joint author. II. Title.
JC73.W66 1978 320.5'092'2 78-17121
ISBN 0-19-520100-0

Printed in Great Britain

For our
York University Students

Contents

Preface

This book has been written primarily from the standpoint of political theory rather than as a work of classical scholarship. We look upon the book as a study of the founding texts in the long tradition of Western political thought, and as a statement on the nature of political theory. Our view is that the classics of political theory are fundamentally ideological, and that to be understood and appreciated as fully as possible, they must be much more closely and systematically related to their social contexts than they often have been in the past. In the case of Socrates, Plato, and Aristotle no analysis of the kind we have attempted has been done. While A. D. Winspear's ground-breaking studies have certainly helped to place Plato (and much less successfully Socrates) in socio-historical perspective, our book approaches the problem somewhat differently. Our point of departure is a particular conception of the Greek polis and its significance in the development of Western social organization, an interpretation that departs from most standard treatments of the subject. Among other things, we take issue with the proposition that the essence of the polis is to be found in the writings of Plato and Aristotle. Chapters on Socrates, Plato, and Aristotle consider these thinkers in light of their lives, class affiliations, and the social circumstances in which they were writing, and try to establish that their political theories are essentially partisan in origin and ideological in content.

We hope that the book will have an appeal beyond a narrow audience of specialists. By examining the founders of the Western philosophical tradition in the way that we have, we are raising significant questions about the social roots of the Western philosophical enterprise as a whole, questions that should be of singular interest, if, as Whitehead said, the European philosophical tradition consists essentially of a series of footnotes to Plato. Moreover, we are responding deliberately to the ahistorical and abstract character of philosophy —both political and non-political—as it is customarily read, interpreted, and taught in the English-speaking world. The Introduction raises these broader theoretical questions and considers whether relating ideas to their social context deprives them of their universal meaning, or, on the contrary, rescues them from the emptiness of ethereal abstractions which have no human meaning at all. Finally, our study may help to illuminate the aristocratic myth about the character of the *demos* which, immortalized by the Socratics, has been a cornerstone of anti-democratic ideology and social theory in the West ever since these philosophers first recorded their fears of the 'mob'.

Although both of us have criticized and amended each other's work, chapters II and IV were written by E. M. W.; and I, III, and V by N. W. Chapter VI is a truly joint effort. Chapter III is a considerably revised version of an essay published as 'Socrates as Political Partisan', *Canadian Journal of Political Science*, VII (March 1974), 3–31.

We are immensely indebted to Oswyn Murray of Balliol College for his painstaking and perceptive criticism of the manuscript at several stages. Naturally, the responsibility for any defects of the book is solely our own. Thanks are due to those at York University who had the burden of typing various drafts: Ruth Griffin of Glendon College, Thetis Leva and Freda Roberts of McLaughlin College, Jo-Anne Degabriele and the University Secretarial Services. We are also especially grateful to Lily Banjac of McLaughlin College and Mrs. Barbara Cohen of Los Angeles, who typed the many last minute revisions. Lastly, we owe much more than the dedication can possibly express to our undergraduate and graduate students at York for their aid through class discussion and debate in helping us shape our ideas about the ancients.

Toronto, July 1977

Ellen Meiksins Wood
Neal Wood

I

Introduction: Perspective and Problems

1. *The Ideology of a Declining Aristocracy*

Our fundamental argument is that a common ideology inspires, informs, and shapes the political thought of Socrates, Plato, and Aristotle. Their political analyses and recommendations are far from being immune to partisanship in the social world in which they lived and wrote. They were never neutral, disinterested spectators of the conflict that swirled around them. Their theorizing was in response to that conflict, the energizer of the particular mode of intellectual activity they had chosen. From a partisan viewpoint, they attempted to grasp the issues and to indicate a way of resolving the struggle. Out of the chaotic conditions of the time they sought order of a practical and intellectual nature, order clearly reflecting their partisanship. They were partisans who chose a side, making a primary commitment to a position and defending it with all the weapons of their considerable intellectual armoury. To argue that the foundation of their political thought is ideological is not to disparage them, but to offer an explanation for the very existence of their theorizing, the reason for its being. Since they put forward practical proposals concerning political and social institutions and action, it is only common sense to ask whose interests are being served and whose interests are being opposed. In terms of the various contending groups of the time, whose side do the Socratics choose, and against whom? Their position is not identical with that of a particular party or class. Nevertheless their thought does reveal the nature of their friends and foes in the conflict of their age.

The Socratics, to a very significant degree, defend and justify the values, attitudes, and way of life of a rapidly declining and increasingly decadent Athenian social group, the traditional, landed aristocracy in opposition to the growing numbers of traders, manufacturers, artisans, shopkeepers, and wage labourers. The aristocracy consisted of leisured members of noble families, many of whom claimed descent from the gods themselves. Originally a warrior class, they had become well-educated, cultured, and refined, living to a great extent upon wealth from inherited landed property worked by slaves, wage labourers, and tenants. Intermarrying, they formed an interlocking web of great families with a distinctive class culture characterized by proud independence, disdain for labour and the nouveau riche, polished manners, sophisticated form and style of conduct, speech, and apparel, and devotion to sport, music, and dancing. After Pericles' death in 429 BC Athenian politics was no longer dominated by aristocratic values and leadership. A growing disenchantment with civic affairs and withdrawal from active political participation typified the most conservative aristocrats throughout the fourth century. Because of the destruction of the land during the Peloponnesian War, many of the nobility suffered grievous economic losses. In general the country-side was badly hit, many peasants being forced to give up their holdings and to migrate to the city where they became wage labourers. By the end of the fourth century agriculture had ceased to be so central to an increasingly complex and diversified Athenian economy, and the peasantry—so important in the fifth century—had given way to urban artisans, shopkeepers, and wage labourers as the backbone of Athenian democracy. Some country gentlemen attempted to recoup their heavy financial losses and to rebuild their diminishing capital by investment in the business world and the arrangement of profitable marriages with the swiftly increasing class of wealthy commercial and manufacturing families. In such a time of troubles, young bucks of distinguished and venerable lineage were exhausting their already depleted fortunes in extravagant consumption: gambling, heavy drinking, and indulging in a variety of erotic pleasures.

In the midst of their corruption and disintegration Athenians of noble birth appeared to become increasingly conscious of their identity, emphasizing the distinction of 'gentlemen' (*kaloi kagathoi*) and the 'better sort' (*chrestoi*) in contrast to 'bad men' (*poneroi*), prosperous business men (*agoraioi*), and the nouveau riche of the commercial and manufacturing world or *neoploutoi*, a term beginning to be used frequently during the period. Awareness of the growing division between urban and rural life was developing at all levels in Athenian society, not only between gentry and men of business but also between peasants and *kapeloi* or shopkeepers and artisans. From the standpoint of the peasant, an urban dweller or *asteios* came to mean 'city slicker', while to a shopkeeper or artisan the *agroikos* or rural dweller began to signify 'country bumpkin'. Fearing further devastation of their estates as a result of new wars many of the gentry together with the peasants during the first half of the fourth century espoused peace at any price as against the more belligerent stance of the urban classes, and in the second half of the century many of the aristocracy tended to become pro-Macedonian. At the end of the century most of the famous noble family names still common during the first half had disappeared from view.

Obviously, Socrates, Plato, and Aristotle were not crude apologists or simplistic rationalizers of the declining aristocracy. They fully recognized and condemned aristocratic degeneration, but thought that the way of life and values of the nobility could be reformed and revitalized so as once more to become the foundation of civic life in order to stem the levelling tide of democracy, the tyranny of the majority, and the vulgar commercialism that they felt were engulfing Athens and the whole of Greece. In a significant way their political thought can be conceived of as the supreme intellectual expression of the increasing class consciousness of the aristocracy during the fourth century, a consciousness that seemed to become more pronounced as the class was progressively threatened with extinction. If the political thought of the Socratics was by no means identical with the values and attitudes of the Athenian aristocracy, there was a commonly shared perspective, an ideological core, or set of socio-political beliefs also held in part by non-aristocratic members of the upper classes like Isocrates who attempted to emulate the nobility. An important component of the ideology shared by the Socratics with many aristocrats was a deep-rooted hatred of democracy. The people were held to be ignorant and incompetent, motivated by narrow selfish interests, contemptuous of law, disrespectful of their superiors, insolent and vulgar, irresponsible and fickle, a rabble subject to the blandishments of demagogues, and the envious victimizers of the noble and wealthy. Denouncing democratic politics, many of the nobles considered it to be a sign of gentlemanly virtue to remain aloof and detached from civic life, a trend culminating in the aristocratic Epicurus' withdrawal into the Garden. Likewise many denounced the esteemed aristocratic leaders of the people of the fifth century like Pericles who were considered to be traitors to their class and responsible for the current mob rule. Many nobles were Laconizers although not necessarily completely uncritical admirers of Sparta as a model of law and order, patriotic solidarity, and aristocratic authority. Again there was widespread nostalgia for the ancient constitution of Solon with its respect for law and the governing privileges that it reserved for the upper classes. Increasing sentiment for enlightened monarchy, felt to be necessary for curbing the excesses of democracy and the civic disorders arising from the rule of the people, took such diverse forms as sympathy for Macedonia and the idolization of Philip II and Alexander the Great, the Platonic philosopher-king, and Xenophon's romanticized ideal of Cyrus the Great. Finally, there was a condemnation of commercialism, closely associated with democracy, and of commercial and urban values. Rural life and aristocratic values were eulogized—at the time they seemed most threatened—with a stress upon the country as a nursery of virtue and manhood in contrast to the corrupting influence of the banausic callings of the city.

All these attitudes became integral parts of the outlook of the Socratics, fundamental to the elaborate intellectual constructions of Plato and Aristotle. They weaved them together into coherent and persuasive formulations buttressed by a philosophic idealism that had long seemed to attract thinkers of probable aristocratic origin like Parmenides and Pythagoras. The philosophic idealist could offer transcendence of the vulgar and materialistic world of sensory experience to which the masses were confined, and comprehension of such transcendence as the exclusive privilege of a cultured and leisured few, the men of golden souls, of nobility and inherited wealth—the *kaloi kagathoi.* Thus, philosophic idealism served to convey their readers aristocratic, antidemocratic, and agrarian values and beliefs, giving them the stamp of absolute intellectual authority and authenticity. In addition to being the paramount intellectual expression of the consciousness of a decaying social class, Socratic political thought was a powerful weapon that might well have been designed to convince upper-class readers of the basic rightness of their attitudes, the urgent need for self-reform and regeneration, the character of the common enemy, and the ideal of a 'rational' polis as a guide for social and political change through concerted action. Among other things, therefore, Socratic political thought was an intellectually sophisticated and ingenious justification for counterrevolution in democracy and maintenance of the status-quo in oligarchy.

Today, these aspects of Socratic political thought are seldom emphasized. Hegel's pervasive influence has perhaps been partially responsible, especially among German scholars. His distorted idea that Plato's philosophy was the apotheosis of Greek life, values, and thought, both symbolizing and terminating an epoch, has misled generations of students. Of greater significance is the fact that some influential classicists, because of a basic sympathy for the social values and attitudes of the Socratics, have been more than ready to accept rather uncritically their account of the situation in Athens and throughout the Greek world. More recently, the problems have been compounded by scholars who have been persecuted and forced to flee from totalitarian regimes and have tended to read their own fears and predilections into the Greek experience. Fourth-century Athens is thus seen as a kind of undeveloped prototype of so-called 'totalitarian democracy' and a warning of the inexorable consequences of the 'tyranny of the masses' with its widespread mediocrity and levelling, social atomism, disrespect for traditional authority, breakdown of law and legal order, resort to violence, and replacement of absolute moral standards by extreme subjectivism and relativism. Socratic political thought, therefore, from this viewpoint, becomes a highly relevant analysis of and admonition against the dangerous potential of mass democracy and democratic culture in the twentieth century. Finally, two other developments seem to account for the type of one-sided reading still usually given to the Socratics. The first is the kind of antipathy to history that since the Second World War has arisen among philosophers and social scientists, even including some Marxists. A second and not unrelated factor is the resurgence of an interest in the 'absolute', a quest for the 'infinite', in an age of religious decline and widespread political and intellectual disillusion. Socratic political thought proves to be tailor-made for just such a nostalgia for the 'philosopher's stone'.

2. *The Charge of Historicism*

The most fundamental objection that will be made against the general nature of our approach to Socratic political thought is that it suffers from historicism. From this critical perspective a variety of questions may be asked. If a political theory is so firmly rooted in a specific social context, as we have shown with the Socratics, how do we discriminate between political theories? Is not one theory as good as another, equally valid and true? Since all theories are basically ideological, what can we say of them by way of comparison, other than that they may represent different and contending social interests? Moreover, if every theory is so embedded in its particular social context that it is time-bound, what is its universal value? Where are its transhistorical elements and implications? Why bother to study and understand the great political theories of the past if their historical specificity prevents them from transcending their own time and place? Has not intellectual activity been so relativized that the result is the elimination of all standards and criteria by which we can judge and act? By removing any permanent grounds for choice, does one not consign men to the flux of extreme subjectivism and personal preference? Moreover, does not the logic of such radical historicizing of thought mean that the approach itself is relative and historical? How can the sociology of knowledge itself transcend the historically contingent?

While these questions focus upon the central problem of historicism, they tend to be rather extreme formulations of the either/or kind. The position that all political theory is essentially ideological does not radically historicize it in the sense suggested by such questions. At the most elementary level of understanding, our position assumes a certain commonness or universal quality in human experience and more specifically among men of Western European culture regardless of time or place, a commonness with ourselves of the experience, conditions, and characteristics of the Socratics and of the men about whom and for whom they wrote. The assumption concerning similarity does not ignore the significant differences between the ancient Greeks and ourselves, but it does much to mitigate the possible charge of complete and radical historicism. To begin with, whether ancient Greeks or twentieth-century English are being discussed, in a broad sense both share a common and familiar physical environment consisting of days divided between light and darkness, and a world of earth, water, sky, plants, and animals; of birth, life, decay, and death. Furthermore, human beings then as now are of a comparable physical make-up: they are born, eat, sleep, drink, feel, sense, reproduce, labour, and die, although even the most basic physical needs are always satisfied through specific socially sanctioned means. Over the centuries men have created different cultures and ways of life in which language has been central. Each of the principal Western European historical cultures has interpenetrated the succeeding one, for example in respect to practical techniques of living, leaving an important residue for the future. So the Englishman like the ancient Greek knows what it means to bathe, to sit on a chair, to recline on a bed or couch; to walk, to run, to swim; to plough, to sow, and to reap; to tie a knot; to boil water, roast meat, weave cloth, carve wood, etc., etc. Perhaps most significantly, in each of the cultures in which political theory has arisen some kind of social division of labour has existed and with it a system of human domination and control that have been the objects of human consciousness and self-awareness, and particularly a central subject for the reflection of the political theorist. Hence, in spite of the historical specificity of a classic political thinker like Plato or Aristotle, a certain commonness exists among men transcending the immediate social context, that renders their political thought intelligible and meaningful to succeeding ages. We are by no means solipsists completely isolated in respect to culture, ideas, and values from our forebears. We are men living in society as they were men living in society, sharing common experiences and states of feeling and appreciating common problems, although our perceptions of many things and out attitudes may be quite different. So to emphasize the historical specificity of a past political theory should not imply that it is completely alien, valueless, and incomprehensible to us living under different circumstances in a different age.

Directly connected to this commonness is the question of context. If knowledge in general and political theory in particular as one mode of knowledge are related to their social contexts or frameworks of reference, the meaning of 'social context' or 'frameworks of reference' should be clearly established. Perhaps, instead of speaking of a specific social context, it might be more accurate in each case to refer to a manifold of social contexts, and to knowledge and ideas as possessing different degrees of historical contingency and universality depending upon the various social contexts to which they are related. For example, to what social contexts can we relate Plato's ideas? The most obvious one is the immediate Athenian context of his life-span, 427–347 BC. But it is important to remember that his own Athens was intimately related to Athens as it existed before 427 and Athens as it developed after 347. Plato's Athens in a meaningful way encapsulated all that had previously occurred in the Greek world and was the condition for all that took place afterwards. Moreover, Plato's ideas can be related to an even broader social context, that of Western European culture in which he has been read and understood by different generations and has exerted an influence upon their thought and action. Hence, Plato's ideas are related in different ways to ever expanding social contexts and to contexts within contexts. That his ideas are related to the immediate context of Athenian society during his life-time certainly does not exclude the possibility that they are related to our own social context, albeit in a different fashion. It follows that many of his ideas are not time-bound, of relevance to his age alone and not to ours, although some of them may be. Social relatedness in this sense does not imply any kind of complete relativism. Historical social contexts are not separate, isolated, water-tight compartments. Despite fundamental changes and disjunctions, there is always continuity in the form of a residue of the past in the present, of persistent social structures and arrangements and patterns of human conduct. Social history of which ideas, values, and attitudes are an integral part reveals a complex dialectic of continuity and change, of permanence and flux. The Heraclitean river both changes and remains the same.

However, the crucial point is that Plato is related in different ways to a variety of social contexts only through the specific social context into which he was born. Perhaps, to stress the self-evident, it is nevertheless worth remembering that he is a man and thinker only by virtue of joining mankind at a specific time and place in history. He is and can be related to us only because of his birth, activity, and death in Athens between 427 and 347 BC. Therefore, in order to determine which of the elements of Socrates' or Plato's or Aristotle's thought are of universal value—not in any absolute sense, but only in relation to larger contexts—and which are related to their age alone, we must possess a rich understanding of the immediate social contexts in which they lived, thought, and acted. What were they attempting to say to their fellow-Greeks? Under what conditions were they saying it? Why and in whose interests were they saying it? So, to ascertain the transhistorical value of their ideas—again not in any absolute sense—we must always in the first instance be concerned with their historical specificity. In addition we should recognize that what may be of value in their political thought tends to vary from age to age, and we must ask why this is the case and whose interests are being served by the different emphases and perceptions in different periods of history. Their truths, far from being universal in any absolute sense, simply transcend their immediate social contexts to become related to greater social wholes.

A political theorist is able to transcend his immediate social context not only because of what we have identified as a certain commonness of man and the related persistence and continuity of some social arrangements and patterns of behaviour, but also for another reason. Out of the social specificity of a theory some things may be perceived in a new dimension, illuminated from a different perspective. The logic of a system of ideas energized by the theorist's partisanship in the conflict of his age may very well generate, even without his awareness, novel ideas and concepts that in the future become important parts of fertile theories or at least stimulate fruitful lines of speculation.[1*] For example, Aristotle's distinction between natural and unnatural acquisition, between production for use and production for profit, which he made to justify a traditional agrarian aristocratic society, in the hands of Marx became a conceptual weapon to attack capitalism and to provide the theoretical basis for the idea of a non-exploitative society. Similarly, when divorced from its source of inspiration in the aristocratic notion of proportionate equality, the Stagirite's concept of distributive justice can be extremely insightful. Or Plato's view that the economic division of labour, so basic to all human societies, entails in advanced social formations a hierarchical relationship of domination and subordination, when detached from his idea of the moral inequality of

* Notes for this chapter begin on p. 12.

men, may be pregnant with theoretical possibilities. A sophisticated and complex system of ideas, consequently, will secrete provocative and challenging insights that when abstracted from their original contexts can serve as intellectual stimuli in the future or basic components of different systems premised upon different values.

Many students of ancient Greek political thought might agree that up to a point an understanding of Plato's ideas requires a knowledge of his social context. And they might also recognize that like Hobbes and Locke and other thinkers of the past, he can provide us with valuable insights and concepts. But some argue that he transcends his context in a way that Hobbes and Locke, whom they view as little more than ideologists of emerging capitalism, could not. While Plato may begin as a dedicated partisan in the struggles of his age, this is little more than a point of departure, the stepping stones out of the cave of obscurantism that result in an almost mystical stroke of genius or imaginative intuitive leap enabling him to rise above ideology and the immediacy of mundane affairs and to postulate social and political truths impervious to time and change. Of course it is easy to assert this, as Plato does himself, but the mere assertion that such truths exist neither validates nor identifies them. The precise nature of these eternal truths and their relevance to social reality are never explained in a coherent and explicit fashion either by Plato or his latter day defenders. Indeed we seem to be asked to accept the existence of such absolute truths as the quintessential articles of faith of a cult of true believers. Apart from its irrationalism the danger of such a perspective, of course, is that it tends to obscure the basic assumptions about the existential social world on which the Platonic position rests and its implications for concrete political practice. Whatever the character of the Platonic truths may be, they most certainly are not any less ideological than the ideas of Hobbes and Locke if it is acknowledged, for example, that the *Laws* represents a project for the practical implementation of the principles of the *Republic* whose source is the eternal matrix of absolute social and political truth.

Classic political theory, however, is not solely a treasury of fertile notions to be selected for the purpose of building our own imaginative systems of ideas. Political theorists like the Socratics, as we have argued, are dedicated partisans who attempted to devise effective guides for political action. Theory and practice are a unity. They cannot be separated arbitrarily or simplistically by the abstraction of past concepts, and applied to contemporary conditions. If our rich historical heritage is to be of benefit in constructing theories of relevance for the urgent political problems of the present, then we must learn to appreciate the unity of theory and practice in the past, the relationship of ideas to the realms of social action within which they were conceived. Only by grasping the connection between ideas and action in the past, can we ever hope to relate theory to practice in a meaningful and useful way today. To do otherwise is to engage in sterile and scholastic exercise both in regard to past and present.

3. *The Poverty of Philosophy*

It has become popular in recent years, perhaps in part due to the influences of analytic and linguistic philosophy, to treat classic political theories as if they were systems of disembodied ideas unrelated to the concrete historical circumstances in which they were conceived and for which they were written. A text, so the claim goes, should be analyzed philosophically in order to clarify its internal meaning, establish the logical connections between concepts and ideas, point out inconsistencies of argument, and reveal illuminating insights that may be of analytic value today. Philosophical analysis of this kind self-consciously attempts to discard history with the implication that philosophy and philosophical analysis can be divorced from history and historical analysis. Indeed, there is the distinct impression from such work that philosophy is intellectually superior to history, and that the philosopher dirties his hands by attempting to explore the historical roots of the text.

The poverty of such a philosophical approach to classic political theory is clearly illustrated by the fact that its proponents can never escape history in spite of their self-proclaimed rejection of history and historical analysis. In the explication of a particular text history is always admitted by the back door in a variety of ways. First and most obviously the particular text to be analyzed is usually related chronologically to other classic thinkers. Plato lived and wrote before Aristotle; Aristotle before Hobbes, and Hobbes before Kant. Few philosophical analysts are so foolhardy as to proceed as if Aristotle were writing in the eighteenth century and Hume in the fourth century BC. Second, the same must be done in reference to the works of a single theorist. The student of Plato never treats the *Republic* as if it were written after the *Laws*. Third, the analyst can never disregard the historicity of language, of metaphor, imagery, references, examples, illustrations, concepts, and categories. Classical Greek is no longer a living language, nor is seventeenth-century English identical with modern usage. In both cases the analyst must refer to the historical meaning of words and phrases—often by way of translation—and must identify names and events in order to establish the meaning of the text. To treat the polis of the Socratics as if it were the nation-state of Hegel or Mill is simply to misunderstand a matter of fundamental import in reading a text. At this point, then, it is clear that a philosophical analysis of a text, if it is to be at all worthwhile, must entail historical perspective and reference to the immediate social context of the theorist.

However, apart from these patently obvious observations, it appears that historical understanding must play a far greater role if justice is to be done to the meaning of a text. How are we to recognize the unexpressed assumptions, values, and beliefs of the author which he takes for granted and consequently never explicitly articulates unless we know something in detail about his social context? The same may be said about the significance of the social types, the human ideals, the heroes he puts forward. Does the author distort and misrepresent a fact or the idea of another thinker, and if so, why? Without some knowledge of the author and his social context, how do we know whether he is writing ironically or satirically? Before we can determine whether he is saying something of novelty or importance we must be familiar with the intellectual world as part of the social context in which he is writing. Does the form or order of the text have any particular significance? How, for example, is the relative value of each line and proposition of the author to be judged except through historical and biographical investigation? Otherwise a text would be read as if all words, phrases, and statements were on a par. In other words how are the emphases of the author ascertained unless consideration is given to his life and times? Frequency counts of words and themes may simply distort the meaning. Furthermore, it would seem to be vital in reading a text to know the circumstances of its composition, something about the author's purposes in writing as best we can ascertain them, something about his intellectual and political friends and foes, and the nature of the immediate audience he is addressing. Perhaps most importantly, how can we ever understand the relationship between thought and action, deal with past theories as any more than sterile abstractions, and ourselves create meaningful guides for contemporary political practice unless we connect what the classic theorists had to say with the concrete historical circumstances in which they said it? Once the value of these kinds of knowledge for reading a text is admitted, the floodgates of history and historical analysis have been raised. No longer can it be maintained that philosophical analysis can be kept separate from historical analysis, or at best that the latter is a very junior partner of the former. Instead, the very contrary can be argued: any sound philosophical analysis of a text presupposes historical analysis; the latter is the foundation of the former. At the most elementary level, would the philosophical analyst of classic political theory take the same ahistorical liberties in determining the meaning of a political speech of a statesman today? Unless his analysis in the latter case is to verge on the nonsensical, he must bring to his task a wealth of historical knowledge and understanding, both conscious and unconscious.

Reading the work of a classic political theorist out of its appropriate historical context has serious intellectual consequences. By approaching the work in this way we tend to overlook that we are observing an individual of faith, emotions, passions, commitments, follies, and foibles—in other words, a living human being who wrote with certain intentions and purposes as a partisan in an arena of fundamental social and political conflict. The result is that the work is sterilized and neutralized, and the author, in fact, is dehumanized. Furthermore, to forget that the theorist under consideration was an active partisan who mobilized all his intellectual talents and resources to argue for a specific course of political action for his own time, is in reality to depoliticize it. With what sense of immediate practical urgency are the ideas of a theorist conveyed to the reader in much of the commentary on classic political theories? Do we ever really grasp that from the standpoint of the theorist fundamental social and political issues of the utmost urgency are often at stake, that vital interests may be on the block, that a valued way of life may be in jeopardy, or that a promise of the future must be realized? Finally, by examining a political theory with little or no attention given to its social origins, it is studied as if it were written in our own times. We approach it from our own historical vantage-point, bring to it our own time-bound values and assumptions, our own conceits, with little or no feeling of knowledge of the past. Such an analysis becomes in itself ideological in a basic sense. Paradoxically, we radically historicize past political theories in the most unhistorical way, by simply dehistoricizing them. They are transformed from living political works into mere passive vehicles for our own values to be exploited at our own will and to serve our own ideological purposes. If one of the chief purposes of reading the works of the classic political thinkers like Socrates, Plato, and Aristotle is to help in liberating ourselves from our own unexamined assumptions, then we cannot afford to dehistoricize their theories, simply appropriating them to our own uncritical standpoint. To do so is to deprive past political theory of its liberating effect, its capacity to generate critical thinking in the present.

Notes to Chapter I

1. See the analysis in István Mészáros, 'Ideology and Social Science', *The Socialist Register 1972*, esp. pp. 57–66.

II

The Nature of the Polis

It is not the least of historical ironies that Socratic philosophy should have come to represent the apotheosis of the polis, the unique form of human association that is the Greeks' most remarkable legacy. In his highly respected book on the Greek state, Victor Ehrenberg expresses the rather common view that the essence of the polis has survived in the works of the great philosophers. As the polis was destroying itself in reality, he argues, 'the idea of the Polis retreated into the realm of the spirit', and 'the nature of the Polis, however magnified, was reflected in those books', the works of Plato and Aristotle.[1]* Yet in the same book, Ehrenberg gives us what must surely be regarded as the best reason for rejecting this view of the Socratics as the trustees of the Athenian political legacy:

> The Polis was the state of its citizens, the *Politai*. There was always identity between state and citizens, but only the full citizens possessed unrestricted rule in the state, roughly what we call sovereignty. Democracy, then, as the rule of the whole people meant the perfection of the Polis.[2]

If democracy is the essence, the 'final cause', the *telos* of the polis, it is not in the works of Plato and Aristotle, or in the ideas of Socrates

*Notes for this chapter begin on p. 74.

which inspired them, that the nature of the polis is to be found. On the contrary, their doctrines must be understood as a negation of the polis.

If the 'Owl of Minerva' is at work in Socratic philosophy, it is not to explicate and idealize a dying polis, but to idealize a polis that never was, to attack the principle of the historical polis at a moment when it seemed to come too close for Socratic tastes to fulfilling its *telos*. The polis idealized by the Socratics is a polis that never was, even in its most oligarchic form—indeed never could have been—because it is grounded in the very principles the historical polis had undermined. The essence, the *telos*, of the Socratic polis is aristocracy and hierarchy, not democracy and equality; and as sadly imperfect as the historical polis was in realizing its 'tendency' toward equality, it represented a very real and concrete attack on the principles and the social realities of aristocracy and hierarchy.

Even in oligarchies, the civic principles of law and citizenship represented tendencies *away* from hierarchy, and their establishment was a response—albeit limited—to demands for equality. It can perhaps be said that hierarchy flourished precisely to the degree that the civic principle was imperfectly developed; and oligarchic poleis appear almost as cases of arrested development. For example, it is precisely in oligarchic poleis like Sparta that tribal vestiges are strongest. In other words, in Greece there seems to have been a direct relationship between the extent of democratization and the extent to which civic principles overshadowed more traditional social principles.

The Socratic polis, as described for example by Plato in the *Republic* and concretely in the *Laws*, assumes the existence of a fully developed civic community and the virtual disappearance of tribal institutions, even a weakening of kinship ties—to a greater extent than even in the most advanced polis; but in Plato's polis the whole elaborate civic apparatus is used to *reinforce*, not to weaken, hierarchy, and to establish and enforce inequality and social immobility more rigidly than the historical oligarchies could ever have done. In short, Plato uses the very institutions that undermined inequality and hierarchy to sustain inequality and hierarchy. The Socratic polis, then, runs counter to the historical experience of Greece in which 'politicization' and 'democratization' appear to have gone hand in hand; and it is in this sense that the Socratic polis never was and never could have been.[3] It is not only counter-historical in the sense that any utopia must be, but is deliberately antithetical to the principles and values of the polis whose ideal expression it is often said to be.

The aristocratic polis of the Socratics is a contradiction in terms, not because it violates some abstract essential definition, but because it violates the historical reality of the polis and deprives it of its significance in the evolution of human social organization. A brief historical survey of the polis, particularly as it developed in Athens, should permit us to make an attempt at discovering its 'essence', or rather, at identifying what is most unique and significant in the social developments it represents. The remainder of the book, devoted to the doctrines of Socrates, Plato, and Aristotle, will, among other things, seek to demonstrate that the Socratic polis is a negation of the historical polis in fact and principle.

1. *The Emergence of the Polis*

The evolution of the Greek polis, then, is marked, above all, by an intimate connection between politicization and democratization. At a certain point in this development, the status and strength of the demos began to rise in proportion to the displacement of the traditional principles of tribe and household by new *political* principles of association. Since archeological discoveries and the decipherment of Linear B have revealed important aspects of Mycenaen political organization, it has become impossible to speak of the rise of the polis simply as an evolution from tribe to state, as many historians once did, without considering the prior existence of an elaborate state apparatus in Greece very different from the political organization of classical times. Nevertheless, the collapse of the Mycenaen social order was so complete, the break between its mode of organization and what followed is so clear, that there is some degree of truth in the old picture. Although cultural continuities can be traced between Mycenaean civilization and its successors, its distinctive social structure, characterized by a number of small highly centralized palace-dominated states, each with a powerful king and a complex bureaucratic apparatus which exercised total control of the economy, disappeared completely. The absolute collapse of this form of social organization is most dramatically illustrated by the disappearance of writing from Greece for a considerable time. Writing had apparently been used exclusively for administrative purposes, and disappeared with the demise of the administrative system. The collections of villages which had constituted the Mycenaean kingdoms were no longer dominated by strong central powers and seem instead to have reverted to some kind of tribal organization, a form of organization which may, in fact, never have died at the village level and which may simply have reasserted itself when the super-imposed palace-bureaucracy was destroyed. In any case, while it must certainly be assumed that the polis somehow bears the mark of the Mycenaean state, the evolution of the new form of state may be described as a process by which tribal principles gave way to civic or political principles of association and a system of civic law.

Two aspects of this evolution must be stressed. The development of a specialized social division of labour and class stratification, in Greece as elsewhere, was inimical to tribal principles. At the same time, however, those remnants of tribal forms that survived this social differentiation became the instruments of the very ruling class whose emergence had undermined the traditional organization, acting as supports of aristocratic power, which is grounded in ties of kinship and hereditary property. Thereafter, conflict between classes expressed itself in a tension between tribal, kinship, and household principles, on the one hand, and on the other, communal or political principles. These political or civic principles were based on ties of *citizenship* rather than kinship, the rule of law instead of tribal custom or the commands of a master, and increasingly the equality of citizens instead of the hierarchy of the household. The *demos*—the middle and lower classes—found the political principle to be an effective weapon against their hereditary rulers, once they had become strong enough to wield that weapon; while the aristocracy, whose emergence had marked the destruction of the tribal community, relied on the vestiges of tribal order to buttress its declining power. It is in this sense that the triumph of the political principle and the democratization of society were simply different aspects of a single development.

The evolution of the polis can, unfortunately, be traced only from its roots in the society which emerged out of the 'Dark Ages' following the Mycenaean collapse—a society often called 'Homeric'. The term 'Homeric society' is of course, a misleading one, since the society described in the Homeric epics is clearly an amalgam of elements drawn from more than one age. Archeological evidence and the decipherment of Linear B have made one thing clear, however: the poems do not describe the Mycenaean civilization which purports to be their theme, even if certain myths, legends, and even material objects surviving from that civilization may have found their way into the poems. The social structure and the social values of the poems are clearly those of a later age; and if they do not reflect the society in which the poet(s?) himself (themselves?) lived, they are not as far removed from it as they are from the Mycenaean state. Even if the Homeric poems do not describe exactly any society that ever existed, if many details are anachronistic, the social structure and values depicted probably do accurately reflect in general outline those of the aristocratic society which had gradually evolved after the end of the Mycenaean age and was itself coming to an end during the age of Homer with the rise of polis civilization.[4]

The destruction of the Mycenaean hierarchy, which left the communities depleted in numbers and wealth, seems to have affected not only the kings but the warrior-aristocrats who surrounded them, and produced a much less clearly stratified community. The new aristocracy which eventually emerged from the ruins was of a very different nature. The palace-controlled, 'redistributive' economy indicated by the archeological evidence and especially the testimony of Linear B inscriptions suggests that the Mycenaean kings, either actually or effectively, owned most if not all arable land; that their subjects were in effect their serfs, bound to transfer surplus product to the king for unequal redistribution among his subjects; and that the apparently wealthy aristocrats who joined the king in ruling his subjects were probably not large landowners in their own right but rather men who occupied positions in the state hierarchy which entitled them to a greater share of the goods distributed by the king and sometimes to land allotments associated with their offices. If the beginnings of private property existed, if the aristocrats or the peasant subjects had any independent claims to land, the dominance of king and palace over land and men remained the essential characteristic of the society. The new 'Homeric' aristocracy, on the other hand, is one whose power clearly rests on property, on ownership of the best land. It is not at all an aristocracy of royal officials or palace-dominated warrior-nobles; rather, the Homeric lords have something in common with tribal chieftains, but chieftains who have gradually become divorced from their community by the acquisition of property and whose unchallenged claim to political, military, religious, and judicial functions and to the labour of others, is already a matter of hereditary property rights. It is possible that the developments that produced this new aristocracy had already begun under the Mycenaean kings; but the full evolution of this new phenomenon had to await the disappearance of palace and king (the Homeric 'kings' hardly deserve the name); and the reversion of land to the community, giving way to the dynamic that transformed communal property into private or class property, the tribal community into a class-divided society, and chieftains into an aristocratic ruling class.

Homeric society, then, lies somewhere between the tribal society based on kinship and the community of citizens embodied in the polis. Its principal social and economic unit is the *oikos*, the household, and more particularly the aristocratic *oikos*, dominated by its lord, with his kin and retainers, and supported by the labour of various kinds of dependents. The *oikos*-system is, in one sense, more particularistic than the tribal community, reflecting a gradual privatization and individuation of property; but this also means that the foundation for a wider community based on new, civic principles is being laid. Although there is a community of sorts among households and a limited recognition of *public* matters, which are taken up occasionally by a communal assembly, the community beyond the household is of secondary importance. Most matters of concern to the members of the community are private matters, to be dealt with among kinsmen and friends. Duties are primarily to the members of one's household, kinsmen, and friends; rights are 'strictly private rights privately protected'.[5] At the same time, however, households are bound together not only by bonds of kinship among household lords, but by ties of class interest among them, reinforced by the traditional ceremonies and obligations of 'guest-friendship'. The society is tribal in the sense that kinship is still crucial. Tribal law still prevails in the sense that essential social functions—the disposal of property, the punishment of crime—are dictated by customary rules of kinship. Property is largely inalienable, transmitted strictly according to traditional rules of inheritance, and to that extent is still tied to the tribal community rather than to an individual propertyholder. Crime is essentially a family matter, to be avenged by kinsmen according to the ancient customs of blood-vengeance. On the other hand, the community is anti-tribal in the sense that it is already bound together by a territorial principle that transcends kinship ties, with an urban centre as the focal point of the territorial community. There are also other principles independent of kinship dictating relations among members of the community: the potentially antagonistic relations between master and servant, and the bonds *among* masters—in short, relations of class, particularly the ties among members of the ruling class, the household lords, whose common class interests gradually override tribal and household bonds. In this sense, class is the foremost anti-tribal force; and even 'tribal' law is administered in an anti-tribal way, once jurisdiction becomes the exclusive prerogative of the ruling class instead of a communal function belonging to the tribe as a whole.

The growth of class out of tribal relations and its consolidation in the *oikos*-system is a turning-point in the establishment of the political principle, its triumph over traditional principles, and the birth of a community of citizens. At first, as the aristocracy increased its power through a growing monopoly of land, the effect of this consolidation of class was simply to fragment the community. The aristocracy became more and more an isolated ruling society, its members increasingly bound together by class interests and cut off from their non-aristocratic associates. Eventually, however, the very conditions of this fragmentation became the basis of a new kind of community, more focused on the *city*, the urban centre, the polis. Initially, the urban centre in most Greek communities had been largely the focal point for activities of the ruling society, its meeting place, the centre of jurisdiction and government; but as the city grew in economic importance, it also became the focal point of a new community, which encompassed the isolated nobility and, ironically, undermined its power, acting as an arena for the struggles of the lower classes. The significant economic changes that took place during the period following the Homeric age can be generally characterized as a decline of the self-sufficient household economy and the growing economic importance of market-place and city, together with an increase in the number of people whose livelihood was not derived from possession of land, tenancy, or service in a noble *oikos*—an increase to which the consolidation of aristocratic power itself contributed, as Ehrenberg suggests:

> ... the nobles appropriated to themselves small private properties, thus robbing the peasants of their economic and political basis ('*Bauernlegen*'), and trade and handicraft rose to be factors of increasing importance. The issue of these two tendencies was that a steadily growing class of men without landed property worked its way into the state—a shift of emphasis in politics and social life that began in the age of colonization and found vigorous and direct expression in the sixth century.[6]

As polis replaced *oikos* as the primary economic unit, the city, born as a centre for the governing activities of the ruling class, became the natural home of the growing classes that depended on it for their livelihood; and gradually it became the source of their power, economic and political, as the *oikos* had been for the landlords. It was in the polis, which brought them together and in so doing created in them a heightened consciousness of their position, that the aspirations of the economically and politically dispossessed classes—the peasants, then the growing classes of craftsmen, traders, and landless workers—found their expression. And, while the nobles continued for a long time to dominate the political life of the polis, in it their monopoly of power was increasingly undermined. The rise of the polis meant that the civic community replaced the exclusive ruling class as the source of law and justice and the arbiter of social order, and the rule of law replaced the arbitrary expression of aristocratic will:

> The unquestioned validity of the noble code was replaced by the will to a justice that extended to all (δίκη). The Greeks had taken

> the road by which the state, as a community at once political and religious, became the one and only power to form rules of life, to create a tradition of jurisdiction, and to establish a system of legislation with written codes of law.[7]

It was, of course, in democratic poleis like Athens that this process came closest to fruition.

As the polis became a source of power for the lower classes, the tribal principle reasserted itself among the nobles as the basis of their authority and class cohesion, as is perhaps to be expected in a class whose power and authority depend on birth and ownership of land based on kinship principles. The clan played an increasingly important role in the social life of the nobility and particularly in their political activities. Not only did the clan help to create a sense of class solidarity and to focus the feeling of exclusiveness and superiority associated with noble descent, but as W. R. Connor has shown, it also served the purposes of a political organization, almost of a political party.[8] In a very important sense, then, tribalism, or its remnants, had become an aristocratic principle opposed to the civic principle with its democratic implications.

Some readers may object to this opposition of tribal principles to those of the polis, in view of the important role tribal and kinship associations continued to play in the social and religious life of the polis, and the extent to which membership in the civic community entailed membership in these associations. The following discussion of Solon and Cleisthenes should make clearer the sense in which the civic community established bonds and identities distinct from, and even opposed to, those of kinship group, household, or tribe.

A more serious objection may be raised on the grounds that Athenian citizenship itself was 'tribal' in principle, that it simply extended kinship to include all Athenians, who still regarded themselves as an exclusive community of blood. To a certain extent this is true. The exclusiveness, even the racialism, of Athenian citizenship may be regarded as a vestige of tribalism. But if in their relations with others, especially non-Greeks, Athenians saw themselves as a kinship group whose superiority of birth gave them license even to enslave those outside their community of blood, in their relations with each other they were characterized by a civic identity, by bonds of law and citizenship, which were intended to overshadow the differences of quality based on birth and family connections. The civic principle, then, tended toward democracy and was opposed to aristocracy and hierarchy, while, as the community evolved into a complex and stratified society, tribalism—or what remained of it—was transformed into a support for inequality and hierarchy.

2. *The Reforms of Solon and Cleisthenes*

Since tribal institutions had assumed an antidemocratic form, it is not surprising that attacks on aristocratic power, as we shall see in discussing the reforms of Solon and Cleisthenes, so often took the shape of attacks on the tribal principle, on the role of clan, phratry, and tribe. Democratic reforms were often directed at diluting the clan and the phratry, creating new social groupings to assume the political functions of traditional tribal groupings, and in general relegating tribal associations to a secondary and superficial role in political life while new associations based on anti-tribal principles were brought to the fore.

There is little agreement among historians concerning the intention of Solon's reforms, whether they were the acts of a democrat seeking to undermine the power of the aristocracy and strengthen the demos, the concessions of a pragmatic aristocrat offering something to the demos in order to keep the peace and salvage whatever he could of aristocratic power at a time of social unrest and rebellion, or simply the compromises of the disinterested mediator that Solon himself claimed to be. Whatever Solon's intentions may have been, however, the consequences of his actions are more easily determined; and it is clear that, whether he was motivated by democratic conviction or aristocratic pragmatism, the demos was the driving force that impelled his actions and gave his reforms their particular character and direction. The general effect of his basic reforms was to strengthen the position of the demos by elevating the status of the *individual citizen* and, correlatively, the status of the *civic community*, at the expense of the traditional associations of birth, blood, and heredity which had evolved from their tribal origins into mainstays of aristocratic authority.

The most famous of Solon's reforms introduced early in the sixth century BC is, of course, the Seisachtheia, the lifting of the burden of debt which had driven many a Greek into exile or servitude, and the prohibition against loans on personal security which had hitherto permitted a man to lose his freedom in default of payment on a debt. As profoundly important as this act was—we shall later examine its truly revolutionary implications—its effects would have been less significant had it not been accompanied by other measures that strengthened the hand of the common man against his hereditary rulers. Among these measures was the introduction of a system of classification according to which citizens were divided into four purely economic categories or property groups for purposes of determining their political rights and duties, especially their access to certain offices. Although this system had mixed consequences and was far from democratic or egalitarian, giving a decided advantage to men of wealth, it did have the important effect of undermining the most basic principle of aristocratic rule, replacing qualifications of birth with the more open-ended and fluid qualifications of income.

Before Solon, the population of Athens had been divided into *eupatridai* (the aristocracy of well-born clans), *agroikoi* or *geomoroi* (farmers), and *demiourgoi* (artisans). Solon, without destroying the old categories, transferred their political functions to the new system of classification. The Solonian classes with the addition of a new category at the top, the *pentakosiomedimnoi* or '500 bushel men', corresponded to the military categories—*hippeis*, *zeugitai*, *thetes*—which had by that time been established and which themselves were to a great extent based on economic standing: the *hippeis* consisting of wealthy knights or cavalrymen; the *zeugitai*, those who, as hoplites, had sufficient means to arm themselves; and the *thetes*, those at the bottom of the economic scale. Before the establishment of the new political categories, the eupatrids had exclusive access to high political office and official priesthoods and formed the ruling class of Athens. Men of small property at best had access to the assembly whose functions were very limited, while those with little or no property—those who for military purposes were classed as *thetes*—probably had no political rights at all.[9] Solon's new classifications opened certain offices to members of the higher economic categories who had previously been excluded by their non-aristocratic birth and, apparently, for the first time gave the *thetes* access to the assembly, whose powers gradually increased as those of the aristocratic council declined, and to the new people's court of appeal.

The old division of the Athenian population into *eupatridai*, *geomoroi*, and *demiourgoi* illustrates how tribal principles had survived largely as supports for aristocratic power, combining with economic realities to reinforce the authority of the hereditary nobility of large landowners over the powerless labouring peasants and craftsmen. It is not difficult to understand why, in order to break the political monopoly of the aristocracy, it became necessary to attack tribal principles and to replace them with new civic principles. In the aristocratic age that preceded the time of Solon, the clans were exclusively associations of noble families. 'The clans with their patronymic names,' writes Ehrenberg, 'were the natural units of the aristocracy.'[10] Moreover, according to Ehrenberg, only members of these noble clans had access to the phratries, the tribal subdivisions through which a man became a full citizen.[11] It was for the eupatrids, self-consciously an association of *clans*, that connections of blood and descent were crucial; it was their position that was based on inheritance and blood ties; and, while they remained for a long time after Solon's reforms a dominant political force as wealthy landowners if not specifically as nobles, it was only they who stood to lose by an attack on the principles of birth and blood that had made their authority so exclusive. Solon's new class system, therefore, certainly represents an attack on aristocratic power; and it was probably Solon, too, who further weakened the tribal supports of that power by finally extending access to the clans—and thereby to full citizenship—to the non-nobles who had till then unsuccessfully sought to gain full citizenship rights through their private cult associations not connected with clan cults. Although the tribal categories of clan and phratry survived, they were already becoming associations whose members were not bound together by blood, even in principle through a mythical common ancestor, but rather by ties of common *citizenship*. In short, Solon weakened the aristocracy and extended the political rights of the non-aristocratic majority in part by diluting the clans and phratries and in part by depriving them of certain political functions. To the extent that the system strengthened the *civic* identity of each individual and the *civic* bonds among Athenians at the expense of traditional identities and bonds, it also weakened the qualitative differences among them and tended toward equality and democratization. The admission of the *thetes* to the assembly and the people's court, the most genuinely democratic aspect of the new system, must have appeared less unnatural in a community in which inflexible qualitative distinctions of birth had given way to fluid, so to speak merely quantitative, distinctions which were far less absolute and which opened the way for the attribute of Athenian *citizenship* to overshadow both qualitative distinctions of birth and quantitative distinctions of wealth.

The democratic implications of the civic principle are reflected in another, in some ways even more radical, Solonian reform: the transformation of the judicial system. Not only did Solon's law permit citizens to have their cases transferred to a people's court, thereby weakening the aristocracy's monopoly of jurisdiction, but just as significantly, any citizen could now bring charges against anyone else on behalf of any member of the community who had been wronged. Traditionally, according to the tribal customs of blood-vengeance, the kinship group always had the initiative in avenging wrongs committed against its members; and in the aristocratic society that had grown out of the old tribal community, aristocratic priests and judges had become the exclusive and arbitrary agents of the surviving tribal laws. Now, not only was a crime clearly identified as a wrong against a member of the civic community, not necessarily a kinsman, but it was the individual citizen quā citizen who had the initiative, and the civic community, in the person of citizens' courts, that had jurisdiction. Again, democratization took the form of elevating the individual citizen and the civic community at the expense of traditional, non-political associations.[12]

In the reforms of Cleisthenes, at the end of the sixth century, the inseparability of democratization and 'politicization' is even more apparent. It is difficult to believe that Cleisthenes was not deliberately and consciously attacking the traditional tribal associations and strengthening the principles of citizenship and polis in order to enhance the position of the demos. His approach was so beautifully simple as to suggest true genius. Without destroying the old four tribes of Attica, Cleisthenes simply created ten new ones to assume the political functions of the old, for example as the organizational basis of elections. With this reform the principle of locality superseded the kinship principle as the fundamental bond among citizens.[13] The basic units of the new tribes or *phylai* were the demes into which the population of Attica was divided on a purely territorial basis. Attica was further divided into three sections—city, coast, and interior—and each phyle was composed of three *trittyes*, that is, groups of demes from each of the three sections, so that each phyle would represent a cross-section of the population and apparently so that the weight of the landowning class in each phyle would be overbalanced by citizens from other sectors of the population. The old phratries and tribes continued to exist, but they were simply made politically irrelevant. As H. T. Wade-Gery explains:

> The three juxtapositions—Demes beside Phratries, Solar year beside Lunar [as the basis of rotation of political functions E. M. and N. W.], Strategoi beside Archons—reveal his [Cleisthenes'] method: to make the religious structure politically insignificant, by creating alongside it a secular structure.[14]

He might have added that the religious structure and aristocratic power were closely linked. It is also worth noting that the introduction of the solar year, which was divided into ten periods, corresponded to the new system of ten tribes. In both cases, the decimal system replaced a duodecimal system for political purposes, confining to religious functions the twelve-month lunar year and the tripartite four tribes. Ehrenberg argues that the decimal system, 'with its freedom from traditional bonds, representing a union of political and scientific thought, became a symbol of democracy'.[15]

The new divisions, then, cut across tribal and class ties, establishing new bonds among the people, bonds specific to the civic community. Even more significantly, it was by virtue of a man's inscription in a deme that he became a citizen. It was no longer as a member of the traditional phratries—although they were preserved largely for cult purposes—but as a member of a deme and one of the new artificial *phylai* that a man was identified as a member of the civic community. This new civic identity was symbolized in the rule according to which a man was no longer to be designated simply by a patronymic following his name, but by his *demotikon*, the name of his deme. The democratic implications of this rule are clear: there were to be no distinctions of quality among citizens based on their family connections and the 'nobility' or 'commonness' of their blood. Each Athenian, as a demesman and citizen in his own right, was like any other; and it is not surprising that the nobles clung so tenaciously to the old system of identification by patronymic. Moreover, since the demes became the basis of Athenian political organization, through them the ordinary citizen acquired a genuine role in the political life of the city, not simply a symbolic equality. After the reforms of Cleisthenes with their emphasis on the equality of citizens and the unity of the civic body, even Solon's four class system, which distinguished among citizens on grounds of wealth, although it was never explicitly abolished, was increasingly ignored as a basis of differential political rights—so much so that Plato in the *Laws* treats the Solonian class-system as an institution that, regrettably for him, belongs to a by-gone age. Again, the civic principle and the notion of citizenship stood opposed to traditional inequalities, to the hierarchical principles of aristocratic society.

In the reforms of Solon and Cleisthenes, then, the opposition of the *political* to the *aristocratic* principle is clear. The polis may have been aristocratic in its origin; but insofar as it evolved principles of association and social order unique to it—citizenship, civic ties, the rule of law—it tended toward democracy; and aristocratic power, even the principle of hierarchy itself, suffered in exact proportion to the victory of these civic or political principles over more traditional social principles. Citizenship meant autonomy and equality, and the rise of the autonomous individual was correlative to the rise of the civic community. It is in this sense that the political principle and the aristocratic principle can be regarded as essentially antithetical.

3. *The 'Essence' of the Polis: An 'Association Against a Subjected Producing Class'?*

The reforms of Cleisthenes gave the Athenian polis the form that was to characterize it throughout its 'Golden Age', in the fifth century BC, though of course there were further developments in consolidating the democracy—most notably, the weakening of the Areopagus. Having traced the evolution of the polis this far, we can go on to look for the 'essence' of the polis, that which constitutes its most significant and revolutionary contribution to the development of social organization. Unfortunately, the greatest admirers of Athens have not always been the most helpful in identifying its most remarkable characteristics. Indeed, there has been a tendency among classical scholars to obscure the most significant qualities, even to regard Athens as corrupt precisely to the extent that these qualities were developed. We can, however, begin by accepting certain aspects of the prevailing interpretation.

It is generally agreed, first of all, that the polis represents a new concept of social organization, different from that of any other contemporary civilization in the known world. More particularly, it is not the kind of social structure characteristic of the other advanced and stratified civilizations of the Mediterranean world and the East. The typical pattern for all these civilizations, as it apparently was for the Minoan and Mycenaean civilizations of ancient Greece, was some form of monarchy, in which king and palace dominated men and land and the essential 'political' relationship was that of master and subject. The advent of the polis marks a radical break with this mode of social organization. Palace and king are replaced by a community of free men or *citizens*; it is not the king but the citizen-body—whatever portion of the population it constitutes—which represents and embodies the *state*. It is this principle of citizenship, which submerges the qualitative differences among men in a common civic identity, and the identity of state and citizen-body that are the most obviously unique characteristics of the polis. That is why, for example, Ehrenberg suggests that democracy, as the most perfect identity of citizen-body and state (both in the sense that a greater portion of the population has citizenship and in the sense that there is an identity of citizenship and sovereignty insofar as the citizen-body consists entirely of citizens with full, not unequal, rights), is, so to speak, the *telos* of the polis; why it can be argued that the polis, having established the principle of citizenship and the identity of citizen-body and state, has a tendency toward equality and democracy.

Greek writers often appear to distinguish between *politics*—as the life of a community of citizens—and other kinds of social relations that we have come to call 'political'. If *politics* represents a truly distinctive form of association, then it is with the polis that politics was born—not simply in the etymological sense, but as a new form of communal relationship which is neither tribe (though it bears certain similarities to early tribal democracy) nor, like the Eastern state, a patriarchal and hierarchical household writ large. The social relations and modes of governing in states other than the polis are not, in this sense, 'political'. Political relations exist where kinship and tribal custom, as well as the relation of master and subject and the arbitrary will of the master, have been overtaken by civic bonds, a territorial organization, and the rule of law as the fundamental principles of social order; where the command and obedience relations and the arbitrariness of the master–subject nexus have at least in principle been superseded by deliberation by a free citizen-body within a framework of law; where reason and *persuasion* rather than the force of a master or the violence of the tribal vendetta are regarded as the essence of social order. In all these respects, too, democracy can be said to be the most perfectly *political* form of state, the form in which these departures from traditional associations are most developed.

There can be no doubt that these developments in political institutions and ideas represent a significant innovation in human social organization; but there is more to the Greek invention of 'politics' than this conventional account suggests. Perhaps the most important aspect of 'politics' as it evolved in Greece—particularly in the democratic polis, which is the most 'political'—is that it constitutes a crucial development in class relations, a milestone in the relations between appropriators and producers.

The Greek polis, at least in its democratic form, was a radical departure from all other existing states, not only in its form or its modes of organization but in its essential purpose. Before the emergence of the polis, in every known civilization of the ancient world where the state had replaced tribal organization as the dominant social system, the state was essentially a means of organizing and extracting labour from largely dependent labouring populations, a means of maintaining a fundamental division between producers and appropriators, an instrument for the exploitation of the former by the latter. The democratic polis may have been the first form of state to be based on a different, even antithetical, principle.

This may seem a surprising statement, since it can so easily be argued that the essential purpose of the Greek state was precisely to consolidate domination of dependent labour, notably of the slave population in Athens and the helots in Sparta. It can hardly be denied that the polis did serve such a purpose, but to argue that this was its essential or primary function is to ignore the radical uniqueness of the form of social organization created by the Greeks and its profound difference from the other traditional states of the ancient world. The powerful imperial states of the East, for example, evolved elaborate bureaucracies and military organizations largely for the purpose of commanding, administering, and exploiting, not only a dependent labour force, but whole subject populations from whom labour and resources were extracted not only as a means of distribution or to sustain necessary public projects but also to maintain a small privileged ruling group and a highly complex and luxurious civilization. The object of their political institutions was to sustain and enforce this hierarchy of exploitative relations. The situation in Greece was very different, if only because of the very small size of the Greek political units. None of the Greek poleis, of course, ever evolved anything like the complex and powerful bureaucratic and military apparatus used by Eastern states to exploit dependent labour, nor did they ever come close to the luxurious conditions created by the extraction of surplus labour in these states; and Greek political institutions, with their emphasis on *citizenship*, instead of reinforcing hierarchical relations, undermined them. Indeed, the purpose of the political innovations of the Greeks appears to have been to eliminate, or at least to weaken and control, rule rather than to consolidate it. This is to a certain extent true even of Sparta, which comes closest to a state in which social organization was determined by the conditions of exploiting a subject population. It can perhaps be argued that the establishment of the principles of law and citizenship in Sparta and the drive for equality that they express simply served the purpose of creating a sense of community in the ruling society so that it could act more effectively to exploit the non-Spartiate population. If this is true of Sparta, however, such an analysis does less than justice to the democratic polis in which the same social principles gave to the productive classes an unprecedented power and freedom from exploitation, as the discussion that follows will seek to demonstrate. Certainly in the case of Athens, as we shall see, with its citizen-body composed in greater part of 'producers' and with no clear division of labour between citizens and slaves, it is difficult to speak of a state whose essence is the exploitation of labour. The very least that can be said is that, if the polis served the purpose of dominating slave labour, it equally had the function of strengthening free labourers against their erstwhile rulers; and the principles of social organization created by the polis, those which were unique to it, were more clearly directed toward the latter purpose than the former. In that sense, the principle of the polis is directly opposed to that of the ancient state.

A consideration of Athenian history, then, compels us to reexamine Marx's characterization of the ancient Greek and Roman state as 'an association against a subjected producing class',[16] at least as it applies to Greece and specifically to the democratic polis. At the same time, Athenian history confirms the fundamental premise of Marx's argument that the evolution of the state must be explained in terms of the relation between producers and appropriators. What is unique about the democratic polis is that is appears to have evolved, not as an association against a subjected producing class, but as an association for the liberation of a producing class in the process of being subjected. The issue, for the moment, is not whether slavery was essential to the Greek polis, especially in its democratic form. What is at issue here is the motivating principle of the polis and the social needs in response to which it evolved. Did the polis evolve to its democratic perfection in order to meet the demands of maintaining power over a subjected labouring class, or did it, on the contrary, evolve in order to free a subjected labouring class from the power of its exploiters?

Let us look more closely at the ways in which the Greek polis differed from other states of the ancient world. The advanced civilizations outside the Greek world—Egypt, Persia, Babylonia, even China—appear to have been founded on an economic base similar to that of the Mycenaeans, though on a larger scale. They were, in varying degrees, centralized states dominated by palace or temple, which exercised control of the economy through a vast bureaucratic and military apparatus. Land seems to have belonged in large part to the central authority, which to a great extent also controlled manufacture and trade. The crucial fact from our standpoint is that in general surplus labour belonged to the central power, which used its elaborate military and bureaucratic establishment to organize and enforce the appropriation of surplus product and to redistribute it, very unequally, to the population, largely to the non-productive elements—officials, soldiers, priests, and other privileged groups. The rigidly hierarchical social division of labour, as well as the often highly luxurious condition of the court and the upper strata, was based on this very effective system of extracting surplus labour. So, too, of course, were often impressive feats of civil engineering and public works—like the Egyptian irrigation system; but if this mode of economic organization served to provide useful, even necessary, public services which enabled the subject populations to exist, it also ensured that they did little more than exist, often in conditions of extreme hardship, while creating and maintaining a luxurious culture and a ruling establishment whose condition of life was in sharp contrast to this minimal existence. There were, of course, differences among the various states in the degree to which they departed from this simple model. Private property and independent labour in the form of urban crafts and trade had no doubt developed to some extent in all of them, more in some than in others. Money and a system of commodity production and exchange developed to some extent alongside the palace-controlled system of production for use and redistribution in kind. Nevertheless, the dominant fact of economic, social, and political life in all these states was the centralized, appropriating despotism. Egypt and Persia, two states which were to figure most prominently in Greek political consciousness, were perhaps the most true to type.[17]

There are, then, two overwhelmingly central facts about this economic formation as it concerns the nature of the state. First, the *state* was the direct appropriator of surplus labour; this was, indeed, its essential function. In other words, the state was not simply a 'third power' designed to bring order to the class struggle between appropriating and producing classes; nor was it even, as in a fully developed class state, an instrument acting on behalf of an appropriating class but entering only indirectly into the process of class exploitation. It *was* in effect the appropriating 'class', the direct master of a huge dependent labour force, with the apparatus of the public power directly engaged in the process of surplus-extraction. This meant, secondly, that to be a *subject* of the state, for the great majority of subjects bound to render labour services or transfer surplus product on demand and virtually without condition to the public master, was immediately and by definition to be a dependent labourer, a servant, a serf. Slaves were owned by the palace, the temples, and the privileged groups, sometimes on a large scale; the primary form of dependent labour, however, was not chattel slavery, but a kind of 'general slavery', as Marx calls it, in which whole populations, continuing to live in village communities and occupying if not owning land, laboured as virtual serfs of the central power to whom their surplus labour belonged. In a sense, the state was a household writ large, in which the fundamental 'political' relationship was that between producing servant and appropriating master.

The deciphering of Linear B appears to prove that the civilizations of Bronze Age Greece were variants of this palace-centred economic formation in which most members of the rigidly hierarchical community were in effect serfs of the king. It is clear, however, that by the time of Homer this form of social organization had long been absent from Greece, and a new social form, a new mode of production and a new form of exploitation had evolved out of the tribal system which had reestablished itself on the ruins of Mycenaean civilization. There was no longer a centralized palace-dominated system of communal property supported by a population of dependent labour. Instead, the state described by Homer was a collection of smaller agricultural units, each of which was a self-contained exploitative system. The *oikos*-system was dominated by an aristocracy of powerful lords who, as a class which owned most of the land and had a monopoly of power, were in a position to exploit the labour of others and to be free of the necessity of labour themselves. As master of a household, which aspired to self-sufficiency, the lord commanded the services of retainers and the labour of slaves, servants, and hired labourers. As a member of a powerful class, which was increasingly becoming a cohesive community transcending the boundaries of the household, he was increasingly in a position to exploit lesser independent land-holders and gradually to subject them, in one way or another, to virtual dependence.

In fact, there is considerable evidence that, as the *oikos*-system gave way to a more unified state in which the loose society of independent household lords was transformed into an aristocratic ruling class, the free peasantry was gradually being transformed into another type of dependent labour. Hesiod, of course, testifies at least to the oppression of the peasantry in the aristocratic society of eighth-century Boeotia, likening the lord to a hawk who clutches the nightingale in his claws, and in response to her cry for pity answers:

> Why do you cry? Your master holds you fast,
> You'll go where I decide, although you have
> A minstrel's lovely voice, and if I choose,
> I'll have you for a meal, or let you go.[18]

The reforms of Solon, however, tell us more than anything else about the condition to which the lower classes had fallen in Attica.

In his account of Solon's reforms, Aristotle sums up the situation with which Solon was called upon to deal by saying that the people were in revolt because the many had become slaves to the few;[19] and the evidence surrounding the reforms suggests very strongly that a large proportion, perhaps the great majority, of the poorer landholders had been reduced to serfdom, bound to the land and to service to aristocratic lords. By Solon's time, 'the poor of Athens were on the way to being reduced to something like helots. . . .'[20] The wealth and power of the aristocracy was such that it could treat free small-holders as dependent labour, indeed, force them into outright dependence. Quite apart from the opportunities for general oppression and exploitation of a 'free' population available to a ruling class with a complete monopoly of power and able arbitrarily to interpret and execute the 'law' in its own interests, there had evolved explicit relationships of dependence, formalized and enforced by law, which transformed many peasants into serfs in law as well as fact.

The most straightforward kind of dependence was probably debt-bondage, a condition to which a poor peasant might be forced to submit in order to borrow—or as a result of borrowing and failing to repay—seed, equipment, or whatever he needed to maintain a farm that barely yielded a subsistence for himself and his family. The status of *hektemoros*, which may or may not have been a form of debt-bondage, was probably the most common form of dependent labour in Attica.

The condition of the *hektemoroi*, the 'sixth-parters', has been a matter of considerable dispute. It is, for example, uncertain whether hektomorage was, as is most commonly believed, the result of unpaid debt, or a relationship entered into without prior debt by a poor farmer unable to maintain his farm, or even a simple condition of serfdom binding a landless labourer to work the land of his master.[21] What is clear, however, is that *hektemoroi* were farmers who were bound to a piece of land with an obligation to transfer a part (most likely one-sixth, possibly—though not probably—five-sixths) of their produce to a wealthy landowner. The land was marked with a stone (*horos*) which indicated that the land together with its occupant and his heirs was under pledge. Although a one-sixth obligation appears modest enough, it must have been very oppressive in the prevailing conditions of poverty aggravated by the increase in population and the poor quality of Attic soil, and given the very small size of peasant holdings. Perhaps even more important was the condition of bondage which tied the *hektemoroi* to the land and their masters, and even prevented them from seeking the other means of livelihood made possible by the growth of trade and the increasing importance of craftsmanship. Moreover, failure to make the required payment meant being sold into outright slavery. The status of hektomorage appears to have been a long-standing one passed down through generations by inheritance.

The question is further complicated by the uncertainty that surrounds Attic land tenure and the question of the alienability of land.[22] All that can be said with a reasonable degree of certainty is that, whether or not property and particularly family holdings were in principle inalienable, the pressures—traditional, religious, and practical—against alienation or division of land were very great, although peasants were probably often forced to divide their lots among several sons, until many farms were too small for further division and were barely large enough to sustain the farmer and his family. In any case, it must be assumed that peasants were reluctant to abandon their farms, even if they were alienable; moreover, it is probable that those who would be most likely to acquire them, the wealthy landowners, would have more to gain by forcing the peasant into dependence, thereby gaining not only his land but his labour, a solution preferable even to outright expropriation. Even if peasant land was alienable, then, these two factors might combine to produce a situation in which, rather than sell his land at the first sign of trouble and be subject to the uncertainties of propertylessness, the peasant would borrow or even enter immediately into a relationship of hektemorage.

Whatever the origins of hektemorage, Aristotle's is probably an accurate description of its effects:

> For the whole political setup was oligarchical and, in particular, the poor together with their wives and children were serfs of the rich. They were called Pelatai and Hektemoroi ['sixth-parters'], for it was at this rent that they cultivated the land of the wealthy. All the land was in the hands of a few, and if the serfs did not pay their rent, they and their children could be sold into slavery.[23]

And if Aristotle's account exaggerates by speaking of pre-Solonian Athens as if it consisted of only two classes, lords and serfs, it at least suggests the magnitude of the problem. There can be little doubt that a large sector of the Athenian population had become, or was becoming, a class of dependent labourers. It is clear that a very large proportion of the poor had become serfs in constant danger of becoming slaves, and that land together with command of dependent labour was effectively in the hands of a few. It is also clear that the power of the few was such that they could force free peasants into subjection, and could easily exceed the legal boundaries of hektemorage. That they did so is suggested by Solon himself. To these subjected peasants must be added many other Athenians who, having taken loans on personal security, were sold into slavery by their creditors for failing to repay their debts, as well as those who fled Attica to escape slavery. Solon's testimony suggests that many were sold into slavery 'unlawfully', presumably because the powerful few needed no unpaid debts to authorize the sale of their dependents into slavery, when they were strong enough to do so at will.

This was the situation, then, that created the revolutionary climate for Solon's reforms, supported no doubt by the growing number of Athenians whose livelihood did not depend directly on the land at all. However incomplete Solon's reforms may have been, however concerned he may have been—as he himself suggests—to restrain the demos and to grant it no more than was necessary to maintain peace, his reforms were revolutionary in their implications. As Andrewes suggests, if the *hektemoroi* were, in fact, serfs who had never owned land, then Solon's abolition of hektemorage meant a significant redistribution of land and the creation of a new free peasantry. Nevertheless, even if, as is commonly believed, the *hektemoroi* were free peasants who had fallen into dependence, Solon's reforms meant the restoration of the free peasantry; and more important, his abolition of hektemorage together with his prohibition against loans on personal security meant, in effect, the legal abolition of the forms of dependent labour to which Athenians had been subject.

These reforms alone, however, would not have been enough to liberate Athenians from the condition of dependent labour if the ruling class had retained the political and judicial power that had given it such absolute control of the lower classes. The aristocratic state provided ample means of oppressing and exploiting the poor without a formal recognition of their dependent status. The strengthening of the political principle by Solon himself and by his successors, the extension of the principles of citizenship and the rule of law, must, therefore, be regarded as extensions of the revolution which legally liberated Athenian dependent labour; and the steps by which the democracy was progressively established can be looked upon as attempts to consolidate the independence of Athenian labour. Even if individual reformers were not themselves motivated by a desire for the independence of Athenian producers, the interests of these classes gave direction to the reforms; and the statesmen who undertook them were those whose power rested to a great extent on the support of the demos.

It would appear, then, that the process that brought the polis and its characteristic social principles to their fullest development was impelled by '... a kind of class-war ..., when noble landowners forced peasants into dependence and into serving as labourers on their estates.'[24] It is possible that Sparta developed some of these principles earlier than did Athens, effectively replacing monarchy by a citizen-body and at least a rudimentary rule of law, and perhaps also partly in response to a conflict, not only between king and nobles, but between an aristocracy of wealthy landowners and the Spartan peasantry; but here the process was arrested by the unusual situation in which Sparta stood with respect to dependent labour—a situation unusual even among oligarchic poleis. Sparta, of course, had a ready-made dependent labour force in the form of a subject population acquired by conquest; and although there were elements of class conflict within the Spartiate population itself, the basic relationship between exploiters and exploited, appropriators and producers, was less in the form of a class-war than war in a more literal sense, a situation in which a conquering people commanded the labour of another, ethnically distinct, population by sheer force and virtually in the conditions of a military occupation. The ruling population, despite its internal conflicts, remained united in its oppression of the helots and continued to survive as a ruling class to whom the surplus product of the subject population belonged. Although inequalities and conflicts reemerged within the ruling community, so that even among the Spartiates there were citizens with inferior rights, these conflicts did not assume the character of a full-fledged class struggle, since the citizen body was deliberately excluded from productive occupations. These functions were reserved for the helots and the *perioikoi* (who were free, but not citizens), and the Spartiates remained united as an appropriating class. It need hardly be added that the rigid education and military training, the severe restrictions on all aspects of Spartan life, were designed to maintain the unity of the appropriating class in the face of constant danger of revolt by the subjected producers.

The very different situation of Athens was more fraught with possibilities of a significant social revolution precisely because the relationship between appropriators and producers there took the form of a *class*-relation. Here the fundamental conflict occurred *within* a community, united at least in principle by blood and ancient tribal connections, and perhaps with a cultural memory of ancient rights and equality. The political institutions which in Sparta were established to deal with inequalities within the exploiting community, in Athens were called upon to deal with the more fundamental division between exploiters and exploited and therefore assumed a more radical character. If in Sparta these institutions served, if only indirectly, to consolidate the ruling population's command of dependent labour by unifying the rulers, in Athens they served to liberate a dependent labour force; and in the process, the institution of the polis developed its essential characteristics far beyond the rudimentary form they had in Sparta.

Even if we assume, then, that the purpose of Spartan reforms was to unite the ruling community against a subjected producing class, it cannot easily be argued that the motivating force in the evolution of the Athenian polis was the same insofar as it united the citizen-body in its domination of slaves, since slavery was an insignificant factor in the economy of early Athens and the slave population a small section of the total population until the democracy was well-established. Even at its highest point, the ratio of slaves to citizens was never remotely like that of helots to Spartiates; and more important, since the majority of the citizen-body themselves continued to engage in productive labour, dependent labour of any kind never had the importance in the economy of democratic Athens that it had in Sparta. At the very least, in Athens unlike Sparta, political reforms did not have the effect of drawing a rigid line between a non-labouring, appropriating citizenry and a dependent labour force. If at the time Athens was forging its political institutions, slave labour (particularly the labour of non-Athenian slaves) had been a sufficiently significant force in the economy to suggest itself as a feasible alternative to free labour, it is possible that Athens, like Sparta, might have taken the occasion to create a citizen body which was exclusively a non-labouring, appropriating class; as it was, slavery was probably not important enough at that stage to be an essential consideration in the development of Athens' basic constitution. Perhaps it can be said that, paradoxically, the incomplete 'liberation' of Athenian producers—incomplete because unlike Spartan citizens they remained producers in the absence of an alternative labour force—is what gave the Athenian situation its revolutionary implications. Instead of creating a class of non-labouring appropriators whose freedom rested on the labour of others, the Athenian revolution created a radically new kind of class—a producing class that was free in a very different sense. One is even tempted to ask why, once an alternative to citizen-labour became available in the form of a sizeable slave population, Athens did not become the city of Plato and Aristotle's dreams, ruled like Sparta by a free citizenry completely relieved of the necessity of labour by its command of a subjected producing class. If the Athenian polis was in its essence an 'association against a subjected producing class', it was a singularly ill-defined and imperfect one; on the other hand, it was more successful as an association for the liberation of a subjected producing class, having created what in the historical context was a radically new phenomenon—a sizeable class of free producers, whose independence lay not simply in their freedom from personal bondage but in their role in self-government. It is perhaps not excessive to say that the labouring citizenry of Athens came as close to being *free* and independent labourers as is possible where a *class* of labourers exists at all—more independent, of course, than the free proletariat of the modern age, and, because of their political role, more free even than later 'petty-bourgeois' classes of independent producers.

How, then, are we to assess the place of slavery in the evolution of the democratic polis, since slavery did become the dominant form of dependent labour in Athens as Athenian labour was liberated? It can, of course, be argued that, if slavery was not the *cause* of Athenian political development—that is, the condition for the evolution of the polis, as an 'association against a subjected producing class'—it was a *consequence* of that development. Since the importance of slavery rose with the progress of democracy, it seems reasonable to suppose that slavery became the predominant form of dependent labour precisely because other forms were no longer available. Of course this proposition is true; but it is almost tautological. If we agree that slavery became the dominant form of dependent labour because other forms were abolished, we are still left with the question of why dependent labour continued to exist at all, and eventually on such a large scale. The answer to this more significant question is not so self-evidently to be found in the liberation of Athenian labour, especially since that liberation did not mean *abolition* of free Athenian labour or even a clear division of labour between citizens and slaves. Historians are still divided, not only about the size of the slave population, but more significantly, about how essential to the economy of democratic Athens slavery was even at its height, and to what extent Athenian citizens—most of whom continued to labour, often side-by-side with slaves—would have had to alter their way of life had slave-labour been unavailable. It is to be doubted that these questions will ever be resolved, and this is certainly not the place to attempt even a tentative resolution. If, however, our purpose is to determine the nature of the polis in relation to other forms of state, and if we look at Athens against the background of the ancient world in general, we should perhaps be even more struck by the existence of a sizeable *independent* labour-force than by the existence of slavery. 'Throughout most of human history', writes M. I. Finley,

> labor for others has been performed in large part under conditions of dependence or bondage; that is to say, the relation between the man who works and his master or employer rested neither on ties of kinship nor on a voluntary, revocable contract of employment, but rather on birth into a class of dependents, on debt, or on some other precondition which by custom and law automatically removed from the dependent, usually for a long term or for life, some measure of his freedom of choice and action.[25]

To Finley's remarks should be added the observation that, throughout history, in societies where the productive capacities have sufficed to support a complex culture requiring production well beyond subsistence, labour has in large part been 'labour for others', and that the state has generally, in one way or another, been an essential means of enforcing such labour. The condition of its independent producers is essential to the uniqueness of the democratic polis; and if we are to understand that polis and its relation to the status of labour, the condition of Athens' independent producers must be gauged not simply against that of slaves, but against the other more predominant forms of dependent labour which seem to have prevailed throughout the advanced civilizations of the ancient world. Seen against this background, what distinguishes Athens is the importance of its free producers; and what distinguishes these free producers, what constitutes their freedom, is not simply their freedom from personal bondage to individual masters, but their freedom from 'general slavery' in the form of helotage, or subjection to an appropriating despotism, and even submission to an exclusive ruling class of dominant property-holders. It is important to remember, too, that this freedom extended to labourers without property, not only to peasants and 'petty-bourgeois' craftsmen and artisans, but also the growing class of workers, agricultural and urban, who owned no means of production at all. Finally, we should remember that, if widespread slavery was in some sense a consequence of the liberation of Athenians, that liberation did not consist in establishing a leisured appropriating class of Athenian citizens against a non-citizen, dependent producing class; and that there was no clear division of labour between citizens and slaves.

Apart from the fact that slaves, like citizens, engaged in virtually every kind of occupation, even the most skilled, it can be argued that the function of slavery was often to free citizens *for* rather than *from* productive labour. Slaves often filled the non-productive roles which citizens tried to avoid on the grounds that such activities usually involved long-term salaried employment and hence, in Athenian eyes, *dependence*. This meant that slaves might undertake not only service jobs but managerial occupations—for example, as business managers, bankers, civil servants, or policemen—while citizens engaged in manual work not only as independent producers but as casual wage-labourers. The lack of any clear social division of labour between citizens and slaves, or between a citizen class of appropriators and a slave class of direct producers must be kept in mind in an assessment of the contention that the polis was an 'association against a subjected producing class'. Moreover, in light of the inadequacy of this contention, if the nature and function of the polis are still to be judged in terms of its role in relation to slavery, it might be worth considering the extent to which *pre*-political factors like the remnants of tribalism sustained the Athenian commitment to the enslavement of foreigners *against* the equalizing tendencies of the civic principle.

What is significant about the absence of a division of labour between citizens and slaves is, again, not so much the fact that slaves and free men often worked side-by-side at the same tasks. This occurred elsewhere too, even in societies where dependent labour was the chief productive force. The democratic polis was unique in that free labourers (other than metics) were full citizens; and that there was no clear division of labour, not simply between free men and slaves, but between *citizens* and slaves. Instead, the very real gulf between the labouring citizen and the slave lay, of course, in the freedom of the former; and, again, that freedom was to a great extent a function not simply of his freedom from personal bondage but of his *citizenship*. The condition of the free but *powerless* labourer tends to merge into the bondage of the slave; and in societies where the free labourer has worked side-by-side with the slave, but where the free labourer has been subject to a powerful ruling class, he has had little to distinguish him from his captive companion. In fact and in the eyes of his master, he has been as much a servant as the slave; and this fact is reflected in the lack of clarity which even the *concept* of free labour has often had in such societies. The conceptual distinction between the free labourer and the slave is, for example, obscure in the poems of Homer, which describe a society dominated by an unchallenged landed aristocracy and a powerless labouring class consisting of both free labourers and slaves. As M. I. Finley writes:

> Not even so simple a contrast as that between slave and free man stands out in sharp clarity. The word *drester*, for example, which means 'one who works or serves,' is used in the *Odyssey* for the free, and the unfree alike. The work they did and the treatment they received, at the hands of their masters as in the psychology of the poet, are often indistinguishable.[26]

In the late Roman Empire, to cite another example, slaves and free men 'merge into a common condition of servitude, in fact if not in law',[27] and to a considerable extent even in law.

In short, where free labourers are *subjects* rather than *citizens* in the Greek sense, their condition tends to approach that of slaves, and the distinctness of free labourers tends to fade in the eyes of observers in proportion to the degree of their subjection. When Athenians spoke, as they typically did, of subjects of a monarch as slaves and kings as masters, when they adopted the word for a master of slaves, *despotēs*, to describe the absolute ruler characteristic of the Orient and even sometimes a Greek tyrant, when they opposed their democratic polis to a condition of slavery, they were probably not speaking purely metaphorically, but expressing their recognition of the connection between the nature of the state and the status of labour. Euripides was certainly not alone among Athenians when, in his eulogy of democracy in *The Suppliants*, he asked what good it is to labour in a city not ruled by the people, 'merely to add to the tyrant's substance by one's toil'.[28]

If the idea of the state was probably inseparable in the minds of Athenians from the condition of labour, it is certainly true of their concept of individual freedom, surely one of their most important cultural legacies. Finley has suggested that 'Only when slaves became the main dependent labor force was the concept of personal freedom first articulated (in classical Greece), and words were then created or adapted to express that idea. It is literally impossible to translate the word "freedom" directly into ancient Babylonian or classical Chinese ...,'[29] languages of societies in which forms of dependent labour other than chattel slavery were dominant. If Finley is correct in pointing to a coincidence between the rise of slavery in Greece and the appearance of a concept of individual freedom, however, it may not be only because that concept appeared in response and in contrast to the condition of those whom the Greeks enslaved. It is possible that, since the growth of slavery followed upon the liberation of native labour, the concept of personal freedom was born among the Greeks out of their own experience of dependence and liberation, not simply in contrast to the dependence of others; although certainly the idea must have acquired greater clarity and sharpness as the condition of slaves became a salient fact of Greek life. At any rate, it seems very likely that the idea of individual freedom was invented in reference to the condition of labour. For the Greeks, moreover, civic or political liberty was essential to true personal freedom; and in the democratic polis, civic liberty meant not freedom *from* labour, but freedom *of* labour, insofar as it is possible in a class society.

In this respect, then, the democratic polis was opposed in its essence and purpose to the traditional state as a means of enforcing the hierarchical social division of labour and exploiting dependent labour. If the polis like other 'states' was created and shaped by the relations between appropriators and producers and served as a means of dealing with the problems generated by the social division of labour, it is far too simple to view the polis as an instrument of the ruling class, designed to extract labour and to maintain and protect the property and status of the ruling minority against depredation and rebellion by the dispossessed. No doubt it served these purposes too (in part by making certain concessions to the dispossessed in order to maintain peace); and no doubt it is true that the polis, like other forms of state, provided a 'whole machinery of law, accounting, and administration ... to enforce the sanctity of property and contracts'.[30] On the other hand, our survey of the evolution of the polis should suffice to indicate that it was as much—if not more—a weapon for the subject classes in their struggle against their rulers, and that it was the rulers who had reason to resist the political principle. The polis as a form of state certainly played a role in the class struggle, as the Marxist interpretation of the state suggests; but which side of the struggle it served best is at least an open question. Nor would it do justice to the revolutionary significance of the polis to argue that, while the polis may have served the wealthy middle or moneyed classes—who are most in need of legal devices and contractual security—in their struggle against the landed nobility, it also served them in their own subjection of the lower classes. Aside from the fact that, as we shall see in a moment, the distinction between bourgeoisie and proletariat is not so easily made in the mode of production and class structure of ancient Greece, this interpretation fails to recognize that the most far-reaching consequences of the polis lie in its effects on the labouring, productive classes.

The democratic polis, in its elaboration of the 'political' principle, its extension of active citizenship to the lower classes, established a realm in which the social division of labour and the fundamental division between labourer and non-labourer was non-essential. It is all very well to dismiss citizenship as a fictional, ideal substitute for real social equality, but the fact is that in Athens it was more than that. It gave the labouring class a freedom and power that it had never possessed before and in many respects has never regained since. We cannot judge the importance of this civic revolution for the condition of labour simply in terms of citizenship in a capitalist society, which plays a more peripheral role in determining the status of the working class. In modern capitalist society, the appropriation of surplus labour by a propertied class is inseparable from, essential to, the process of production itself. In pre-capitalist societies, 'non-economic' means of control, more or less extraneous to the productive process—tribal, religious, legal and political authority and military coercion—play a more central role in extracting surplus product, in the form of forced labour, rents, or taxes. This form of exploitation can be applied not only to the serf but to the 'free' peasant who is not, in principle, like the modern proletarian deprived of the means of production and therefore not so clearly dependent on an appropriating class for access to the very conditions of his labour. Therefore, access to 'non-economic' power may have far greater significance. The polis at least so far modified the traditional social division of labour that it began to undermine its *hierarchical* nature by attacking the perfect coincidence of economic position and political power, thereby attacking one of the traditional instruments of economic domination and the command of labour. Furthermore, the political role assumed by the labouring class of the polis meant that, despite the contempt for labour which is often said to characterize the ancient world, the radical idea of a labourer capable of self-government had entered Western culture.

4. *Class in the Democratic Polis*

Before pursuing our argument on the significance of the polis and in order to put it in perspective, something must be said about the class structure of Athens at the height of its development; and this requires some explanation of what we mean by 'class'. The concept of class and objections to its use in the case of Greece will be discussed later. The problematic place of slavery in the class structure of Athens will be dealt with, as will the significance of the distinction between citizen and non-citizen, and, in general, the question of the relation of class to other forms of social stratification such as *orders* or *estates*. For the moment, the following will serve to explain the concept of class that underlies our account of Athenian social structure:

Class is a *relationship* among human beings in which the parties to the relationship are defined and define themselves in terms of their respective positions in the process of production and, more specifically, in terms of their relations to the means of production, especially insofar as that relation determines their positions with respect to *labour* (e.g. are they obliged to labour for a livelihood; are they obliged to *sell* their labour; are they in a position to *buy* labour-power and extract surplus value; are they in a position to live passively on the product of others whose labour they command by right of certain kinds of landownership? etc.). Although the objective conditions that constitute the phenomenon of class exist in any social situation where the social division of labour has taken the form of hierarchical relations that permit certain social groups to exploit the labour of others, it is more meaningful to talk about class where some objective conditions are accompanied by some sense of common experience among those who share a common position in the relations of production, some sense of common interest that is distinct from, even opposed to, the experience and interests of those in different positions. Therefore, the phenomenon of class entails not only a set of objective conditions inherent in a mode of production, but also the various ways in which those conditions are experienced and defined by the human beings who live them; and the class experience, the nature of class itself, will vary not only according to differences in the mode of production but according to the particular cultural and historical experience of the men who live it.[31]

In the discussion that follows, we shall for reasons of convenience speak of class as a 'category of stratification'. It should be understood, however, that we share E. P. Thompson's reservations about sociological concepts of class as a 'structure' or 'category', to the extent that such concepts treat class as a disembodied, abstract, rigid, independently existing structure or social *role* that human beings happen to *occupy* —a *thing*, rather than a *relationship* which is a fluid historical phenomenon experienced and defined by living, conscious human beings. As Thompson writes,

> ... the notion of class entails the notion of historical relationship. Like any other relationship, it is a fluency which evades analysis if we attempt to stop it dead at any given moment and anatomize its structure. The finest-meshed sociological net cannot give us a pure specimen of class, any more than it can give us one of deference or

love. The relationship must always be embodied in real people and in a real context. Moreover, we cannot have two distinct classes, each with an independent being, and then bring them *into* relationship with each other. We cannot have love without lovers, nor deference without squires and labourers.

If we stop history at a given point, then there are no classes but simply a multitude of individuals with a multitude of experiences. But if we watch these men over an adequate period of social change, we observe patterns in their relationships, their ideas, and their institutions. Class is defined by men as they live their own history, and, in the end, this is its only definition.[32]

In this chapter, we are attempting to shed light on the history of the polis by considering it in terms of the particular class-experience of the Greeks, and specifically, the Athenians. Certainly the objective conditions of class existed in Athens; and it is the premise of our argument that there was a considerable degree of class-consciousness—certainly at least to the point that Athenians were very much aware of themselves as belonging either to a group of men who were compelled to work for a living or to a group who were freed from the necessity of labour by their command of the labour of others, and that this awareness was central to their social experience. In short, it is being suggested here that the creation and evolution of the polis and its unique civic principles constitute the particular way in which the Greeks defined and handled the experience of class.

Here, then is an outline of Athenian class structure.[33] The ancient Homeric world, as Finley points out, had been marked by a 'deep horizontal cleavage':

Above the line were the *aristoi*, literally the 'best people', the hereditary nobles who held most of the wealth and all the power, in peace as in war. Below were all the others, for whom there was no collective term, the multitude. The gap between the two was rarely crossed, except by the inevitable accidents of wars and raids. The economy was such that the creation of new fortunes, and thereby of new nobles, was out of the question. Marriage was strictly class-bound, so that the other door to social advancement was also securely locked.

Below the main line there were various other divisions, but, unlike the primary distinction between aristocrat and commoner, they seem blurred and they are often indefinable. Not even so simple a contrast as that between slave and free man stands out in sharp clarity. The word *drester*, for example, which means 'one who works or serves', is used in the *Odyssey* for the free and the unfree alike.

> The work they did and the treatment they received, at the hands of their masters as in the psychology of the poet, are often indistinguishable.[34]

Though within this undifferentiated labouring multitude a distinction was recognized between, on the one hand, relatively independent skilled workers, peasants, and herdsmen, and, on the other hand, landless *thetes* and slaves who worked directly for others, it is clear that the fundamental division, the only one that 'stands out in sharp clarity', was the division 'between those who were compelled to labor and those who were not' in order to live.[35]

Centuries later after considerable economic change, this fundamental dividing line was still apparent in fifth- and fourth-century Athens; but of course, with the decline of the *oikos*-economy, the class structure had become considerably more fluid and somewhat more differentiated. And, in the democracy, at least for those who were independent producers, the division between labourers and non-labourers was no longer so clearly and directly a relation between producers and appropriators. The old nobility no longer had such a rigid monopoly of landed wealth; a wealthy non-noble class had developed, but the tendency was to use wealth to acquire land, less as an investment than to join the ranks of the landed aristocracy. While commercial activity was a source of wealth and even the old land-owning aristocracy was not above engaging in it, it still remained true that, as always in the ancient world, 'land ownership on a sufficient scale marks "the absence of any occupation",'...;[36] and this condition of traditional aristocratic leisure was still probably the primary object of wealth. Large land-holdings, which were not typically concentrated in plantations but consisted of several smaller and often widely scattered farms, were probably worked to a great extent by tenants and day-labourers, not primarily by slaves and certainly not by slave-gangs like those of the Roman latifundia.

The bulk of the free population was a fairly homogeneous class of craftsmen, traders, peasants, and labourers which had not yet become clearly differentiated into bourgeoisie and proletariat. The typical productive unit was the small shop whose proprietor produced and sold his own products. Often, the labouring proprietor was assisted by co-workers, whether slaves or free labourers; but there seem to have been very few large enterprises owned by a non-labouring capitalist and employing a sizeable workforce of slaves or wage-labourers. Athens was not fundamentally a market economy, and production was on a fairly limited scale.[37] Both urban craftsmen and peasants generally sold as well as produced their own products, and in this sense can be said to compose a single class of small producer-traders; but if any further division can be made within this petty bourgeoisie, it must be between rural and urban workers—although the town-country dichotomy was not so clearly defined as it was later to become. Beyond that, it is difficult to identify any sharp differentiations within the mass of small producers. The difficulty of drawing further distinctions is augmented by the fact that many ostensibly independent producers were often forced to supplement their earnings by casual wage-labour; and in general, the line between small, often poor, independent producers and propertyless labourers was vague and fluid. There was perhaps an incipient bourgeoisie in the owners of the few larger enterprises—even though they were more rentiers than capitalists—whose numbers were negligible but growing. At this stage, however, they were too few to constitute a distinct class, and in any case, it is difficult to isolate them as a separate interest, opposed to both the traditional landed class and to the majority of small producers and labourers. Some of them joined the aristocratic-oligarchic party in its attack on the democracy; but the popular leaders of the new democracy after Pericles—notably Cleon—came out of this group of more prosperous producers with more leisure for political activities. In the eyes of anti-democrats, there was little essential difference between the 'leather-monger' Cleon and the small peddler, shopkeeper, or craftsmen with his stall in the marketplace. He was simply a more prosperous version of the same social type.[38] Moreover, it is apparent that the demos at this stage identified its interests with these new leaders who represented the productive classes in the conflict with the aristocratic-oligarchic classes and whose leadership, as we shall see, marked a radical departure from the old pattern of aristocratic rule. In the eyes of the demos (and its aristocratic enemies) it seems to have been more a case of being led by its own that being guided by its 'betters'; and it is certainly true that under the leadership of these new men the demos had unprecedented power.

It is also possible, perhaps, to identify an incipient proletariat, consisting of citizen wage-labourers and perhaps even part of the slave and metic populations; but in view of the nature of the productive process and the typical productive unit, the division between wage-labourers and small and often poor independent producers engaged in manual labour cannot be as clear as the proletarian-bourgeois dichotomy suggests. The position of slaves and metics in the class structure is even more problematic. The difficulty lies in the fact that there was no clear division of labour, not only between freemen and slaves, but also between citizens and non-citizens, even citizens and slaves.

It cannot be emphasized enough that, contrary to a very popular myth, slaves and metics did not constitute, for all practical purposes, the labour force of Athens. To begin with, most Athenian citizens worked for a living, many if not most of them in 'banausic' occupations, some as wage-labourers;[39] and while only citizens were permitted to own property, ownership of property was *not* a condition for citizenship. The importance of slaves to the Athenian economy and probably their number have been exaggerated until recently, and the role of citizens in the productive process underplayed. It must be remembered not only that the majority of citizens were compelled to earn their livelihood and were engaged in productive activities, but also that, on the other hand, there was virtually no occupation in which slaves did not engage.[40] Not only were citizens labourers, many slaves were not. Slaves occupied every possible position from mine-worker to banker or businessman, even labour contractor, to civil servant. Finley, in fact, reports that Pasion, 'the manager of the largest banking enterprise in fourth-century BC Athens', was a slave, later freed and granted citizenship.[41] 'Free and slave-labour stood on the same economic level,' writes Ehrenberg.[42] Some slaves were actually wage-earners, and in any case, slaves and free men worked side by side at the same tasks. Citizens avoided long-term service to a single employer in the form of regular wage-labour or salaried employment, preferring, if possible, to leave such dependent roles to slaves; but the effect of this was not a division between labouring slaves and non-labouring citizens. On the contrary, the consequence was often that citizens remained common labourers—even casual wage-labourers—while slaves undertook managerial functions. Competition between slave and free labour does not seem to have been a significant factor. If anything, the availability of slaves may, by encouraging the ambitious public construction projects undertaken by the democracy, actually have created work for otherwise unemployed citizens, many of whom worked beside slaves on the famous monuments of Athens. In any case, slave-labour did not constitute a different form of production in competition with free labour. In particular, there was no opposition between independent small-scale craft-production, on the one hand, and on the other, some kind of large-scale 'factory' production with a specialized division of labour within an organized, integrated labour force consisting of slave-gangs. The latter type of production simply did not exist. Instead, slaves, like citizens, even in the relatively few cases where many slaves worked for one master under one roof, generally worked as independent small producers or craftsmen, labouring in a sense on their own accounts and paying a 'body-rent' to their master.

Metics, too, engaged in virtually every possible occupation; and while they played a very important role in certain crafts and trades, 'the modern view that practically all trade, banking and craftsmanship were in the hands of metics is false....'[43] It is not correct 'to speak of a "deep social gap" between citizens and metics, for both, whether rich or poor, were on roughly the same social level, and actually formed one and the same social body',[44] the same more or less homogeneous class of producers and traders that constituted the mass of the Athenian population. Ehrenberg sums up the role of citizens in relation to others in the economy of Athens this way:

> The barrier of political privilege was high, but social life flowed over it. This is shown not only by the fact that non-citizens had won, in some degree, a position of social equality, but also by the fact that the activities of the citizens were not exclusively political. From the middle-class came most of the political leaders after Perikles as well as some of the State-officials, but the class which earned its living by trade and craft was also largely composed of citizens. Manual labour was not looked down on, though of course those who worked as workmen, paid by, and dependent on, a master, were not very highly esteemed. In the assembly and the courts there were only citizens, but many of these citizens were also workers. This is the true meaning of the statement that the demos was lord of the market, of the harbours and of the pnyx.[45]

The difficulty of placing slaves in the class structure and of regarding the relation between citizens and slaves as a class relation is complicated not only by the lack of any clear division of labour between these groups, but also by the complexity of the slave condition itself. It must be said, to begin with, that Athenian slavery differs from 'absolute' slavery—if we use as our criterion the slavery of the American South, which may be the closest approximation to absolute slavery in the history of the world[46]—not only in the variety of functions which slaves performed and the extent to which they were engaged in skilled and even managerial occupations, but also in the degrees of freedom they enjoyed. What makes the condition of Athenian slaves so difficult to define is that there was, at least *de facto*, such a broad spectrum of conditions with respect to freedom of choice and movement. Even in law there were differences of condition, notably between public and private slaves, the former having legal rights comparable to those of metics (with the all-important qualification that public slaves could apparently be transformed into private slaves by sale to a private master). In *fact*, if not in law, slaves occupied any number of positions along a continuum from bondage to freedom.

There appear to have been, for example, a large number of slaves, usually engaging in craft occupations, who lived on their own, rather than with their master or in slave barracks, and who moved freely about the city like free labourers, offering their services as wage-earners, often with little supervision from their masters—though, of course, they could not themselves enter into legal contracts of employment. Wages received by slaves seem to have been equal to those of the free labourers by whose side they often worked; but they owed a certain 'rent' to their masters from their earnings. In certain respects, the condition of these slaves was *de facto* if not *de jure* more comparable to that of serfs who work independently but owe a portion of their produce to their lords; but in other important respects, these wage-earning slaves were more free than agrarian serfs, since their freedom of choice and movement was greater than that of the serf who is bound to a given plot of land. Again, those slaves in managerial positions, those who worked independently—albeit with obligations to their masters—as businessmen, bankers, labour contractors, were not only in a position of relative *de facto* freedom, but would also be in a position to superintend the labour of others, and not necessarily under the eyes of a master. Some were able to amass considerable wealth, which was, of course, likely to be used for manumission. Finally, there were the public slaves, the most striking example of which were the police, whose freedom extended to the power of arresting free citizens.

The condition of Athenian slaves, then, represents a continuum from the bondage of the mineworker to the relative freedom of the bank manager and the policeman. Add to this the possibility of manumission (there even existed in Athens what might be called benefit societies or loan associations which lent money to slaves to buy their freedom) and the existence of the transitional condition of those manumitted slaves who retained a certain legal relation to their former masters, merging into the condition of the free metic, who had no political rights, but who might be anything from a labourer to a very wealthy businessman, and the result is a fluid picture that makes a precise class distinction between slaves and citizens impossible to draw. The basic criterion of relation to the means of production is no more decisive. While only citizens were permitted to own land—at least without special dispensation, which may sometimes have been granted to metics—not all citizens did own property; and while a significant proportion of citizens did own some property, many of these owned only a house, or perhaps a tiny garden plot, and nothing which could properly be called the means of production. At the same time, non-citizens, metics, although not entitled to own property outright, might as shopkeepers or businessmen who rented or leased their business premises have, so to speak, a much closer relation to the means of production than the citizen-*thetes*; and even certain slaves might at least perform functions more typical of an owner in command of labour, in contrast to the wage-earning citizen. At any rate, the critics of the democracy who, like Plato and the Old Oligarch, complained that it was virtually impossible to distinguish the slave from the free citizen in democratic Athens, were no doubt exaggerating, and the Old Oligarch is surely wrong or speaking ironically when he suggests that the Athenian law against striking a slave (presumably other than one's own) was established because of the danger that one might be striking a citizen when the two were so alike; nevertheless, the remarks of these conservatives undoubtedly express an important truth about the social structure of democratic Athens.

All this may help to explain why slavery in the eyes of Athenians was apparently not necessarily the worst form of bondage. The condition of Sparta's helots, for example, may well have appeared to them a more abject servitude than that of Athenian slaves. Sometimes even the free non-citizens of an oligarchic state, and especially the subjects of a monarch such as the Persian king, may have seemed more servile and dependent. What the slaves themselves thought of this is impossible to determine. It would be childish to think that they were in any way satisfied with their condition of bondage; and the absence of slave revolts is, as Finley and others have pointed out, to be explained less by the humane treatment of Athenian slaves than by the fact that unlike Sparta's helots they were uprooted foreigners from many different lands who did not constitute a community. Nevertheless, the fact remains that the relations between citizens and slaves was not clearly one of class-war between a class of exploiting appropriators and a class of exploited producers. This is not, of course, to say that the distinction between citizens and slaves was not a very sharp one for Athenians, nor to minimize the crucial difference between legal freedom and legal bondage; but the sharpness of the distinction based on legal and political rights does not quite so clearly correspond to visible differences of social condition or conditions of labour; hence the difficulty of identifying the distinction as a class-division.

Although the position of women does not fit neatly into the question of class relations, it should be mentioned in this connection not only because the status of women was affected by class oppositions, but also because women constituted an important part of the Athenian labour force, at least as domestic labourers, and can be regarded as a group of producers whose labour was appropriated by others.[47] The status of women in Athenian democracy, like the position of slaves, is an ambiguous and paradoxical one. In some respects, the low status of women itself testifies to the growth of democracy, freedom, and equality in Athenian society—although it must be said immediately that the evidence of a decline in the status of women as democracy advanced is not unequivocal and is still a matter of controversy. It must also be stressed that one cannot speak of the 'status of women' as a single, undifferentiated condition, since circumstances even among citizen women varied according to class.

Generally, the legal status of women was low in democratic Athens. They were treated by the law virtually as children; and the attitude of society was on the whole paternalistic, which also often meant protective: for example, the law strictly guarded a woman's dowry from being disturbed by her male relations or anyone else. Women could not, of course, participate in the political life of the democracy; and though they could inherit property, their male guardians managed it for them. Their primary civic duty was to propagate citizens, and to a certain extent to preserve property. It has often been pointed out that the development of private property, the closer association of property with the individual household which accompanied the rise of democracy, was a prime factor in depressing the condition of women. Their freedom was restricted by the demands of property to the extent that a woman whose family lacked a son was regarded as 'attached to the family property' and could be obliged by law to marry her next-of-kin, in order to preserve the family property and maintain the independence of the *oikos*. It is even suggested that in such cases the kinsman could oblige her to divorce, if she were already married at her father's death, at least if she had no son. The very complicated law of heiresses, however, reflects one of the ambiguities of the woman's position. For example, while the law was certainly nothing but restrictive in the case of wealthy heiresses, it probably improved the condition of the poor 'heiress', who may have inherited only her father's debts, since her nearest kinsman was obliged to marry her or to provide a dowry sufficient to attract another husband.[48] The truly paradoxical nature of the situation is illustrated by the fact that it was precisely in more restrictive and far less democratic societies like Sparta and Gortyn that the position of women in relation to property was more independent. In Sparta, for example, the laws of marriage for heiresses were probably less rigid; in any case, women had considerable control over their own property and often managed estates. It is also worth noting that Plato, whose political doctrine is profoundly aristocratic and anti-democratic, proposes a considerable degree of freedom and equality for women—at least women of the ruling class.

Indeed, it can be argued that the position of women generally declined in Athens precisely as a result of the democracy's attack on the aristocracy.[49] For example, the laws of Solon, which regulated and restricted the behaviour of citizen women, may have been instituted for the purpose of strengthening the citizen community, reducing conflicts among men, and limiting the power of the aristocracy, partly means of sumptuary laws which, among other things, restricted the ways in which the rich could employ the services of the poor. As Sarah Pomeroy argues, 'The curbing of the aristocrats by the democracy of the fifth century BC entailed the repression of all women, but leaned especially heavily on the aristocrats who had the time and the means to make and enjoy displays of wealth.'[50]

In general, then, aristocratic women probably lost more in the democracy than did lower class citizen women; and though all women found their behaviour restricted, the status of citizen women as a whole gained in relation to non-citizen women—notably the slaves who worked in state brothels. Again paradoxically, on the other hand, the freedom of non-citizen women was in some respects greater than that of citizens, since they were not subject to the regulations which tended to keep citizen women in the home and out of sight. The most famous example of the position attained by some non-citizen women in the political and intellectual life of Athens is, of course, the courtesan Aspasia, mistress and companion of Pericles.

The very fact that Athens was an increasingly urban society, one of the largest cities in Greece, tended to depress the status of women to the extent that their activities, in contrast to those of women in agrarian societies, were driven indoors and out of sight.[51] The division of labour between men and women was accentuated by the contrast between the woman's domestic functions and the expanding political life of her male compatriot—though women did have important religious functions in the city. Even marketing, which would have taken her out of the home more, was considered to be a man's task. The less advanced, agrarian society of Sparta, which never progressed beyond a collection of villages, again presents a paradoxical contrast, allowing its women more visibility and freedom of movement. Again, however, a distinction must be drawn among classes. Poor citizen women often went out to work, for example as washerwomen, woolworkers, and as workers in other clothing industries, as sellers of food or home-spun and woven articles, as nurses of children and midwives.[52] Thus, while poor women engaged in work outside the home which was in great part an extension of their domestic functions, work which was regarded by many as demeaning, they did as a consequence move in the community more freely than their wealthier counterparts.

It is perhaps worth noting, too, that as a result of this freer movement, and in the absence of the pressures of preserving property, in Athens there were apparently more love-matches in lower class marriages than was usually the case in traditional societies or among the upper classes.[53]

It is difficult, therefore, to make any generalizations about the status of women in democratic Athens, except to reiterate the paradoxical fact that not only did democracy fail to include women in political life, but many social developments designed to strengthen the democracy, expand the political realm, and enhance freedom had the effect of restricting the freedom of women.

To summarize what we have said about class in Athens, then, if we are to divide fifth- and fourth-century Athens into classes based on the social division of labour and position in the productive process, the clearest division we can observe is still that between the landed leisure class living passively on property and the labour of others, and the bulk of the population who lived on their earnings. The formation of what might be called a capitalist class or bourgeoisie and a proletariat, the buyers and the sellers of labour-power, was only in the most rudimentary stages; the market economy and production for the market remained undeveloped. An incipient bourgeoisie, such as it was, might be seen in the commercially active landowners and the larger and more prosperous producer-traders; while a proletariat of sorts was growing out of the wage-labourers and the impoverished small producers, especially the peasants (who became increasingly impoverished in the latter stages of this period and thereafter), who were being forced to join the wage-earning ranks. At the time with which we are primarily concerned, however—that is, roughly up to the Macedonian conquest—this process of differentiation had not gone very far. The division between labouring and non-labouring classes was the *class* distinction that figured most prominently in the literature and philosophy of the democratic age as well as in the civil strife of the democracy, the political conflicts between the aristocratic-oligarchic faction and the democrats. The old essentially agrarian class opposition principally between aristocratic and peasant landholders, which had been the motivating force of early political development, had now been transformed into a new conflict focused on the polis: a conflict which expressed itself particularly in a political opposition between, on the one hand, rich citizens, who felt victimized by the democratic polis, the role it gave banausics, its redistributive function extracting funds from the rich and conferring public payments on the poor; and on the other hand, poorer citizens who stood to gain from the institutions of the democracy, its checks on the rich and its diversion of surplus product to subsidize the political and judicial activities of the poor. This class division, however, though it played a significant role in the relations among citizens, did not determine the distinction between citizen and non-citizen, or even free man and slave.

It is precisely the fact that political standing is *not* determined by a fundamental class division between labourers and non-labourers, or even producers and appropriators, that makes the democratic polis so important in the history of class relations and particularly in the history of the working classes. That a distinction between citizen and non-citizen—especially citizen and slave—exists at all, as distasteful as it is, should not obscure the significance of the fact that the distinction is not based on the division of labour and that the status of labourer, no matter how 'base and mechanical', even dependent labourer (since wage-earners may be citizens), does not determine exclusion from the political realm. Paradoxically, the very sharpness of the conceptual and legal difference between free man and slave inherent in Athenian citizenship may suggest a significant change in the status of labour, if one recalls the vagueness of the distinction between free labourer and slave to the Homeric aristocrat for whom all labourers are natural inferiors and servants. In an important sense, a similar vagueness is implicit in any rigidly hierarchical society where all labourers, free men or slaves, are merely *subjects*, at the complete mercy of an economically dominant and hereditary ruling class, a class of masters. The fact that Athens has *citizens*—that is, full and active members of the body politic—not merely 'free' subjects and that the distinction between citizen and non-citizen does not correspond to the social division of labour must, in light of previous historical experience in Greece and other advanced civilizations, be regarded as a revolutionary development, even if the fact that the distinction between citizen and slave survives at all indicates a tragically incomplete revolution.

What is important about the Athenian case is not only the immediate fact that the 'banausic' classes achieved unprecedented power in their struggle against domination and that, as we have said, the principle of a hierarchical social division of labour was thereby weakened, but also that a new attitude toward labour and the labourer was introduced into European consciousness. The attitude of Plato—and other aristocrats, Xenophon, even Aristotle—towards the *banausos* and his incapacity for a fully rational, moral life should illustrate, by contrast, the significance of the Athenian reality. This attitude will be discussed at some length in the subsequent chapters. For the moment, suffice it to say that the whole of Plato's political philosophy is grounded in the conviction that to earn a livelihood, and especially by means of manual labour, corrupts the soul and disqualifies a man for politics, making it not only justifiable but necessary for him to subject himself to the command of others. Moreover, the incapacity of the *banausos* for politics and self-rule is not simply a consequence of his lack of leisure time, but inheres in the corruptive nature of labour itself, so that even granted sufficient time for political participation—which many 'banausic' Athenians had—he would be disqualified. Plato's attitude is typical of his class and in general seems to have characterized—if not always so extremely—all non-democratic cultures; but while commentators sometimes like to regard Plato's view as typical of Athens in general and often make reference to the Athenian contempt for labour, the reality of Athens suggests that a very contrary attitude is also at work. No culture in which the working class has the kind of political role the 'banausics' played in Athens—a role in many ways unequalled in most, if not all, modern democracies—could have retained such contempt for the labourer. The attitude expressed by Protagoras (or even Pericles), who, if Plato's testimony is to be believed, affirmed the fundamental capacity of shoemakers and smiths for politics, is clearly more typical—if the realities of Athenian political life were not enough to prove that Plato's view is a *class* prejudice and not a cultural ideal.[54]

It is one thing to say that everyone, landowner and labourer alike, regarded a life of leisure as preferable to a life of toil; it is quite another to suggest that the kind of contempt for the *banausos* expressed by Plato and his fellow-aristocrats was a universal cultural prejudice. Whatever the average Athenian may have thought about a life of poverty and labour, the political role of the *banausos*—even the wage-labourer or the landless *thes*, who was often a casual labourer—indicates a very different attitude from one which relegates the working classes to a sub-human status virtually devoid of reason and moral worth. One need not glorify a life of labour, which the Athenians certainly did not, to recognize the labourer as a fully rational and moral being, qualified for access to the political realm and self-rule. It is important to distinguish in Greek attitudes between a recognition of the woes of labour or the pleasures of leisure—an attitude that was no doubt widespread—and an aristocratic contempt for the labourer and his moral capacities. The conventional attitude toward labour among the common people of Athens is probably reflected in the ethic of craftsmanship, the concept of *techne*, the emphasis on the technical arts and skills, as the mainsprings of civilization, which figure so prominently in the writings of the democratic age.[55] It is also worth noting that the Greeks appear to have been the first to rescue craftsmen from anonymity, in sharp contrast to the great civilizations of the Near East and Asia.[56]

It may even be necessary to qualify somewhat the commonplace that the Greeks were careful to distinguish between dependent and independent labour and that, even if contempt for labour was only a class prejudice, contempt for dependent labour was universal. To begin with, it must be said that for aristocrats like Plato, Xenophon, and Aristotle, *all* necessary labour was dependent; in their eyes, anyone who was compelled to earn a livelihood, even the independent craftsman, was dependent on others, if only to buy his wares. As for the labourers themselves, no doubt they all preferred to be independent and would perhaps work as casual labourers rather than 'take even a black-coated job as a regular employee . . .';[57] but this 'contempt' for dependence, in contrast to the aristocratic disdain of Plato or Xenophon, does not constitute contempt for labour as such. In fact, there is a sense in which the opposite is true. The scorn for dependence felt by a labouring man who may at the same time have taken pride in his work was, in the democratic climate of Athens, as much an assertion of his freedom from those above him as contempt for those below; and it expressed what in the historical context was a fairly revolutionary idea: that labour need not be, as aristocrats like Plato would have it, by definition dependent and servile. In any case, Athenians did take jobs as regular wage-earners and this did not prevent them from being full citizens. In this sense, whether a man was considered 'free' enough to be permitted to participate in self-rule did not depend on whether he worked for himself or for another man.

Not only did Athens grant full political rights to the 'banausic' classes, it encouraged their participation by payment for attendance at assemblies and juries as well as the theatre, which might be called a school of politics;[58] and these classes eventually achieved a remarkable degree of power—to the extent that critics of Athenian democracy created the myth, which has survived to this day, of Athens' decline into 'mob rule'. It is also worth noting that the Athenians were so consciously protective of the status accorded to labourers, so wary of the aristocratic attitude, that they instituted slander laws to punish insulting references to a person's trade.

The significance of the polis may be obscured in part by the reluctance of certain social historians to speak of the ancient world in terms of *class* at all. It is sometimes argued that, while class analysis suits the conditions of modern capitalism, it is inadequate to the realities of, say, classical Greece or Rome; and in such cases it becomes necessary to recognize other social categories, such as 'order' or 'estate' and 'status'. These arguments, however, are often beside the point. Even the existence of other social classifications does not necessarily render the category of class less essential; indeed, it may be that these other categories cannot themselves be understood except in light of class.

Certainly the significance of Athenian social structure and the role of the polis, not to mention the meaning of philosophies of the polis, is obscured if we refuse to recognize the truly fundamental importance of class.

A brief examination of one such treatment of class by a major social historian in a recent study of ancient Greece and Rome may serve to illustrate our point. In *The Ancient Economy*, M. I. Finley writes:

> Half a century ago Georg Lukács, a most orthodox Marxist, made the correct observation that in pre-capitalist societies, 'status-consciousness . . . masks class-consciousness'. By that he meant, in his own words, that 'the structuring of society into castes and estates means that economic elements are *inextricably* joined to political and religious factors'; that 'economic and legal categories are objectively and *substantively so interwoven as to be inseparable*'. In short, from neither a Marxist nor a non-Marxist standpoint is class a sufficiently demarcated category for our purposes. . . .[59]

Other terms must be found, then, to deal with the various legal, political, and religious categories that 'mask' class-consciousness and sometimes overlap each other, as well as the less clearly defined social distinctions of inferiority and superiority within these categories. Finley accordingly identifies two systems of social classification which he regards as most relevant to the situations of ancient Greece and Rome: *order* and *status*. An order or estate Finley defines as:

> . . . a juridically defined group within a population, possessing formalized privileges and disabilities in one or more field of activity, governmental, military, legal, economic, religious, marital, and *standing in a hierarchical relation to other orders*. Ideally membership is hereditary, as in the simplest and neatest ancient example, the division of the Romans in their earliest stage into two orders, patricians and plebeians. But no society that is not wholly stationary can rest on that simple level, especially not if, as was the case in Rome, there was no way to replace a patrician house that lacked male heirs.[60]

In addition to the early Roman division of the population into patricians and plebeians, he cites as examples of classification into orders the Solonian system of economic 'classes', and even the distinction between citizens and non-citizens. *Status* is a less clearly defined category, 'with a considerable psychological element',[61] not necessarily corresponding to explicit legal boundaries or to class, encompassing various distinctions of rank which have no juridical standing but which are nevertheless socially recognized. In Roman or Greek society, for example, at a time when noble birth no longer carried exclusive legal standing and when the *class* of large landed proprietors was no longer coextensive with the nobility, the nobility was still recognizable as a distinct status group. In Greece, argues Finley, largely because of the development of democracy, there occurred the most complete shift from orders to status-groups, that is, from rigid legal classifications and restrictions to vague social distinctions.[62]

There is no need to quarrel with Finley's introduction of these categories into an analysis of Greek society, since they obviously played a recognizable role in the social structure of the ancient world. Lukács' point is undoubtedly well-taken. It is Finley's treatment of *class* and the relationship between class and other social categories which is inadequate, suggesting, perhaps, that he has ignored some of the implications of Lukács' remarks. For example, Lukács goes on to say: 'This is not of course to deny the objective economic foundations of social institutions. On the contrary, the history of [feudal] estates shows very clearly that what in origin had been a "natural" economic existence cast into stable forms begins gradually to disintegrate as a result of subterranean, "unconscious" economic development. That is to say, it ceases to be a real unity. Their economic content destroys the unity of their judicial form.'[63] In other words, at the very most, status-consciousness merely 'masks' class-consciousness; it does not erase the objective reality of class or its fundamental influence on status itself, nor is the 'mask' sufficient to preserve the integrity of a social category that has ceased to correspond to 'subterranean' economic realities. Indeed, Lukács' very language demands that we look beneath the mask for the underlying reality. The present argument goes somewhat further than Lukács, however, in attributing an 'unmasked' class-consciousness to the Greeks, perhaps because unlike Lukács, we do not assume that large numbers of Athenian citizens took no part in the economic life of the community and in the productive process. This is an important disagreement because according to Lukács, the failure of class-consciousness 'to achieve complete clarity' in pre-capitalist societies is explained by the fact that class interests in such societies 'never achieve full (economic) articulation'; and (again according to Lukács) in Greece this failure to achieve full articulation is in great part due to the total independence of a large portion of the population from the economic life of the community.[64]

Finley quite rightly criticizes modern historians who assume the existence of the same class divisions in the ancient world as prevail in a capitalist, market economy, so that they feel compelled to assume, for example, 'that there must have been a powerful capitalist class between the landowning aristocracy and the poor'.[65] An error of this kind, however, cannot be attributed to an emphasis on the concept of class as such. If anything, the kind of dynamic historical perspective that Marx's analysis of class entails is the best antidote to this sort of ahistoricism. Oddly enough, Finley's own failure to deal adequately with the concept of class and to put it into some kind of perspective in relation to other social categories may itself result from a certain lack of historical perspective. Although he obviously hesitates to argue that the concept of class has no relevance to the ancient world (in other works—such as *The World of Odysseus*—he makes illuminating use of it), he has very little to say about the class structure of Rome and even less of Greece, except to point out that *order* and *status* do not coincide with class, as if this were enough to indicate the relative insignificance of class divisions. A historical perspective, however, immediately makes it plain that neither order nor status can be understood in isolation from class.

Finley's discussion of the Roman orders illustrates the point perfectly. In his account of the changes that the simple division between patricians and plebeians underwent, he seems almost unconsciously to demonstrate how the system of orders gradually adapted itself to changes in the underlying economic realities and class relations. As Rome grew, 'The original patrician–plebeian dichotomy had lost its relevance.'[66] The new senatorial order, now the highest, was increasingly plebeian. Surely it is impossible to deny that this change, this 'irrelevance' of the old division, was a consequence of its growing lack of correspondence to basic economic realities and the new class divisions to which these realities gave rise—the most obvious expression of which, as Finley himself suggests, was the emergence of rich plebeians. Surely the fact that, though 'The patriciate continued to exist for centuries thereafter, . . . its practical significance was soon reduced pretty much to certain priestly privileges and to ineligibility for the office of tribune, . . .' is not unrelated to the fact that the patriciate no longer had a monopoly of economic power. The legal, religious, and political categories with which the class divisions were 'inextricably interwoven' had a certain life of their own and tended to develop and proliferate to a certain extent by their own momentum, even contributing to the shape of economic categories; but they could not remain intact when they ceased to correspond to economic realities. If they survived, it was in severely restricted, even superficial, sometimes ceremonial, form, their important practical functions gradually taken over by new and more 'relevant' categories. The somewhat vague 'status' of the nobility in democratic Athens was also a survival of an earlier class division between a rigidly exclusive hereditary leisure class of large landowners and a mass of labouring peasants, herdsmen, craftsmen, and dependent labourers. When economic realities demanded that wealth in general and landownership in particular become less restricted and the nobility began to lose its character as a distinct class, surviving as a status group, it also began to lose its relevance as a separate social category, with fewer and fewer definable privileges, duties, and distinctive characteristics. Being a large landowner, noble or not, was more important, more relevant, than being a noble.

If there is a time lag—sometimes a very great one, as has been the case also in more recent times with the modern British aristocracy, for example—between changes in class relations and changes in 'status' and 'orders', and if non-economic categories have a way of surviving and proliferating on their own, there can be no doubt that ultimately their character and importance are inextricably linked to the underlying class realities. If class in the ancient world cannot be understood in isolation from political, religious, and legal categories that do not directly correspond to class, it is even more true that these categories cannot be understood apart from class. Nor would it suffice to say that class, order, and status are coequal and overlapping categories; since, while there is no direct correspondence between class on the one hand, and order and status on the other, and while order and status may contribute to the shape of class, the relation of these non-economic categories to class is too much that of 'dependent variables' to an 'independent variable'.

To argue that class is the ultimate social category in a stratified society is not to suggest that human motives are largely economic. For that matter, to speak of class as an economic category is not necessarily to suggest that class interests are purely economic. In order to appreciate the significance of class, the simplistic economism of classical liberal economics must be avoided;[67] and this kind of economistic reductionism can perhaps best be avoided simply by beginning with a definition of 'economic' that is not itself simplistic and reductionist. 'The substantive meaning of economic,' writes Karl Polanyi, 'derives from man's dependence for his living upon nature and his fellows. It refers to the interchange with his natural and social environment, insofar as this results in supplying him with the means of material want-satisfaction', the means of maintaining his physical existence.[68] If such a definition of 'economic' is kept in mind, Marx's concept of class, for example, can be better appreciated. According to Marx (and Polanyi), man enters into a relation with nature in order to obtain the means of sustaining his life, and he enters into relations with other men in the process of deriving his livelihood from nature. The most basic social divisions are those that are most immediately related to this most basic process of sustaining human life, those that express most immediately the 'interchange' with the natural and social environment through which man obtains the means to maintain his existence. Needless to say, different societies at different stages of history are characterized by different modes of sustaining human life, different kinds of relations to nature and among men; and within each society, each mode of sustaining life, different groups of men will—once a social division of labour evolves—occupy different positions in the fundamental process of obtaining the means of existence. *Class*, where it exists, is the category of social stratification that is most immediately determined by the 'mode of production' which supplies the means of existence, and by the relations among men that characterize that mode. There can be social classifications, even divisions of labour, without class. Class is a category of stratification, which emerges out of the social division of labour that is *hierarchical* and exploitative, that is, when the division of labour takes the form of differential relations to the means of production permitting certain social groups to exploit the labour of others. Where it exists, this kind of stratification, which is a direct expression of the hierarchical social division of labour, underlies other systems of stratification; and even systems of classification that do not directly reflect the process of production and have a certain life of their own are ultimately dependent on and conditioned by the social divisions that do directly reflect that process, as Lukács' observation, cited above, suggests.

The nature of class divisions will, of course, vary according to the particular mode of production, just as the nature of any particular class will vary according to both the mode of production and the specific role in the process of production—particularly the 'relationship to the means of production'—occupied by that class, as well as the specific nature of the means of production to which the class is 'related'. The class division is the ultimate category of stratification—where recognizable social stratification exists—because it reflects the ultimate fact of human life, the necessity of maintaining life itself; but while the process of maintaining life itself must necessarily condition all aspects of life, it obviously does not exhaust all human endeavour. Moreover, 'economic' drives, in the broader sense, need not be 'economic' in the narrow sense.

It is characteristic of pre-capitalist societies, according to Polanyi and others, that the production and distribution of material goods is not generated—as it is supposed to be in market economies—by the motive of gain, that is, by the 'economic' motive in the narrow sense of liberal economics. The process of supplying material needs is '*ensured by non-economic motives*'.[69] To point out the 'non-economic' basis of pre-capitalist economic systems is, however, not to deny that the ultimate divisions in these societies are those most immediately related to the process of sustaining life, the process of production, or that various non-economic categories that shape the complex network of social relations are ultimately grounded in that process and the class relations that have emanated from it. It may even be true that in all societies,

> Purely economic matters such as want-satisfaction are incomparably less relevant to class behavior than questions of social recognition. Want-satisfaction may be, of course, the result of such recognition, especially as its outward sign or prize. But the interests of a class most directly refer to standing and rank, to status and security, that is, they are primarily not economic but social.[70]

It nevertheless remains true, as even Polanyi's language suggests, that class is the vehicle of these non-economic drives. Where men are divided into classes by their mode of sustaining life, it is through class and in reference to it that they generally seek 'rank', 'standing', 'status', and 'security'; at the very least, the obstacles to the achievement of these goals and the means of achieving them will vary according to class.

To return, then, to Finley's argument on the role of class in the ancient world, it ought to be clear that the existence of other social categories in no way renders the concept of class less essential. A more serious question, which is implicit in Finley's remarks on the relevance of class to the Greek situation, arises from the dissociation of citizenship from class in Athens. On the face of it, if the most explicit divisions of the population, those with the most obvious consequences—the distinctions between citizen and non-citizen, free man and slave—do not correspond to class or to the social division of labour, it would appear that the class division is of secondary importance. Yet it is precisely here that the crucial importance of class becomes most evident. Again, it is a question of looking at the situation historically. It is useless simply to isolate the relationship—or apparent lack of it—between citizenship and class that prevails in the democratic age from the *process* of dissociation that led to it. Viewed in isolation, the independence of citizenship from class in democratic Athens appears to indicate the relative unimportance of class. Seen as a process, the product of a development, even a struggle, that led from the perfect coincidence of class division and political hierarchy in Homeric Greece to the dissociation of class and citizenship in democratic Athens, that dissociation proves the vital importance of class in the social life of Athens. The dissociation of citizenship from class—indeed, the principle of citizenship itself—was clearly the consequence of a challenge by subordinate classes to the exclusive power of the ruling class, associated with the changes involved in the transition from an *oikos*- to a polis-economy. The gradual dissociation of political rights from class and the social division of labour hardly proves the insignificance of the latter. On the contrary, the elaboration of the political principle itself and the principle of citizenship transcending class boundaries was a response to the social division of labour and the conflicts arising from class divisions. The polis with its principles of citizenship and law was a way of dealing with class divisions and the social cleavages brought about by the hierarchical social division of labour—and a radically new and unique way of dealing with what was, and still is, a universal social problem. Again, what is most significant from our point of view about this new method of dealing with class relations is that, by beginning to dissociate political power from the social division of labour, it was beginning to attack the very principle of a hierarchical social division of labour. In all other advanced civilizations, state power was a means of coercing and controlling dependent labour and maintaining the social division between leisured masters and labouring servants.[71] The polis, therefore—particularly in its democratic form in which the dissociation of political power from class had progressed the farthest—represents something very new in class relations and a significant victory for subordinate classes, undermining a traditional instrument of class domination. It is an achievement that cannot be imagined without a considerable degree of class-consciousness, a fairly developed perception of common interests and a common class enemy, on the part of the subordinate classes as well as on the part of their rulers. In that sense, the lack of coincidence between class and citizenship in democratic Athens represents a triumph of class-consciousness, not a proof of its absence.

If the process of dissociation did not progress to the point of abolishing slavery, it can perhaps be argued that it went far enough to undermine the traditional justifications of slavery. In a sense, the Athenian principle of citizenship with its tendency toward equality carried at least a certain intellectual momentum that in principle would eventually have to encompass slavery. As we have seen, the distinction between slave and free labourer was very hazy in the Homeric consciousness; they shared the essential inferiority associated with a life of labour. The democratic polis invented a labourer with a new status and in general challenged the very principle of social hierarchy. Again, even the sharp conceptual and legal difference between free labourer and slave in democratic Athens in a paradoxical way indicates progress in the status of the labouring classes and a tendency toward social equality. Although that tendency was never realized in Athens and the polis continued to be marked by the guilt of slavery, perhaps it was necessary that the tendency should work itself out in the 'realm of the spirit'; and it can hardly be an accident that it was Athens which articulated the revolutionary idea that inequality is a convention and not a natural condition, and that the subjection of any man, including a slave, is not justified by any law of nature or dictate of the gods.[72]

At any rate, it is difficult to see how the significance and uniqueness of the polis can be explained without reference to class. Certainly, it is impossible to deal with the reforms of Solon and Cleisthenes, the politics of the democratic age, the conflicts between the aristocratic–oligarchic party and the democrats, without referring to class relations; and the philosophies of Plato and Aristotle are unintelligible in abstraction from those relations. Finley himself provides an example of how the import of Plato's philosophy, for instance, can be misunderstood if one fails to take careful account of the realities of class in his time. Speaking of the idea, which he argues is practically universal in the ancient world, that wealth is an absolute requisite for the good life, Finley writes:

> There were exceptions. Socrates went so far as to suggest, in his own way of life, that wealth was neither essential nor even necessarily helpful in achieving the good life. Plato went further, at least in the *Republic* where he denied his philosopher-rulers all property (along with other normally accepted goods).[73]

This is a rather misleading account of Plato's ideas, especially in light of his extremely forceful attack on the moral and political capacities of the poor and the labouring classes. It is, of course, possible to say that, strictly speaking, wealth is not a condition for the good life according to Plato; but it is not wealth as such that is at issue. For Plato, as many others who *do* extol wealth, it is freedom from labour and the right to command and live on the labour of others that is the fundamental social condition for the good life. If that freedom can be achieved without wealth—as Plato fancifully proposes in the *Republic*—all well and good; but the most practical way to achieve it is the traditional aristocratic hereditary monopoly of land and dependent labour, and in the *Laws* Plato substitutes this less fanciful solution to the problem dealt with in the *Republic*. As we shall see in the chapter on Plato, he makes it very clear that the system of exclusive and hereditary landownership in the *Laws* is the next best thing to the ruling class 'communism' of the *Republic*, and certainly the more practical of the two, and that both systems are intended to serve the same purpose. For the aristocrat, unlike the bourgeois, it is not wealth as such which is the condition for superiority, not earned wealth or wealth acquired by 'banausic' means, but hereditary landed wealth that implies freedom from labour or vulgar trade. Viewed in the context of aristocratic values and the conflict between the traditional landed aristocracy and the commons, the logic of Plato's argument becomes clear and his 'communism' is recognizable as an idealized expression of aristocratic values, not a revolutionary attack on the importance of wealth.[74]

5. *The Aristocratic Myth of the Polis*

To return, then, to our search for the 'essence' of the polis, it does not seem excessive to argue that its most unique and significant characteristic is its treatment of the social division of labour and class relations and the status it accords the labourer. If the principle of citizenship is regarded as central to the polis, it must be recognized that the most radical consequence of this principle, its most innovative departure from other known forms of social organization, is its extension in democracy to the labouring classes—the perfection, as it were, of the citizenship principle, the culmination of the polis' attack on the hierarchy of the traditional state. It is strange, therefore, that this aspect of the polis, far from being recognized as the essential significance of that unique form of association, is so often treated more as an aberration, a corruption of the polis, even by the greatest admirers of Athens. There often appears to be a tendency to share Plato's prejudices and to admire Athens only insofar as she satisfies those prejudices. A great deal has been written about the corruption of Athens, her descent into 'mob rule', as the polis became more democratic and as aristocrats, like Pericles himself, ceased to dominate; while democratic Athens is often praised precisely for her *aristocratic* character. Like Thucydides, many modern admirers appreciate the democracy only insofar as it was bogus, a democracy in name only, a democracy in which the people allowed themselves to be led by their 'betters'. It often appears that the more democratic Athenian democracy became, the more it departed from its 'essence'.

Oddly enough, even Ehrenberg, one of the most eloquent proponents of the view that democracy is the realization of the polis, seems to share this attitude:

> When the masses were no longer led by aristocrats but by men of their own stamp, the standards of 'the people', that is to say of its majority of *petits bourgeois*, became predominant and general. A people,

however, of 'small officials and cunning beggars' (Aristophanes, *Frogs*, 1084), a people distinguished by economic egotism, narrowness of outlook and good-natured love of pleasure, will never create true and eternal things, either in the political or spiritual field. It will make no decisive difference if this people is excited by its leaders to fanatical devotion or outrage. The peasants and artisans, merchants and workmen represent an often pleasant and lovable part of the people, but they were and are unable to maintain and carry on the traditions of a great past. This can only be done by the famous 'creative minority', an aristocracy of intellect and morals, an upper class, not mere individuals, of a higher level of intellectual and moral education. It is the undying merit of democracy to have found the means for the necessary aristocracy to receive continually new blood from the whole people, and at the same time to have controlled this aristocracy by public opinion.[75]

This kind of attitude seems to be at the root of several conventions that are often encountered in modern images of Athens. Ehrenberg, again, expresses a view which, though not always so clearly stated, is at least implicit in many accounts of Athens' decline. For Ehrenberg, the decline of the polis took the form of a 'great change . . . , the change from a political to an economic outlook, from the political consciousness of a citizen to the economic purpose of an individual human being. . . . Social life became private life, the patriotism of the citizens became the egotism of class-conscious individuals.'[76] This transformation of 'political man' into 'economic man', this degeneration of public-spirited citizen into class-conscious egotist, according to Ehrenberg, accompanied the increasing dominance of the middle and lower classes:

> The fact that the policy of Athens was made by men whose life was not characterized by the passive ownership of property, but by the constant activity of earning—this fact shows unmistakably the process by which the Polis and its citizens, no matter whether they belonged to the rich or to the increasing number of the poor, came more and more under the influence of economics. The nature of Athenian economics, on the other hand, was determined by the insignificance of practically all financial questions. The general standard of life was that of a modest middle-class, and no capitalism disturbed its moderate character. Property and work, not capital, were the basis of economic activity, money was scarce and prices were generally low. Men's outlook was dominated by small-scale activity which resulted, on one hand, in the modesty and frugality of Greek life, on the other in a greedy desire for wealth and an almost complete lack of social conscience.[77]

Ehrenberg's formula does, of course, contain an important truth which has been emphasized by certain economic historians, notably Karl Polanyi: namely, that archaic economies differ from the market economy of the capitalist era in that—to use Polanyi's language—the economy is 'embedded' in society, and production and distribution of material goods, the fulfillment of 'economic' needs, the needs of physical survival, and want-satisfaction are 'ensured by non-economic motives'.[78] It is only in the market economy that an 'economic system', 'economic laws', and an 'economic' motive can be isolated. Only in a market system—a system in which 'the production and distribution of material goods in principle is carried on through a self-regulating system of price-making markets', a 'disembedded economy' 'governed by laws of its own, the so-called laws of supply and demand, and motivated by fear of hunger and hope of gain',[79] in which labour-power becomes a market commodity subject to those same laws—does the 'economy' as a distinct set of relationships and laws, with motives unique to it, come into its own.

In this sense, the economy of ancient Greece has no life of its own, and no purely 'economic' motive can be isolated. Modern capitalist notions of market laws, the primacy of the acquisitive drive, the identification of human rationality with market calculation and the maximization of profit, are not very useful in explaining Greek society. To this extent, Ehrenberg (like others, including Ernest Barker and M. I. Finley) is identifying a real phenomenon when he suggests that Athens during its Golden Age subordinated economics to politics; and to the *very* limited extent that the growing importance of commerce meant the emergence of a rudimentary market mechanism, he is probably correct to suggest a difference between the earlier and later stages of Athenian history with regard to the status of 'economics' as Athens changed from a society dominated by a landed aristocracy to a society in which traders and labourers played an increasingly important role.

There is, however, more to Ehrenberg's remarks. The emphasis in his discussion of the emergence of 'economic man' is on the *moral* transformation this represents for him, the transformation of the public-spirited citizen into the class-conscious and materialistic egotist and the corruption of the polis-principle which is the inevitable consequence of this moral transformation. This aspect of his argument, whatever truth there may be in his remarks about the changes in the role of the 'economy', simply cannot be sustained and reveals a remarkable blind-spot in an otherwise useful analysis. It is a blind-spot he shares with many classicists who make so much of the corruption of Athens, and it is reflected most dramatically in Ehrenberg's opposition of Plato's 'absolute politics'—the union of politics and ethics—to the 'economic desires of the lower classes'.[80] The implication of this opposition is that Plato's politics and the 'economic desires of the lower classes' represent polar opposites on the continuum from 'public-spirited citizenship' to 'class-conscious and materialistic egotism'. There is no hint, for example, of the possibility that this 'absolute politics' may represent, not the opposite of class-conscious egotism, but the idealization of a different class interest, opposed to that of the lower classes and characteristic of a different kind of 'economy' from that which promoted the rise of the lower classes.

If the 'economic' motive—narrowly defined—was born out of the rise of commerce or a market economy, class interest as such certainly was not. The 'economic' motive is not the only possible expression of class interest, nor does the denigration of the 'economic' motive necessarily represent the absence of 'egotism' and class-consciousness. We may turn again to Polanyi to clarify this point:

> *Services, not goods, make up wealth in many archaic societies. They are performed by slaves, servants, and retainers.* But to make human beings disposed to serve as an outcome of their status is an aim of political (as against economic) power.[81] With the increase of the material against the non-material ingredients of wealth, the political method of control recedes and gives way to so-called economic control. Hesiod, the peasant, was talking thrift and farming centuries before the gentlemen philosophers, Plato and Aristotle, knew of any other social discipline than politics. Two millennia later, in Western Europe, a new middle class produced a wealth of commodities and argued 'economics' against their feudal masters, and another century later the working class of an industrial age inherited from them that category as an instrument of their own emancipation. The aristocracy continued to monopolize government and to look down on commodity production. Hence, as long as dependent labour predominates as an element in wealth, the economy has only a shadowy existence.[82]

In short, the class interest of an aristocracy whose wealth and status consists in its command of land and dependent labour will clearly express itself differently from the class interests of those whose status depends on wealth in goods and the ability to *buy* labour-power, or those whose livelihood depends on their own labour. Aristocratic class interest, however, if it is not typically characterized by the 'economic' motive in the narrow sense, is no less 'class-conscious' or 'egotistic' or 'materialistic'—and, for that matter, no less *economic* in the broader sense. The nature of class interest is, needless to say, relative to the particular nature of the class in question and to the kind of economy that sustains its dominance. Aristocratic interests lie in the maintenance of dependent labour and 'non-economic' powers of exploitation for those who command labour, usually by means of a hereditary monopoly of the best land, a rigidly hierarchical social division of labour, and highly exclusive social power based on a deep cleavage between labouring and non-labouring conditions. The fundamental principles of aristocratic class interest are all expressed, as we shall see in Chapter IV, in the 'absolute politics' of Plato. In any case, whether or not one accepts the suggestion that Plato's 'absolute politics' represents an idealization of aristocratic class interest, the fact remains that such a class interest did exist, even if, for obvious reasons, it did not typically express itself in the way that Ehrenberg attributes to the lower classes.

Although Ehrenberg does not quite explicitly, or perhaps even consciously, identify aristocratic values with public-spirited citizenship (indeed he considers himself a great admirer of democracy) his elaboration of the opposition between 'economics' and 'politics' clearly implies this kind of identification. He seems to recognize as an expression of class interest only the 'economic' motive of bourgeois greed or the labourer's preoccupation with his livelihood and the efforts of these classes to defend their respective interests, while he refuses to recognize aristocratic interests for what they are. He admits the existence of class struggle, but only insofar as it relates to conflicts within the non-aristocratic classes as they become more clearly differentiated into bourgeoisie and proletariat; and while he is quite ready to attribute to the bourgeoisie a class interest in the oppression of the lower class, he fails to recognize a similar interest in aristocrats like Plato. In Ehrenberg's case, the problem is not a refusal to recognize the importance of class in ancient Greece—on the contrary, he places considerable emphasis on it, especially in his account of Athens' decline; instead, there is a peculiar kind of aristocratic blindness that makes only bourgeoisie and proletariat appear as classes driven by class interest. It would appear, then, that these classes, according to his argument, are by nature anti-'political'. 'Politics', the ethic of citizen and polis, must lie elsewhere than in the class-conscious 'economics' of the 'pleasant and lovable' peasants, artisans, merchants, and workmen. At the very least, his view is clearly that 'economics' increasingly supersedes 'politics' as the middle and lower classes cease to be led by their aristocratic 'betters' and as their culture increasingly puts its stamp on the polis.

The contention of this book, of course, has been that politics in the special Greek sense which Ehrenberg has in mind was *produced*, not destroyed, by the self-assertion of these classes against their aristocratic 'betters'. It can be argued that the very idea, as well as the reality, of civic-mindedness and public-spiritedness were creations of the demos in its struggle against its aristocratic rulers, while particularism and class-'egotism' were typical of the Athenian aristocracy. If, as Polanyi argues, an aristocracy uses political power 'to make make human beings disposed to serve as an outcome of their status', if the state with its administrative apparatus and its institutionalized methods of coercion was created as a means of sustaining the power of an aristocratic ruling class over dependent labour, then the polis and politics in the specific Greek sense (especially as they developed in Athens) may be said to represent a new kind of political power, a countervailing power, the political response of the non-aristocratic classes to the 'politics' of the aristocracy. The assertion of the community principle against the particularism of tribe and class, and the concomitant rise in the status of the individual, both of which are inherent in the principle of citizenship, were essential weapons in the struggle of the demos against its hereditary rulers.

We have already noted the importance of tribal principles for the aristocracy and its reliance on the particularistic allegiances of clan and friendship-group in the struggle to maintain class dominance, in contrast to the attacks on tribal principles by the democratic reformers. W. R. Connor has shown how the aristocratic clans, ostensibly based on blood relationship, 'were groups formed to look after common interests, in effect privilege groups'.[83] The ties established by these clans or 'privilege groups' were extended by exogamous marriages, and class interests further were served by powerful friendship-groups which also helped to unite members of the upper class into a more cohesive political force. Aristocratic 'politics' was anti-communal, anti-political, both in its ends and in its means, and the idea of obligation to the community as a whole was foreign to the aristocratic code with its emphasis on loyalty to kin, class, and friends—loyalities that were difficult to dissociate from one another as kinship and friendship ties became the instruments of aristocratic class interests.[84] No doubt the subordination of the city to family and friends was still part of the conventional morality of Athenians in general in the fifth century. As A. W. H. Adkins points out, the picture of the *agathos polites*, the good citizen, derived from the literature of the age suggests that he is

> ... a self-sufficient unit, able to defend both himself and his friends, and harm his enemies; as a paterfamilias, able to protect his children, his property, and his wife; and when it is threatened by an external enemy, able to defend his city. The city's claims *may* override others in times of stress; but where the city's interests are not threatened, or seem irrelevant to the case in hand, there is nothing in these standards of value to prevent the *agathos polites* from attempt-

> ing to thwart the laws of the city on behalf of his family and friends, with whom he has closer ties.[85]

The significant point, however, is that while aristocratic interests continued to depend on the strength of these particularistic ties and their assertion against the community as a whole, it was the democrats who developed a notion of civic-mindedness according to which the polis and the demos were granted the status formerly accorded only to friends and kinsmen, apparently in a conscious effort to attack the principles on which aristocratic dominance was based.

In a very significant passage cited by Connor, Herodotus provides a clue to the inseparability of democracy and the idea of civic-mindedness. Describing the unique method by which Cleisthenes gained power, Herodotus notes that 'he [Cleisthenes] made the *demos* his *hetairos*'.[86] In other words, unlike other powerful members of his class, Cleisthenes did not rely on his kinsmen or aristocratic friends to gain power, but was the first leader systematically to appeal to the people, making the *people* his 'friendship-group' or club. This was, of course, a very successful political technique, but it represents something more than a tactical innovation. As Connor demonstrates, Cleisthenes' political technique was the 'origin of a new kind of democracy, a new pattern of politics that was to become increasingly conspicuous as the century went on'.[87] This new kind of democracy, although it began with Cleisthenes' appeal to the demos, did not come to fruition until after the death of Pericles when aristocratic dominance effectively ceased. It was a democracy in which the people were more genuinely the source of political power than they were even during the 'Golden Age' of democracy dominated by aristocrats. The significant fact is that the appeal to the demos as the source of political power, rather than to aristocratic clansmen and friends, also meant the identification of the polis—the 'club' of citizens, as it were—(not the 'state', of course, which was an idea foreign to the Greeks, but the community of citizens), as the primary object of group sentiment commanding 'the kind of loyalty which was formerly promised to friends'.[88]

Certainly Cleisthenes was himself an aristocrat, but it is not the standards of the aristocracy that he brought to Athenian political life; indeed, he attacked those standards. It was the interests and values of the demos that found their expression in his reforms, and it was not until the people were led by men 'of their own stamp' that these new standards came to fruition. Only then were civic virtues given a high priority in the Athenian hierarchy of values. As Connor argues, these new virtues 'form both the natural culmination of a progression toward popular rule, and the essential preconditions for a successfully functioning democratic system'.[89] It was Cleon, the arch-villain of post-Periclean democracy to all its critics, who developed Cleisthenes' notion of 'making the demos his hetairos' and giving the polis a status formerly occupied only by family, friends, and class. Plutarch records an extraordinary anecdote about Cleon which, again, illustrates the close connection between democracy and the civic ethic:

> ... Cleon, when he first decided to take up political life, brought his friends together and renounced his friendship with them as something which often weakens and perverts the right and just choice of policy in political life. But he would have done better if he had cast out from his soul avarice and love of strife and had cleansed himself of envy and malice; for the city needs not men who have no friends or associates (*hetairoi*), but useful (*chrestoi*)[90] and sensible (*sophrones*) men. As it was, he drove away his friends. 'But a snake-like mass of flatterers writhed' [Aristophanes, *Peace* 756] about him, as the comic poets say; and being rough and harsh to the better classes (*epieikeis*) he in turn subjected himself to the multitude in order to win its favour—'The gerontagogue, donor of reiterated wages' [Anonymous fragment of Old Comedy, II]—making the most unpretentious (*phaulotaton*) and unsound elements his associates against the best (*aristoi*).[91]

What is significant about this anecdote (apart from Plutarch's revealing comments on it and what they tell us about the precise nature of Cleon's crimes) is the fact that it reflects an important new development in Greek political values. To quote Connor again:

> Now, in the Athens of Cleon's lifetime, affection for the city takes a new form. Its new expressions convey far more than the venerable feelings of homesickness or pious devotion to a founding and protecting city. The new terminology goes further, affirms loyalty to the city, and even implies that that loyalty is a requirement for political advancement. Thus is marks a new stage in the enunciation of Greek values. For before this time the Greeks had not often or clearly expressed, let alone resolved, the conflict between devotion to the city and devotion to a friend. The new vocabulary did not bring with it an automatic resolution to a persistent and difficult problem, but it did permit a new clarity of discussion and it did imply a new series of priorities. The politican who presented himself as *philopolis*, *eunous toi demoi*, *philodemos*, or the like, implied that he was willing to accord the city the place which friends had so often enjoyed in earlier periods of Greek history, and that he was willing to transfer his

> 'primary loyalties' from the *philia* group to the wider circle of the *polis* or the *demos.*[92]

It was precisely this attitude, this appeal to the demos and the claim of civic loyalty or polis-friendship, that the critics of democracy dismissed as demagoguery in the pejorative sense (almost as if the demos- or polis-lover was for the anti-democrat what the 'nigger-lover' is for the racist).

Ehrenberg suggests somewhere that the rhetoric of civic virtue grew as the reality declined; but this is not a satisfactory explanation of the evidence presented by Connor. There can be no denying the particularism of aristocratic allegiances throughout the 'Golden Age', nor was the claim of civic virtue ever really central to the aristocratic code. There was no shame in subordinating the polis and the interests of the community to one's friends or class; on the contrary, to do so was honourable and just. Athenian aristocrats—at least those who did not become and remain democrats—were never noted in practice for their loyalty to Athens, from the amoral Alcibiades to that paragon of gentlemanly virtue, Xenophon, and all the other friends of Sparta who by other standards could only be regarded as traitors to Athens. However imperfectly the democrats may have lived up to their civic values, these values were *theirs*; and it is one of the significant and exceptional innovations of Socratic doctrine to try to claim the civic ethic for the aristocracy. If there was, as some suggest, a decline in civic virtue and a growing 'lack of social conscience' in the fourth century—and the evidence is at best ambiguous—this cannot be attributed to some kind of class 'selfishness' peculiar to the ethic of the increasingly dominant middle and lower classes. The ethic of the upper class was always more anti-'political', and it was the anti-democrats who increasingly urged a withdrawal from politics after the apparently final defeat of the oligarchs. If anything, 'politics' in Athens was an expression of middle and lower class interests.

It is, in any case, not clear upon what kind of evidence Ehrenberg, and others who speak of the corruption of Athens or the decline of 'politics', are relying. Certainly the demos after the death of Pericles puts its stamp on politics in a way which it had never done during the aristocratic democracy of the Periclean age; but unless one identifies democratization or 'vulgarization' with moral corruption by definition, as Plato does, the evidence of a decline in political consciousness and civic virtue is far from unequivocal.[93] It is no doubt also true that in the fourth century the relatively homogeneous non-aristocratic classes began to differentiate, as Ehrenberg suggests, into a kind of bourgeoisie and proletariat, and that new class conflicts emerged from this differentation; but again, class conflict as such was nothing new, nor is it clear that the new conflicts were more destructive, more devoid of civic virtue, than the old struggles between the aristocracy (joined by elements of the 'bourgeoisie') and the commons that played such a crucial role in the continual strife between oligarchs and democrats, culminating in the Terror of the Thirty Tyrants, the finest hour of aristocratic class-consciousness.

Since one of the most obvious changes in Athenian political life after the Golden Age of Pericles, until the Macedonian conquest, was the declining influence of aristocratic culture, and since much of what we are told by historians who assure us of Athens' moral decline is simple assertion, it sometimes appears that we are to understand that moral decadence and the decline of aristocracy are self-evidently one and the same. There is no question that Athens had serious problems—economic, social, political—in the fourth century; but moral decay is another matter. In any case, it is useless to speculate about the degree of internal decay to which Athens might have been subject, since whatever promise Athenian democracy still held, whatever possibilities, good or bad, might have developed had Athens been left to herself, were brought to an abrupt end by the Macedonian conquest—cheered by many Athenian oligarchs. The important thing is to understand the degree to which the class interest and class-consciousness of the lower classes, whose ethic is often held responsible for the destruction of the glories of Athens, were in fact responsible for their creation, and to be a bit cautious about the aristocratic clichés that have become so much a part of classical scholarship.

The view that the nature of the polis is reflected in the ideas of Plato and Aristotle can perhaps be classed among these aristocratic clichés. Aristotle, whose concept of the polis is probably the most often cited statement of its essential nature, characterizes the polis as a unique form of association by contrasting its principles to those of the *oikos*. And yet, if the distinctive nature of the polis is indeed to be found in this contrast, Aristotle's idea of the polis is plagued with paradoxes.[94] It is the democratic polis, and not Aristotle's ideal city, which is arguably the most perfect contrast to the *oikos*, the most complete—if still very imperfect—denial of the hierarchy of the *oikos*, the relation between master and servant, the principle of rule and subordination which for Aristotle is essential to the nature of the household. And, in fact, despite Aristotle's emphasis on the distinction between *oikos* and polis, his insistence that the polis as an association of equals is not an *oikos* writ large, his ideal polis is certainly modelled on the *oikos*. The ideal polis adheres strictly to the essential division between its 'conditions' and its 'parts'—between leisured landowning citizens and productive subjects—a division which corresponds to that between household lord and his 'animate instruments', slaves. In the ideal polis as in the aristocratic *oikos*, there are means, animate and inanimate, which serve ends; and '... there is nothing joint or common to the means which serve an end and the end which is served by those means—except that the means produce and the end takes over the product'.[95] Like the household, the ideal polis is based on what for Aristotle is the most basic natural principle that in all things there is a ruling element and a ruled. In this respect, the polis is distinctive only in that it has a plural despot, permitting masters to leave behind their inferiors and meet their equals.

The distinction between *oikos* and polis has a more profound meaning as a democratic idea than as an aristocratic one, as a striving for equality among unequals and an effort to overcome the inequality of the master-slave relation essential to the household. In this case, the polis is distinctive only to the extent that productive classes are integral 'parts' of the polis. Historically it was certainly the democrats, impelled by the interests of the 'mob', who alone sought to organize the polis on principles different from those of the *oikos*, undermining the *oikos*-model of the polis, weakening its hierarchical structure as well as its kinship principles insofar as they supported aristocratic power, and opposing the 'isonomia' of the democracy to the 'eunomia' of the hierarchical *oikos*. To argue that the political theories of Plato or Aristotle represent the ideal of the polis, to contend that the productive classes have destroyed the political realm, to suggest that the civic spirit is lost in the vulgar materialism of the 'mob' and its petty preoccupation with daily needs, even to identify the aristocrat as 'political man' and the 'banausic' as 'economic man'—all this is, in effect, to take the *oikos* as the model of the polis and to deprive the Greek state of its unique significance.

Notes to Chapter II

1. Victor Ehrenberg, *The Greek State* (2nd ed.; London: Methuen, 1969), pp. 101–2.
2. *Ibid.*, p. 43.
3. If it is true that 'politicization and democratization' in Greece went hand in hand and that democracy is, as it were, the *telos* of the polis, we can perhaps be forgiven for concentrating almost exclusively on Athens as the model of the polis which best reveals the significance of that unique mode of social organization.

4. Cf. M. I. Finley, *The World of Odysseus* (New York: Viking, 1965), pp. 13–15.

5. *Ibid.*, p. 117.

6. Ehrenberg, *The Greek State*, p. 21.

7. *Ibid.*, p. 21.

8. See Ehrenberg, *The Greek State*, pp. 11, 20; and W. Robert Connor, *The New Politicians of Fifth-Century Athens* (Princeton: Princeton University Press, 1971), *passim*.

9. The contention that *thetes* had no political rights assumes, of course, that they were first admitted to the assembly by Solon, a fact which, if probable, is not absolutely certain.

10. Ehrenberg, *From Solon to Socrates* (2nd ed.; London: Methuen, 1973), p. 52.

11. There is some controversy about membership in phratries. For example, W. G. Forrest, in *The Emergence of Greek Democracy* (New York and Toronto: McGraw-Hill, World University Library, 1966), pp. 50–4, argues that non-aristocrats belonged to phratries; however, he agrees that the *clans* were aristocratic, that the *orgeones* were inferior groups, and that full citizenship before Solon was confined to clansmen.

12. Solon, of course, introduced a number of other equally important measures that are not immediately relevant to this discussion, notably his economic reforms which facilitated trade and commerce and his new law of inheritance.

13. A qualification must be added here. A man continued to belong to the same deme even if he changed his residence, and his descendants kept his *demotikon* wherever they lived. In this sense, kinship continued to play a role and locality lost some of its new importance. Ehrenberg's interpretation in *From Solon to Socrates*, p. 96, seems reasonable: 'If a man still belonged to his deme, no matter where he lived, the neighbourhood principle was no longer in full force, but neither had it been replaced by new bonds of kinship. If anything now counted beside the local principle, it was the individual citizen whose political activity had sometimes few ties left with any larger groups.'

14. H. T. Wade-Gery, *Essays in Greek History* (Oxford: Basil Blackwell, 1958), p. 154.

15. *From Solon to Socrates*, p. 93.

16. Karl Marx, and Frederick Engels, *The German Ideology: Parts I and II*, ed. R. Pascal (New York: International Publishers, 1947), p. 12.

17. This social type can, with certain qualifications, be equated with Marx's 'Asiatic mode of production', in its 'despotic' form. For Marx's most systematic discussion of this mode of production, see *Grundrisse: Foundations of the Critique of Political Economy* (Rough Draft), trans.

Martin Nicolaus (Harmondsworth: Penguin Books, 1973), pp. 472–4 (Notebook IV).

18. Hesiod, *Works and Days*, 205–10, *Hesiod and Theognis*, trans. Dorothea Wender (Harmondsworth: Penguin Books, 1973), p. 65.

19. Aristotle, *Constitution of Athens*, 2 and 5.

20. Antony Andrewes, *Greek Society* (Harmondsworth: Penguin Books, 1967), p. 118.

21. The latter two interpretations can be found respectively in Forrest, *op. cit.*, pp. 147–50, and Andrewes, *op. cit.*, pp. 116–17.

22. For a brief but very useful outline on the problem of alienability in ancient Greece, see M. I. Finley, 'The Alienability of Land in Ancient Greece', in his *The Use and Abuse of History* (London: Chatto and Windus, 1975), pp. 153–60.

23. *Constitution of Athens*, trans. and ed. Kurt von Fritz and Ernst Kapp (New York: Hafner, 1950), 2.

24. *From Solon to Socrates*, *op. cit.*, p. 57.

25. M. I. Finley, 'Slavery', *International Encyclopedia of the Social Sciences*, XIV, p. 308.

26. Finley, *The World of Odysseus*, p. 49.

27. Claude Mossé, *The Ancient World at Work*, trans. Janet Lloyd (London: Chatto and Windus, 1969), p. 111. Cf. A. H. M. Jones, who writes: 'During this period [the reign of Diocletian and thereafter] the social and legal status of slaves and free persons both on the land and in the state industries tended to be assimilated.' 'Slavery in the Ancient World', in *Slavery in Classical Antiquity*, ed. M. I. Finley (Cambridge: Heffer; New York: Barnes and Noble, 1968), p. 14.

28. Euripides, *The Suppliants*, 450, E. P. Coleridge translation.

29. Finley, 'Slavery', p. 308.

30. A. Winspear, *The Genesis of Plato's Thought* (New York: S. A. Russell, 1956), p. 36. 'When a social organization is devised,' writes Winspear, pp. 35–6, 'that will give absolute sanction and complete protection to the right of private and individual property, devising elaborate rules to protect a man's holdings against fraud and theft and individual violence, as well as against the organized protest of the poor and dispossessed, the state will be born.'

31. Cf. E. P. Thompson, *The Making of the English Working Class* (Harmondsworth: Penguin Books, 1968), pp. 9–11, 939.

32. *Ibid.*, pp. 9, 11.

33. The following account of Athenian social structure is based largely on the following works: Victor Ehrenberg, *The People of Aristophanes: A Sociology of Old Attic Comedy* (2nd ed.; New York: Schocken Books, 1962); M. I. Finley, *The Ancient Economy* (Berkeley and Los Angeles: University of California Press, 1973); A. H. M. Jones,

Athenian Democracy (Oxford: Blackwell, 1969); and to a lesser extent, the now somewhat outdated Gustave Glotz, *Ancient Greece At Work: An Economic History of Greece from the Homeric Period to the Roman Conquest*, trans. M. R. Dobie (New York: Norton, 1967), first published in 1920.

34. Finley, *The World of Odysseus*, p. 49.

35. *Ibid.*, p. 70.

36. Finley, *The Ancient Econōmy*, p. 44.

37. Cf. Finley, *Ibid.*, pp. 138–9, and Karl Polanyi, *Primitive, Archaic, and Modern Economies: Essays of Karl Polanyi*, ed. George Dalton (Boston: Beacon Press, 1971), *passim.*

38. See Ehrenberg, *The People of Aristophanes*, *passim.*, for a discussion of the image of Cleon in Athenian comedy and the degree to which the comic exaggerations that turn the wealthy Cleon into a mere 'leather-monger' do actually reflect a social reality and a social consciousness in which Cleon and lesser producer-traders represent the same social type.

39. Cf. Finley, *The Ancient Economy*, p. 68; Ehrenberg, *The People of Aristophanes, passim.*, esp. chaps. V–VII; Jones, *op cit.*, pp. 10–18.

40. Cf. Finley, *The Ancient Economy*, p. 72; Ehrenberg, *The People of Aristophanes*, p. 183.

41. Finley, *The Ancient Economy*, p. 62.

42. Ehrenberg, *The People of Aristophanes*, p. 183.

43. *Ibid.*, p. 150.

44. *Ibid.*, pp. 161–2.

45. *Ibid.*, p. 162.

46. Finley, 'Slavery', p. 308.

47. The following discussion of women is based largely on Sarah B. Pomeroy, *Goddesses, Whores, Wives, and Slaves: Women in Classical Antiquity* (London: Robert Hale, 1975) and K. J. Dover, *Greek Popular Morality* (Oxford: Basil Blackwell, 1974). See also W. K. Lacey, *The Family in Classical Greece* (London: Thames and Hudson, 1968).

48. Pomeroy, *op. cit.*, pp. 61–2.

49. Cf. *ibid.*, pp. 57, 78.

50. *Ibid.*, p. 78.

51. *Ibid.*, p. 71.

52. *Ibid.*, p. 73.

53. Dover, *op. cit.*, pp. 209–11.

54. Of course, in the oligarchic cities, which in varying degrees restricted the political rights of craftsmen, labourers, and traders, sometimes prohibiting citizens from engaging in any occupation, the contempt for labour did more nearly approach a cultural norm—or, to put it

another way, in these cities, the class prejudice exemplified by Plato was that of the *ruling* class.

55. This point is discussed at greater length below, pp. 132–7 in connection with Plato's use of the concept of *technē*.

56. See Alison Burford, *Craftsmen in Greek and Roman Society* (London: Thames and Hudson, 1972), pp. 20, 212 ff.

57. Jones, *Athenian Democracy*, p. 11.

58. It must be stressed that such payments did not and could not support ordinary citizens in leisure, as is sometimes suggested. To quote *ibid.*, p. 18: 'political pay served only to compensate them in some measure for loss of working time'. Cf. Forrest, *op. cit.*, pp. 31–3; Ehrenberg, *The People of Aristophanes*, p. 231.

59. Finley, *The Ancient Economy*, p. 50.

60. *Ibid.*, p. 45.

61. *Ibid.*, p. 51.

62. *Ibid.*, p. 48.

63. Georg Lukács, *History and Class Consciousness: Studies in Marxist Politics*, trans. and ed. Rodney Livingstone (London: Merlin Press, 1971), p. 57.

64. *Ibid.*, p. 55.

65. Finley, *The Ancient Economy*, p. 49.

66. *Ibid.*, p. 46.

67. Cf. Polanyi, *op. cit.*, pp. 139 ff., for a discussion of the 'economistic fallacy', which consists 'in an artificial identification of the economy with its market form'. (p. 142 n.1).

68. *Ibid.*, p. 139.

69. *Ibid.*, p. 23.

70. *Ibid.*, p. 41.

71. In such states, even apparently free and independent labour—the labour of an independent 'petty-bourgeois' craftsman or artisan—often assumes the character of dependent labour, to the extent that surplus labour is extracted by the ruling class through rents, taxes, and so on, with the aid of its complete monopoly of state power.

72. The *nomos-physis* distinction elaborated by the Sophists is significant in this connection. One need only cite the example of the Sophist Antiphon who explicitly argued that all men—including non-Greeks—were essentially the same by *physis*, and unequal only by *nomos*, or Hippias, who explicitly questioned the rightfulness of slavery. As we shall see in Chapter IV, even the aristocratic Plato, who placed so much stress on inequality and attacked the Sophists for their tendency to attribute to mere convention the principles he preferred to regard as natural, did not escape the influence of the democracy and the intellectual climate that encouraged the Sophists. He, too, ascribes

a surprising degree of influence to social environment, education, and convention, rather than to nature, in producing inequalities.

73. Finley, *The Ancient Economy*, p. 36.

74. Indeed, the idea of 'communism', if this is not a completely inappropriate use of the term, was generally an aristocratic idea in [illegible] Glotz, *op. cit.*, p. 155.

75. Ehrenberg, *The People of Aristophanes*, p. 373. There appears to be some confusion in Ehrenberg's use of the word 'aristocracy'. Although he speaks of an 'aristocracy of intellect and morals', this passage clearly reveals that he has difficulty dissociating this 'aristocracy' from a particular economic class.

76. *Ibid.*, p. 72.

77. *Ibid.*, p. 252.

78. See above, p. 60.

79. Polanyi, *op. cit.*, p. 81.

80. Ehrenberg, *The People of Aristophanes*, p. 68.

81. The word 'political' is, needless to say, being used in a broad sense to refer to *state* power in general. 'Politics' in the particular Greek sense, referring to the unique life of the polis, is a special kind of political power, in a sense exercised to *resist* the kind of power Polanyi is describing.

82. Polanyi, *op. cit.*, p. 93.

83. Connor, *op. cit.*, p. 11.

84. See below, Chap. IV, for a discussion of the view of justice as 'helping your friends and harming your enemies', expressed by Polemarchus in Plato's *Republic* and rejected by Socrates, a rejection which his aristocratic friends would find incomprehensible. It will be argued that one of the more noteworthy accomplishments of Socratic philosophy was to transform the civic ethic from a democratic into an aristocratic idea.

85. A. W. H. Adkins, *Merit and Responsibility* (Oxford: Clarendon Press, 1960), p. 231.

86. Herodotus, 5.66, quoted in Connor, *op. cit.*, p. 90.

87. Connor, *op. cit.*, p. 90.

88. *Ibid.*, p. 100.

89. *Ibid.*, p. 106.

90. The word *chrestoi*, like so many other Greek moral terms, refers also to a *class*. The *chrestoi* are not simply 'useful' men; they are gentlemen, the upper classes.

91. Plutarch, *Moralia*, 806–7, quoted in Connor, *op. cit.*, pp. 91, 93.

92. Connor, *op. cit.*, pp. 105–6.

93. For some more balanced attempts to assess the evidence of 'decline', see Finley, *Aspects of Antiquity* (New York: Viking Press,

1969), pp. 55–88; A. H. M. Jones, *op. cit.*, esp. ch. III; Claude Mossé, *Athens in Decline*, trans. Jean Stewart (London and Boston: Routledge and Kegan Paul, 1973). W. K. Pritchett's *The Greek State at War* (Berkeley, Los Angeles, and London: University of California Press, 1974), 2 vols., also sheds light on some of the so-called examples of Athenian moral decay, such as the trials of generals, the alleged dishonesty of officials and the shirking of civic and military duties by citizens in the fourth century. M. I. Finley's 'Athenian Demagogues' in *Studies in Ancient Society*, ed. M. I. Finley (London: Routledge and Kegan Paul, 1974), pp. 1–24, is a particularly useful corrective to the highly misleading picture of these democratic leaders painted by many historians. See pp. 2–4, above, and pp. 111–15, below, for brief discussions of the 'decline'.

94. One particularly ingenious and very recent version of the aristocratic myth, which is based on this distinction between *oikos* and polis, appears in the political theory of Hannah Arendt, who argues that 'politics' has been destroyed by the intrusion of the labouring masses into the public realm. Her case is particularly interesting because she supports her comment on the condition of modern man with a completely mythical conception of the polis, according to which true 'politics' *did* exist in Athens, allegedly because the labouring masses were virtually *excluded* from the 'political space'. The corruption of politics occurred primarily in the modern age, particularly with the French Revolution.

95. Aristotle, *Politics*, 1328a.

III

Socrates: Saint of Counter-Revolution

Far from being a detached, disinterested, and transcendent seeker after truth, Socrates appears to have been a political partisan. To affirm this is neither to belittle him nor to denigrate his philosophy, but to enrich our understanding of his intellect and his intellectual activity, and perhaps of the philosophic enterprise in general. Political partisanship in a broad sense would often seem to be the necessary stimulus and condition for meaningful philosophic enquiry. The two are complementary rather than incompatible. Without Socrates' initial political commitment, some vision of the well-ordered polis, there perhaps would have been no Socratic philosophy. His partisanship apparently provided the impetus and canalized the intellectual energy of his philosophic quest, giving it form, structure, and coherence. Moreover, as we have argued, in a wider sense no philosophy, much less that of Socrates, can escape the influence of society, nor can it be analyzed adequately without full recognition of this fact.

Our thesis, therefore, is that Socrates held a particular political perspective or ideology that can be isolated, described, and analyzed in terms of what little we know of his life and social connections within the historical context of ancient Athens. Moreover, his broad philosophic recommendations concerning the questions of definition, knowledge, and soul, far from being non-partisan and doctrinally pure, are permeated and shaped by elements of his political ideology. If we grant—and few dispute it—that Socrates was an important founder of Western philosophy, then it would seem that philosophy at its very source was ideologically motivated and fashioned. A demonstration that the first philosophy is fundamentally ideological may suggest something of significance about the nature of the philosophic enterprise as it subsequently developed, namely that 'non-political' philosophy may be ultimately ideological and firmly anchored in the political.

In the course of this chapter we wish to establish in two stages the close connection between Socrates' socio-economic position and his political and philosophic ideas. First, we wish to dispel the commonly accepted view that he was a man of the people. If our thesis is correct then Socrates by birth, education, marriage, and income (at least originally) probably belonged to the upper forty percent of the Athenian citizen-body. His intimates, friends, and associates were largely of exalted status; and he had little in common with the life experience of the ordinary Athenian. Second, in view of this hypothesis we find it interesting that his political and philosophic ideas are what common sense would lead one to expect from one of his upper-class affiliations. His political and philosophic stance was by no means an independent one inimical to all existing social groups, but very definitely favoured the aristocratic-oligarchic classes against the values and interests of the lower classes. However, it should be emphasized that our argument is neither predicated upon nor concerned with the crude notion that class and status rigidly and permanently determine the political and intellectual outlook of the individual. Rather, we are proceeding from the common-sense proposition that ideas, to be fully understood, should be considered in the social context in which they are conceived and with reference to the audience to which they are addressed. The nature of the relationship between ideas, on the one hand, and social context and audience on the other, will vary, of course, with different thinkers. In Socrates' case, or so we shall argue, the ideas are remarkably reflective of their context and the audience to which they are addressed.

Before turning to a consideration of Socrates' life, his intellectual context, political ideology, and philosophic recommendations, a general word about method is necessary. It should be emphasized that the Socrates with whom we shall be dealing is the thinker presented by Xenophon in the *Memorabilia* and particularly by Plato in the early so-called 'Socratic dialogues', especially what was perhaps the first, the *Apology*, and the following: *Crito*, *Laches*, *Euthyphro*, *Charmides*, *Ion*, *Protagoras*.[1]* Our generalizations about the opinions of the literary Socrates have been derived primarily from these writings. Reference will also be made to several later works—*Gorgias*, *Meno*, *Euthydemus*,

* Notes for this chapter begin on p. 115.

Phaedo, *Symposium*, *Phaedrus*—largely to confirm conclusions reached on the basis of Xenophon and the early Socratic dialogues, to indicate continuity between the thought of Socrates and Plato, and to suggest how some of Socrates' notions reached fruition in the hands of Plato. Although Xenophon probably scarcely knew Socrates, his portrait does not appear to contradict on any relevant or essential points the characterization of Plato. The *Memorabilia* is part of a literary tradition to which contributions were made by Themistus, Cebes, Phaedon, Aristippus, and Aeschines of Sphettos; and their Socrates tends to confirm the delineation of Plato and Xenophon. At any rate we have relied more upon Plato as a source than Xenophon, and have judged the account in Aristophanes' *Clouds* to be an unreliable caricature.[2] For those who might wish to distinguish the 'real Socrates' from our literary figure, the burden of proof is upon them, since as we shall see, the positive historical evidence is limited to a scant number of rather meagre facts.

1. *Life and Associates Reconsidered*

Most of what can legitimately be said about Socrates' life is the result of informed inference and conjecture and the critical examination of various traditions. Our purpose is not to provide a reassessment of all the evidence available for constructing a convincing account of the life of Socrates. Nevertheless reasonable biographical inference and conjecture must be separated from the less reasonable if his teaching is to be examined in its proper context. We wish mainly to dispel one of the less reasonable assumptions about him. In our opinion he was not 'a man of the people', a 'proletarian' of the lowliest social origins—one tradition is that he was actually a slave. The evidence seems strongly against the view that he came from a poor and humble home and lived in poverty throughout his life.

All we know with absolute certainty about Socrates is that he was an Athenian citizen of the deme of Alopeke, son of Sophroniscus and Phaenarete, who probably participated in some military campaigns during the Peloponnesian War and in the trial of the generals of 406 BC, and who was tried, condemned to death, and died in 399 BC. The only evidence for the story that his father Sophroniscus was a stonemason or sculptor is the references in Plato to Daedalus as his ancestor,[3] and the fact that many stoneworkers lived in Alopeke, which was on the route to the quarries of Pentelicon. That Socrates followed in his father's footsteps, learning the trade at an early age, if indeed Sophroniscus was a sculptor, is only a conjecture based upon the Greek tradition of the son plying the craft of his father. Indeed, Plato, Xenophon, Aristophanes, and Aristotle never refer to either father or son as artisans. Sophroniscus had possibly married above his station, for Phaenarete, a midwife (evidently not in any professional sense), seems to have been of good family. He appears to have been a respected man of some substance in his deme of Alopeke, as is indicated by the statement in the *Laches* that he was on good terms with his fellow demesman, Lysimachus, son of the famous Aristides the Just,[4] an affluent aristocrat supposedly connected with the wealthiest family of Greece, that of Callias, and his son Hipponicus, also of the same deme.

From Plato and Xenophon we learn that Socrates questioned and talked extensively with artisans.[5] But if in fact he had been a stonemason or sculptor or trained in any craft it is truly surprising that Plato records his remark about discussions with artisans: 'I knew quite well that I had practically no technical qualifications myself. . . .'[6] Moreover, it is puzzling that in Xenophon's description of his visit with Cleiton the sculptor, no mention is made of the fact that Socrates had himself been a sculptor or stonemason, or the son of one, had this indeed been the case; nor is there any word of this in the reference in Plato's *Symposium* to his association with another sculptor, Apollodorus of Phalerum.[7] Xenophon also refers to Socrates' visits with Parrhasius, a distinguished painter who wrote on the subject; with Pistias, an armourer, and an unnamed saddler.[8] Although never substantiated by Plato or Xenophon, according to a later tradition Socrates was also a friend of Simon the shoemaker who knew Pericles. All these craftsmen must have been fairly well-to-do hoplites. None of the testimony suggests that Socrates attempted to 'convert' such citizens or bring them as active participants into his circle, that he numbered them among his intimates, with the possible exception of Apollodorus, or that he counted *thetes* and wage-labourers among his friends and acquaintances. If Aristophanes' burlesque of Socrates in *Clouds* at all reflects the attitude of ordinary Athenians, then the philosopher was clearly neither respected not esteemed by the lower classes some twenty years before his trial, nor did he seem to have very much in common with them. Of course, it can be argued that his constant concern with the nature of *technē*, and his application of the idea to statecraft, stemmed from his early background and training as a craftsman. But an inhabitant of Athens, regardless of class or status, could hardly avoid using the language of craftsmanship, so important and pervasive were the crafts and craftsmen in the life of the polis. More important, as we shall see in the case of Plato, Socrates used the notion of *technē* in opposition to the direct democracy of an artisan populace by showing that statecraft was a highly skilled specialty only capable of being mastered by a small, refined, and educated elite. In other words Socrates used the idea of craft to betray craftsmen, an odd, although not impossible, position to be taken by a former craftsman.

Other grounds exist, however, for asserting that Socrates was probably not of the poor and needy and that he had little sympathy for or understanding of them. After receiving the customary basic education in gymnastic and music, he most likely became a student of the successor of Anaxagoras in Athens, the physicist and biologist, Archelaus, who is credited with originating the antithesis between *physis* and *nomos*. Upon his master's retirement, Socrates may even have succeeded to the headship of the 'school', achieving something of a reputation prior to the outbreak of the Peloponnesian War, i.e., before he reached the age of forty. If this is a true account, then he obviously possessed the funds and leisure to devote his life to the pursuit of philosophy, to pay the fees charged by one of the most illustrious teachers of the age, and to support himself and later his wife without charging fees himself. Had he been a penniless proletarian it is also difficult to understand how late in life, probably in the 420s, he could have married a much younger woman of superior social status like Xanthippe. Her aristocratic origins are suggested not only by her name, but also by the name of their eldest son, Lamprocles, and that of the youngest, Menexenus. The second son was named after the paternal grandfather, Sophroniscus.

However, more significant testimony for the estimation of Socrates' socio-economic position is Plato's report that he served in the hoplite class during his last active military engagement in the Battle of Delium of 424. Little has been made of this important fact. Socrates' service with the hoplites meant that his property had been assessed at over twenty minae, that he had provided his own weapons and armour, and that he had been accompanied on the campaign by an attendant (a slave if he possessed one or a young relative) to carry his food and kit. Therefore, at least at the time, he was not a member of the *thetes*, the Athenian masses who numbered about sixty-percent of the citizen body and manned the navy. The *thetes* were the Athenian people, *hoi polloi*, consisting of a very few extremely modest property-holders, many small artisans, and a larger number of casual labourers. Whether Socrates suffered personal loss in the financial crisis of 415 can only be guessed. Whatever happened, his poverty depicted both by Xenophon and Plato evidently occurred only about 424 or afterwards and seems to have been self-imposed, probably the consequence of his intellectual crisis and philosophic 'conversion' sometime during the period. Nothing said by the two authors implies that Socrates had always been poor, or that his poverty was anything more than a consequence of self-renunciation.

If Plutarch's story of the opinion of the late fourth-century Peripatetic, Demetrius of Phalerum, is credible,[9] Socrates possessed a house and capital of seventy minae that was invested by his friend Crito, a wealthy fellow-demesman and exact contemporary. Such an account, for what it is worth, enables us to locate Socrates with much greater precision in the Athenian social structure, at least about 424. Provided his dwelling is valued at about a minimum of twenty minae, his total worth approximated ninety-minae or the not inconsiderable amount of one and a half talents (thirty minae to a half-talent). Hence, Socrates could very well have been among the upper fifteen percent of the citizens, but well below the richest class, an elite of about five percent.

Regardless of the validity of Demetrius' contention related by Plutarch, Socrates was most likely neither of a poor family nor a working-class member of the Athenian masses, and prior to 424 if not later he must have been able to live quite comfortably. Such an image is supported by the fact that the overwhelming number of his friends and associates, mentioned by Plato and Xenophon, were apparently of the aristocratic-oligarchic classes in Athens. Most certainly Socrates could afford a life of poverty among such friends, for they were from among the wealthiest families. The majority were an elite of wealth and influence, interlocked by relations of blood and marriage, centring upon the families of two of his most notable companions, Alcibiades and Plato.

While the Socratic circle included some who were neither wealthy nor noble, the aristocratic-oligarchic group of friends and associates seems to have formed some kind of continuing nucleus. Unless he was saying things they wished to hear, Socrates could hardly have attracted over the course of many years such a following of the rich and well-born, young and old. His practical advice and comments on Athenian affairs must have proved congenial to the considerable number among them who were of the conservative anti-democratic opposition, in order to have sustained their interest and friendship. Although he no doubt never headed a political party of the kind that had proliferated during the Peloponnesian War among those of the aristocratic-oligarchic classes who were attempting to subvert Athenian democracy, evidence exists that the circle of friends was to some extent institutionalized. Plato in the *Apology* portrays Socrates as explicitly denying that he was ever a member of a secret society or political party.[10] Nevertheless, the *Memorabilia* contains two allusions to common meals of some of the associates, including Alcibiades and Plato's cousin Critias, leader of the Thirty Tyrants, evidently meeting periodically and presided over by Socrates.[11] These occasions cannot be counted as party meetings. They did, however, provide a regular forum for the exchange of politically conservative and anti-democratic ideas. To Athenian democrats who had suffered through the counter-revolutions of 411 and 404–3 these gatherings of upper-class neighbours of the deme of Alopeke must have had somewhat sinister undertones.

2. *The Intellectual World of the Sophists*

Before turning to the political ideology of Socrates, we must attempt to place him in the intellectual context of the times by discussing his relationship (and Plato's) to the Sophists and their teachings. A convenient way to begin is with the characterization of Socrates in Aristophanes' comedy, *Clouds*, apart from the portraits of Plato and Xenophon the only extant contemporary account of the philosopher, actually written long before his death and produced in 423 BC. Aristophanes' Socrates is an obvious caricature, quite different from the figure described by Plato and Xenophon, one designed to typify and ridicule the Sophists in general and appeal to the audience by expressing what appears to have been a popular Athenian attitude toward the sage. Socrates was perhaps selected for the role of the Sophist because of all the intellectuals and teachers of the period in Athens his appearance, conduct, and style of life were best known to ordinary theatre-goers. The Sophists as personified by Socrates are a miserable lot: poor, filthy, dishevelled, and barefoot. Unlike the Socrates of Plato and Xenophon the Sophist of *Clouds* is primarily interested in astronomy and meteorology, a researcher in the natural sciences who for payment also teaches the art of persuasion to be used by the wrong-doer for convincing others that he is in the right, and who is an impious disbeliever in the traditional religion and its gods. Sophists according to Aristophanes are no more than charlatans corrupting the youth of Athens by a verbal sleight of hand into thinking that justice is a mere fiction and law an arbitrary convention and that respect is owed to no authority, to neither parents nor elders. Although Socrates may be maligned by Aristophanes, most of the characteristics attributed to him could be found among his contemporary intellectuals. Moreover, the play serves to present the conflict between generations, between the traditional system of education with which Aristophanes and the elders of his audience evidently sympathized and the new educational prescriptions of the Sophists that threatened to captivate the young. Although only a small fraction of Athenian youth were actually educated by Sophists—children of the wealthy classes—there was a widespread fear among elder citizens that the few who had succumbed to the blandishments of these intellectual impostors would set a bad example, exercising a pernicious influence upon the vast majority. Of marked concern to Aristophanes and probably his audience in general was the Sophists' neglect of physical training and health; their 'moral nihilism' which undermined traditional beliefs, sacred custom, received opinion, and authority; and their innovations in music. In another play, *Knights*, presented the previous year and unlike *Clouds* a great success, Aristophanes had launched a spiteful attack upon the popularly supported new self-made men of politics in the person of Cleon and had clearly drawn the connection between the subversive doctrines of the Sophists and these upstart 'demagogues'. Sophistic ideas and political demagogy were, from Aristophanes' vantage-point, mutually sustaining causes of the corruption of the traditional values and venerated way of life in Athens. Much later in *Frogs* (405 BC), which features a contest between Aeschylus and Euripides, the former stands for the old heroic order responsible for Athenian greatness, and the latter represents the way of things and is clearly linked with the Sophists and blamed for the decline of the polis.

While the Socrates of Aristophanes is most probably historically inaccurate and obviously differs from the hero of Plato and Xenophon, it is of exceptional interest for our purpose that he should be used to symbolize the Sophists; for the playwright had perhaps fortuitously and for the wrong reasons correctly associated Socrates with Sophism, an association that few since have been ready to admit. We shall argue that in certain respects the intellectual perspective of both Socrates and Plato was deeply rooted in Sophism, despite their adoption of the name 'philosopher', or lover of wisdom, to differentiate themselves from the Sophists whom they viewed as the fifth-column of the polis.

The Sophists were teachers and writers who began to appear in the Greek world in mounting numbers from the middle of the fifth century evidently in response to the increasing demand for the advanced education of the youth of well-to-do families. Travelling from polis to polis, tutoring and lecturing for fees on general cultural matters and more specialized subjects, in particular the art of rhetoric and oratory, they tended to gravitate to Athens, forming an intellectual community somewhat comparable to the *philosophes* of the eighteenth-century enlightenment. Among the most renowned and earliest was Protagoras of Abdera, the friend and adviser of Pericles. An agnostic, Protagoras was famed for his dictum: 'Man is the measure of all things'. Unfortunately all that remains of his voluminous writings and those of the other Sophists are a few fragments and second-hand accounts of their lives and doctrines. Other notable early Sophists include the brilliant rhetorician, Gorgias of Leontini; Prodicus of Ceos, a perceptive student of language; Hippias of Elis, whose encyclopedic interests were legendary; and Thrasymachus, a principal participant in Book I of Plato's *Republic*. Although much abused, largely on the basis of the oversimplification and distortion of their views particularly at the hands of Aristophanes and Plato, some of the early Sophists were democratic defenders of the Periclean regime and theorists of a pragmatic politics of consensus. Unlike the pre-Socratic philosophers they were less concerned with cosmology and the natural world, directing their efforts to moral and social problems. They developed a naturalistic explanation of man, society, and religion that entailed a conception of cultural evolution embodying a primitive notion of progress and a conventional theory of language. Ethically, they were often relativists; and epistemologically, subjectivists. The early Sophists were followed by a second generation including Lycophron, a formulator of the idea of the social contract; Critias, the urbane litterateur and uncle of Plato; the possibly fictional Callicles, a student of Sophism, used by Plato in the *Gorgias* to represent the radical Sophists' view of justice as the right of the strongest; so-called 'Anonymus Iamblichi', who argued against the radical Sophists that the source of power is in community consensus; Antiphon, the first exponent of the inherent equality of all men, Greek and barbarian; and Alcidamus, the champion of the natural freedom of men. Nor in such a catalogue should one fail to mention the great atomist Democritus, primarily a natural philosopher and not a Sophist, influencing them perhaps in a long life devoted to science and moral reflection.

From our standpoint the most significant contribution of the Sophists was the creation of a radically new intellectual genre, what we would call 'political theory'. Without some conception of man—not necessarily in terms of an abstract inborn essence or human nature—the enterprise of political theory is out of the question; and the Sophists were the first to formulate both: they discovered 'human nature' and thereby were able to invent political theory. Rejecting the age-old Greek intellectual preoccupation with the nature of nature and natural phenomena, they concentrated upon the question of man in society. Their discovery of human nature and the innovation of political theory arose out of the controversy over *nomos* and *physis*. Traditionally *nomos* was a social category, referring to customary law, to the values and way of life of a people. As such the *nomoi* of a polis were thought to constitute divinely ordained, immutable, absolute moral standards, existing as it were by nature. *Physis*, on the other hand, denoted the essential, underlying stuff of natural phenomena that explains change, but itself was changless. Since the early seventh century and the speculations of the father of Greek philosophy, Thales, thinkers had given different explanations of *physis*, some arguing like Thales himself for a single substance, others for a plurality, culminating in the atomism of Leucippus and Democritus. In the latter half of the fifth century, there arose on the isle of Cos a famous school of medicine under the direction of Hippocrates. Among the many writings of the Hippocratic school is an extant treatise, 'On the Nature of Man', that reflects the endeavours of these pioneer medical scientists to define a physical essence or *physis* of man. The early Sophists, possibly influenced by these medical investigations, became concerned not so much with the physiological make-up of man as with his *physis* in a psychical and spiritual sense, and in so doing hit upon the idea of 'human nature'. About the same time, perhaps as a result of travel accounts such as those of Hecateus and Herodotus, and increased exposure of the Greeks to strange and exotic peoples due to commercial expansion, intellectuals were becoming aware of the rich variety of cultures with values often in direct opposition to each other. Consequently the *nomoi* of a particular polis no longer were thought of as sacrosanct and absolute canons of morality since approved conduct in one locality was taboo in another. *Nomoi* began to be conceived as conventions, not necessarily arbitrary, but originally devised by a people out of self-interest, for their security and well-being, and varying from polis to polis. *Nomos*, as convention, could thus be distinguished from *physis*.

So there developed among the Sophists not only the idea of cultural and ethical relativism, but also a number of different conceptions of human nature and of political theories, depending upon the way *nomos* and *physis* were defined and related to each other. Protagoras, for example, seems to have held that man possessed a fairly malleable nature to be shaped by *nomoi*. He viewed the democratic polis as a great school for moulding the citizenry from the cradle to the grave into cooperative, law-abiding, cultured, and virtuous human beings. In contrast Thucydides the historian, not a Sophist but influenced by their doctrines, believed that man by nature was selfish, power-seeking, and anarchic. Hence the peace and order of the polis depended upon draconian measures to curb that volcanic nature from erupting and producing violence and chaos. Although Thrasymachus and the radical Sophists as typified by the Platonic Callicles shared such a view of human nature, they parted company with Thucydides in their claim that *nomoi* were simply artificial obstacles to self-realization. The best polis, then, would be one in which the strongest ruled unfettered by law. Antiphon and Alcidamus disagreed with Thrasymachus and the radical sophists as to human nature, accepting, however, their conclusion that law was an unnatural impediment to human self-fulfillment. But the reasons given were different. For Antiphon *nomoi* were conventions that prevented the fruition of a basic natural equality, and for Alcidamus they hindered natural freedom. With Socrates and in a much more refined form with Plato, we find a position almost diametrically opposed to that of Protagoras. They maintained that man possesses an ideal nature that should be in harmony with the nature of the cosmos.

Laws should be true to that nature by promoting its self-realization and its harmony with the cosmos, unlike the actually existing situation.

In addition to creating a novel man-centred mode for intellectual discussion in the form of the idea of human nature and the genre of political theory, the Sophists also instituted within that mode a unique framework of discourse, one devoted to the question of moral norms. Ironically, Sophistic teaching must have influenced Socrates' quest for moral absolutes and Plato's attempt in the *Republic* to formulate a new moral code. The practical universality and absoluteness of moral norms had in fact long been undermined as, first, the consensus of the primitive community gave way to class divisions, and then the unchallenged dominance of aristocratic values fell before the fifth-century democratic challenge to the political hegemony of the nobility itself. Without this very concrete attack on the practical foundations of a universal morality, there would, of course, have been no need to raise the question on the theoretical, philosophical plane. In this sense the historical situation itself, since the reforms of Cleisthenes and the rise to power of the demos, made the question of ethical norms a problem for theoretical enquiry. It was the Sophists who first explicitly recognized and articulated the demands of the new historical circumstances, who first stated the problem and made the examination of moral norms a matter for philosophical analysis, a subject for rational discourse and argumentation. They pioneered bringing to human social life and the norms by which it was conducted the spirit of investigation hitherto reserved in Greek thought for the non-human universe.

Socrates and after him Plato, therefore, were responding both to the historical situation that had undermined the practical universality of the traditional aristocratic social norms and to the Sophistic statement of the problem, employing the theoretical framework developed by the Sophists to deal with it. Undoubtedly an innovation, Socrates' definitional search for moral absolutes helped determine Plato's novel path to the world of transcendent ideal forms. But the originality of the efforts of Socrates and Plato should not obscure the singular inventiveness of the Sophists who established the ground-rules for Socratic philosophical endeavours. As innovative as Socrates and Plato certainly were, their philosophy was undeniably shaped by the necessity of meeting the Sophists on their own ground. Furthermore, although Plato's thought owes much to other philosophic approaches—notably that of the Pythagorean and Eleatic schools—his interlocutors are often Sophists or their pupils. Not only the substance of Plato's argument and what we can conjecture about Socrates' views, but also their style of presentation, their method, and the reasoning adduced in support of their philosophic principles, are clearly dictated by the Sophistic approach, its rationalism, humanism, and naturalism.

Moreover, it perhaps can be argued that Socrates and to a greater extent Plato are in a sense extending and revising for their own purposes the anti-democratic arguments of some of the Sophists against the views of Protagoras. Thrasymachus' argument in Book I of the *Republic* is sometimes treated as a democratic one, or at least as an argument typical of the moral climate of democratic Athens. In a very general sense it is, of course, true that all Sophistic doctrine—whether in its democratic or anti-democratic form—is an expression of democratic culture. Again, the very necessity of *arguing* about moral norms, the very fact that morality has become a subject for rational discourse, can be attributed in great part to the democratic challenge to the unquestioned norms of an unchallenged ruling class. As for Thrasymachus himself, as long as he confines his efforts to a kind of sociological realism, stating simply that in every society the values of the ruling class tend to be the dominant norms, his argument that 'justice is the interest of the stronger' is at least neutral to democracy. At most, it recognizes the claim of the demos, like any other class, to establish its norms as universal where it is the ruling class. However, to the extent that Thrasymachus' argument takes the form of espousing the 'moral' principle that might makes right and approaches the superman philosophy of Callicles, it becomes an aristocratic-oligarchic argument, perhaps a modernized and extreme version of the heroic ethic, if we accept Adkins' suggestion: 'Scratch Thrasymachus and you will find King Agamemnon.'[12] Certainly, with its principle of rule and subordination, it is an aristocratic-oligarchic principle insofar as it applies to relations among citizens, even if the democratic imperialists accept it as the rule in relations among states; or as Barker has observed: 'It was, indeed, the affinity between oligarchical opinion and the teaching of the radical Sophists which brought the Sophists into such disfavour with the Athenian populace.'[13] Professor Guthrie also remarks that the prohibition against appeals to 'unwritten law', instituted by the restored democracy in the wake of the oligarchic coups, was directed specifically at the views of those who, like Callicles, claimed the authority of the 'law of nature' and the right of the strong in order to justify tyranny by the few. For the democrats, writes Guthrie, '... positive, written law appeared as a safeguard against the return of tyranny or oligarchy based on the new conception of "nature's law". The latter was perforce unwritten and so, finally, the concept of "unwritten law" took on a sinister meaning and was banished from the modern, more nearly egalitarian society.'[14]

The argument of Protagoras is much more obviously a democratic one. His view that moral norms are conventions generated by the collective wisdom of the community, in conjunction with his position that political virtue is universal, that even the most ordinary citizens can and must partake of the virtues necessary to the life of the polis, suggests that democracy is the most viable and stable form of polis. It is the democratic polis in which the norms of the community represent the most direct expression of the collective wisdom and the participation of all men in political virtue, the polis that most closely approximates to the social consensus that gives moral principles a practical universality, the only possible universality. The doctrines of Callicles, and to a lesser extent Thrasymachus, appear to be aristocratic-oligarchic responses to the democratic implications of Protagoras' argument, deliberate attempts to adapt Sophistic doctrine to the interests of the aristocratic-oligarchic party and to provide a new kind of support, in the Sophistic manner, for the old principle of rule and subordination. If Sophism in its Protagorean origins is a democratic doctrine in which the view that morality is merely conventional is used to attack the aristocratic principle of rule and subordination, later Sophism is often an attempt to turn the same idea *against* democracy. Seen against this background, Plato's philosophy can perhaps be regarded as a step beyond aristocratic Sophism, an attempt to correct the deficiencies of its excessively relativistic support of aristocracy, while still in many ways remaining locked into the framework of discourse established by the Sophists. Like Callicles, Plato looks to *physis*—albeit with a new ethical meaning—for a natural principle of rule and subordination and rejects the rule of law to the extent that it acts as an equalizer.

In summary, therefore, it is not too wide of the mark to refer to Socrates and Plato as Sophists from a number of standpoints. First, like the Sophists they focused their intellectual attention upon man and human society rather than upon nature and the cosmos. Second, as was true of the Sophists, they were concerned with human nature, with the spiritual and psychical *physis* of man. Third, they adopted and developed the Sophistic invention of political theory by relating *nomoi* in the form of laws and social institutions to the problem of the self-fulfillment of the ideal human *physis* as they defined it. Fourth, they adapted for their own purposes the general conceptual framework of discourse of the Sophists in respect to moral norms. Finally, their attacks upon democratic Sophists like Protagoras utilized in a more complex and sophisticated fashion the arguments of radical anti-democratic Sophists like Thrasymachus and Callicles. This is not to say that Socrates and Plato did not go far beyond the Sophists or differ from them in many ways. But at least there seems to be greater justification for such an interpretation than E. A. Havelock's labelling the Elder Sophists as

'Socratics' in the sense that their lives coincided with the career of Socrates, that their ideas competed with his, and that any historical consideration of them necessitates thinking of Socrates and Plato.[15] On the contrary it was the Sophists to whom Socrates and Plato were responding, and who so fundamentally influenced the direction, style, and 'ground-rules' of their philosophic enterprise. Quite properly, then, we should not be able to discuss Socrates and Plato without placing them in the intellectual context of Sophism.

3. *Anti-Democratic Political Ideology*

Socrates' political ideology can be characterized as a deep-rooted anti-democratic sentiment compounded from a number of elements, beginning with a basic antipathy to politics in any conventional sense. Apart from service with the Athenian forces in three major military engagements, involvement in two brief political episodes, and his own trial of 399, Socrates did not apparently participate actively in the public life of his polis. As we have seen, he denied belonging to any of the clubs or parties so much a part of the aristocratic-oligarchic milieu of his day. Both Plato and Xenophon record his ready admission of refusing to engage in politics.[16] Nevertheless in the *Gorgias* Socrates likens himself to a 'doctor' of the polis striving to make the Athenians better citizens,[17] announcing that he is 'one of very few Athenians, not to say the only one, engaged in the true political art, and that of the men of today I alone practice statesmanship'.[18] Although Socrates was highly critical of Athenian politics and politicians,[19] he did praise politics and the art of statecraft in principle.[20] He evidently believed that true mastery of politics depended upon self-mastery in the form of temperance and moderation,[21] and Xenophon suggests in this sense that his master prepared his young friends for the political arena, an educational enterprise not to be confused with the Sophist's instruction in the art of rhetoric.[22]

Plato's explanation in the *Apology* helps clarify these thoughts of Xenophon. In the first place, Socrates claims not to have taught the youth of Athens anything. He never had regular pupils so he could not be blamed for how his friends turned out.[23] In the second place, he elucidates his failure to be a participant in politics by saying that his private oracle or sign always prevented him from engaging in such activity, adding that it is just as well for if he had he would have perished long ago.[24] This is a reflection he repeats when toward the end of the dialogue he confesses to being 'too strict in my principles to survive' a life of political involvement.[25] Anyone standing for right, he affirms, must act privately because he cannot go to war with the Athenian people and survive.[26] Previously, he had remarked that the nature of his mission was that of a gadfly to stir into life the great steed of Athens, not by speaking in the Assembly, but by privately questioning fellow-citizens.[27] At the end of the dialogue his meaning is more apparent. There he contends that he has acted for the greatest good of all citizens by going among them as individual to individual in order to persuade them to search for virtue and wisdom and to consider the true nature of the polis and of politics before turning to the pursuit of private interests and public concerns.[28]

Socrates' intention now becomes clearer. Like many of his aristocratic-oligarchic associates he rejects Athenian democracy, together with its ideals, institutions, and procedures. More importantly, he discards its very foundation; the pragmatic politics of equality, common-sense, and consensus, so extolled by Pericles, Protagoras, and probably by Democritus. The politics of Athens, as he sees it, is very simply a false politics premised upon the invalid assumptions of equality and the sovereignty of opinion instead of an absolute standard of right and the axiom of natural inequality. In its place he seeks to substitute what he feels to be the true elitist politics of right, not, however, by the direct political action that assuredly would lead to the destruction of himself and his rich and noble friends as betrayers of democracy and democratic values. Instead he chooses withdrawal from the politics he detests and that threatens all he cherishes, prudently recognizing that he can be far more effective by quietly working for the 'moral regeneration' of the more affluent and less hostile citizens. This last point requires emphasis for neither Xenophon nor Plato offer any very convincing evidence that Socrates tried to work among the lower classes or to convert any individuals among them to his point of view.

Socrates' anti-political position conforms to the behaviour so perceptively described by Connor as characterizing many members of the Athenian aristocratic-oligarchic classes in reaction to the new style of politics beginning after Pericles' death in 429 and continuing with Anytus through Socrates' last years.[29] The new politicians so different from Pericles and his predecessors were not aristocratic land-holders, but largely *nouveau riche*, wealthy middlemen and manufacturers who, priding themselves upon plain speaking and lack of decorum, jettisoned many of the traditional aristocratic social and political values. In the main they repudiated a politics based upon an interlocking network of friendship groups, the clubs or *hetaireiai*, used to such advantage by Pericles, Thucydides, son of Melesias, and others. Rather than attempting to achieve a balance of power among the friends or *philoi* belonging to such upper-class groups as was the custom, the new politicians strove to forge a mass alliance by appealing directly to the *demos*, to find their *philoi* among the common people and to combine them into a potent political force. Only after Pericles had oligarchic politics actually been replaced by democratic politics in Athens. The new politicians succeeded in democratizing politics by becoming leaders of the people or 'demagogues', a term of abuse in the speech of their aristocratic-oligarchic opponents. Allegiance to the polis had at last replaced loyalty to one's friends as the political norm. Connor concludes:

> These changes had something fresh and exciting about them, a sense of healthy innovation. And, as we have noted, they were badly needed modifications, for the formal constitutional structure of Athens was not well suited to carry out the complex and continuing business of the imperial city. Expert leadership was needed—the new politicians promised it, and sometimes provided it. Moreover, their statements and gestures of devotion to the city must have seemed a step forward, toward a higher and clearer ethical standard. They asserted more clearly than ever before that the first duty of a politician was to the city, not to some small clique within it. They professed civic virtues and civic concerns, and moved beyond the provinciality of family and faction that had so often characterized Greek politics in the past. They seemed to foretoken a new era in which the interests of all citizens would be equitably represented, in which ever closer ties would bind the citizen to the *polis*. . . .[30]

According to Connor the widespread response of wealthy and cultured families was twofold.[31] One was escape from the polis, withdrawal from politics 'into private circles of like-minded friends, small informal gatherings. . . .' The other 'aimed at a new kind of political arrangement in which the "better" people would again be dominant'. Both responses assumed the form of small clubs, the *hetaireiai* that had traditionally characterized aristocratic-oligarchic politics. In the case of those who wished a radical change in government the *hetaireiai* were transformed into revolutionary cells or *synomosiai*, 'bands of sworn revolutionaries, determined to overthrow the democracy'.[32] The serious domestic troubles and upheavals plaguing Athens between 412 and 400 were not the responsibility of the *demos* or their new style leaders, but of the subversive activities of these upper-class malcontents.

So it can be speculated that out of a sense of helplessness and rejection, Socrates, himself a member and friend of the upper classes, experienced his conversion and began his self-imposed poverty at a time when it was evident that the new politics was to be more than a temporary phenomenon. He withdrew from politics, along with many of his upper-class friends, because of his opposition to the new political developments and his realization that any direct action might be extremely foolhardy. His circle of friends would appear to be similar to one of the *hetaireiai* of the wealthy and cultured who sought refuge from the polis in the time of the new politics, although it is highly unlikely that it ever became a revolutionary cell.

While Socrates opposed the vulgar and uncultured democrats and obviously cherished some of the traditional aristocratic values, his viewpoint was scarcely identical with those of many of his oligarchic-aristocratic friends. He departs from them and their 'anti-political' politics and in a sense sides with the democratic opposition by giving precedence in his hierarchy of values to loyalty to the polis and obedience to its laws over allegiance to friends and friendship groups, as indicated in the *Crito* by his decision not to escape. But he did evidently share with his conservative friends at least one over-riding interest: the replacement of the new-style democracy by the rule of an aristocratic-oligarchic elite. Socrates' self-perceived role in this effort appears to have been his devotion to the idea of individual persuasion, to the attempt to regenerate morally the affluent and aristocratic youth who one day might hold the reins of power in a reconstituted Athenian order. If democracy was to be replaced by a regime of the aristocratic, the wealthy and the cultured and if the new order was to be conserved effectively, then the future leaders would have to be as upright, intelligent and knowledgeable as possible. Socrates evidently thought he should convince them that the foundation of the true politics was a morality of exclusiveness, the province of the few, not the many. Such teaching would certainly provide them with greater self-assurance for the part they might have to play. He was the only true politician because he tried to mold the souls of a future ruling class, and in this he proved to be one of the supreme ideologists of all time.

An assessment of the anti-democratic cast of Socrates' political views must include a consideration of his undisguised contempt for the common people. He shows an almost callous disdain for the masses, an attitude in keeping with his class origins and affiliations. His words suggest little to indicate either understanding or sympathy for the *thetes*. Toward them he is critical, condescending, and patronizing. His speeches abound with deprecating references to the *hoi polloi*. Would anyone with an iota of genuine concern for the ordinary man label members of the assembly the 'most stupid and weak', composed of 'cleaners, shoemakers, carpenters, blacksmiths, farmers, merchants', not fit to examine themselves, much less to look after the affairs of others?[33] Or could he cry, as Socrates does: 'Good heavens, Euthyphro! Surely the crowd is ignorant of the way things ought to go.'[34] And later in the *Gorgias* he exclaims: 'with the many I will not even enter into discussion'.[35] The *Alcibiades I*, judged by some specialists to be an excellent presentation of Socratic doctrine although the former attribution of authorship to Plato is now disputed,[36] presents Socrates' condemnation of the many as teachers.[37] He declares that in those who manage Athenian affairs one 'may still see the slaves' cut of hair, cropping out in their minds as well as on their pates',[38] and adds: 'The husbandmen and the other craftsmen are very far from knowing themselves, for they would seem not even to know their own belongings. When regarded in relation to the arts which they practise they are even further removed from self-knowledge. . . .'[39]

How does one account for Socrates' excoriation of the people, if it is not an expression of his social status and connections? Obviously he believes that democracy had corrupted Athens. Like most of the upper classes, including Plato, and unlike the Sophist Antiphon who preached egalitarianism and the unity of all men, Socrates never suggests a belief in anything but the inequality of mankind. Men are of unequal moral value, each capable of being fitted into a natural hierarchy denoting the degrees of moral superiority or inferiority. Nowhere does he condemn the idea of slavery—some men are inherently suited to perform only menial tasks—or the notion that the Greeks are by nature superior to non-Greeks who are naturally suited to be enslaved. So much do these views seem to be taken for granted by Socrates and his associates that they are never explicitly formulated by Xenophon, or by Plato, at least in the early dialogues. Finally, as we shall see, the masses possess corrupted souls, according to Socrates, by virtue of the menial tasks and physical labour they perform, and their lack of leisure. But how much of human inequality, for Socrates, is genetic and how much is environmental is not clear.

Nevertheless the charge that Socrates is anti-democratic in his political outlook rests upon more than his rejection of conventional politics and distaste for the common man. He also continuously attacks the cherished institutions and leadership of Athenian democracy, expressing a fairly clear preference for the Spartan mode of government. Generally he dismisses the opinion of the majority because 'a good decision is based on knowledge and not on numbers'.[40] In a passage critical of existing governments, he opposes choice by lot, so beloved by the Athenian *demos*; and also popular election, a device favoured by oligarchs: '. . . kings and archons were not those who held the sceptre, were elected by the electorate or chosen by lot, or gained power by force or treachery; rather they were those who knew how to rule'.[41] Socrates' antipathy to choice by lot and popular election is emphasized by his seeming to place them on a par with gaining power by force and treachery. He also complains about payment of citizens for attendance in the Assembly.[42] Besides disapproving of such venerated procedures, he seldom hesitates to castigate the hallowed heroes of the past. Pericles, Themistocles, Cimon, Miltiades, and others were good men, but they failed to teach their sons virtue and to elevate the moral quality of the citizens.[43] Socrates concludes 'that we do not know of any man who has proved a good statesman in this city',[44] and that Athens 'is swollen and festering through these statesmen of old. For they have paid no heed to discipline and justice, but have filled our city with harbors and dockyards and walls and revenues and similar rubbish. . . .'[45] Although in his various discussions of the problem Socrates may merely be trying to argue that virtue cannot be taught in any ordinary sense, to Athenians his words must have sounded like an intemperate onslaught against their democratic tradition.[46]

During Socrates' denunciation of Pericles in the *Gorgias*, Callicles accuses him of passing on gossip that originated with the pro-Spartan or Laconizing set.[47] Socrates was probably not one of the run-of-the-mill Laconizers, common enough among the Athenian upper classes; nonetheless he unquestionably admires Sparta and Spartan institutions.[48] Xenophon, himself a friend of Sparta, represents him in conversation with Pericles acknowledging the decline of their polis and holding that its former virtue could only be recovered by a return to a superior ancestral constitution, a cherished article of faith of the Laconizers.[49] More interesting is Socrates' subsequent eulogy of cities that are the most law-abiding because he insists obedience to the law is the necessary condition of unity, strength, and prosperity, singling out Sparta in this regard and its legendary law-giver, Lycurgus.[50] While in the *Protagoras* he is obviously indulging in irony when he comments that there were more philosophers in Sparta and Crete than elsewhere, he may be praising an aspect of the Spartans, overlooked even by the Laconizers, namely, their shrewd native wisdom, a kind of primitive philosophical style of discourse.[51] Finally in the *Crito* he confesses that Sparta and Crete are his 'favorite models of good government. . . .'[52] No wonder that the Athenians had reservations about him!

Socrates denounces the democratic politics of his polis because he believes the ordinary man, merely because he *is* a 'common' man, a shoemaker or blacksmith, a 'banausic', lacks the specialized knowledge necessary for sound political judgment and decision. He encourages Charmides in the *Memorabilia*:

> . . . you feel ashamed to speak before the most stupid and weak! Do the cleaners, shoemakers, carpenters, blacksmiths, farmers, merchants, or those who make exchanges in the marketplace and worry about

> buying something cheap so as to sell it at a profit, do these make you feel shame? These are the men who make up the Assembly. You are no different from a professional who fears an amateur![53]

Then he comments: 'The Assembly swears to look out for the affairs of others and is not fit to examine itself.'[54] Elsewhere in the *Memorabilia* Socrates expresses concern that officials, particularly generals, elected by popular vote lack the qualifications and skills requisite for responsible public office.[55]

Expert knowledge, not votes, must be the criterion for the selection of governor or ruler. Again, the governing of a polis—'the greatest of all works'—is not an art to be easily mastered, any more than skill in the lesser arts.[56] Judging from the few who are proficient in governing compared to the many qualified in the lesser arts, politics must require the most complex and specialized knowledge of them all.[57] The emphasis in the *Protagoras* is similar:

> Now when we meet in the Assembly, then if the state is faced with some building project, I observe that the architects are sent for and consulted about the proposed structures, and when it is a matter of shipbuilding, the naval designers, and so on with everything which the Assembly regards as a subject for learning and teaching. . . . But when it is something to do with the government of the country that is to be debated, the man who gets up to advise them may be a builder or equally well a blacksmith or a shoemaker, merchant or shipowner, rich or poor, of good family or none. No one brings it up against any of these, as against those I have just mentioned, that here is a man who without any technical qualifications, unable to point to anybody as his teacher, is yet trying to give advice.[58]

Socrates at his trial, according to Plato, laments that artisans who are masters of their respective crafts seem to believe that their skill gives them 'a perfect understanding of every other subject. . . .'[59] Politics for Socrates is a *technē* no less than weaving or shipbuilding, and necessitates a specialized skill no less than they do. If the weaver lacks the knowledge for shipbuilding, why does he imagine that he is an expert on politics any more than on shipbuilding? And his incapacity for politics is not confined to governing or ruling in a narrow sense. Socrates' point, it must be stressed, is that the 'ordinary' man is not fit to participate in politics and self-government at all.

Since politics is the supreme art or *technē*, entailing the highest knowledge and skill attainable only by a very few, Socrates believes that the polis should be ruled only by those few. Democratic politics and institutions, therefore, rest upon false assumptions. Mastery of the supreme art of government does not depend upon choice by lot or majority vote, nor are the many capable of acquiring it. The common man, whose labours—so necessary for the proper functioning of the polis—weaken and taint his soul, is excluded by Socrates from any knowledge of politics and consequently from any role in governing the polis. The educated man of leisure, however, can devote himself to learning the political art that will qualify him for ruling. Hence, the Socratic ideal of the well-ordered polis is apparently one governed by an aristocracy of talent, that with certain qualifications seems to correspond to an aristocracy of birth and wealth, by those proficient in the *technē* of politics. Such a polis would be characterized by a functional hierarchy in which merit as defined from the Socratic point of view determines one's status, the lower serving the higher, and the higher commanding the lower. The operating principle of this ideal socio-political organization, hinted at by Socrates in the *Charmides* as the principle of temperance,[60] would be each man tending to his own business, no one interfering with another's function in the hierarchy, except that part of the ruler's function would be to direct the function of the ruled. All of this translates into the axiom that the superior should dominate the inferior who must submit to their domination, just as soul should command body, and body should obey soul. In both cases the relationships are conceived of as existing by nature and hence by right. The Socratic ideal contains a built-in bias for the upper classes of his age. The common man is disenfranchised and depoliticized, placed under the unlimited authority of a select few from the aristocratic-oligarchic classes. Ultimately meritocracy, if not identical with the rule of the existing upper classes, would favour some of its members (not an Alcibiades, a Charmides, a Critias, or even a Xenophon) who had truly examined their own souls like the noble Plato. Socrates may have condemned tyranny in the ordinary sense,[61] but whether a meritocracy such as he probably had in mind would be any improvement can be seriously questioned.

In order to round off our evaluation of Socrates' anti-democratic political position brief reference must be made to his deep respect for law and order and firm belief in the strict observance of the law. On this point, as has been noted, he must be differentiated from many of his aristocratic-oligarchic associates for whom allegiance to Athens was subordinated to loyalty to friends. Perhaps Plato's approach in the *Republic* suggests an explanation for Socrates' deviation on this score from aristocratic values and for its role in his anti-democratic doctrine. Like his disciple, Socrates seems concerned to attack any idea or action that in principle threatens to fragment the community or to deny its organic unity, precisely because his vision of a meritocracy consists of a hierarchy of all classes in a single harmony. And up to a point his admiration for the unity of Sparta and for Spartan law and order would seem to confirm this explanation. Far from being democratic his respect for law was integral to his anti-democratic ideal and his fundamental opposition to contemporary Athenian democracy.

Socrates was always the staunch upholder of legality. His only recorded 'political acts' prior to his own trial were both in defence of the letter of the law. In 406 he, alone of his fifty tribesmen who were serving as *prytaneis*, opposed the illegal collective trial of the generals who had failed to rescue the Athenians manning the ships wrecked on a military mission against Arginusae. Again, during the reign of terror of the Thirty Tyrants he was unwilling to be a party to what amounted to the judicial murder of the wealthy metic, Leon of Salamis. He refused to act illegally in both cases: the one in resistance to democracy; the other, against oligarchy. The Xenophonic Socrates contends with Hippias that obedience to the law is the decisive factor determining the supreme political ends of unity, strength, and prosperity.[62]

His passion for obedience to the law is best known from his remarks in the *Apology* and *Crito*. Confronting his accusers, he defends what he considers his divine mission of being the 'gadfly' of Athens by stating that he will obey God rather than his fellow-citizens and never cease his philosophic questioning if, for example, they should discharge him upon the condition that he forsakes it.[63] Although in this instance he threatens to disobey a legal act if it is passed by the Five Hundred, something never put to test, in the *Crito* he leaves little doubt that his reason for refusing to circumvent the death penalty by escape and exile is a deep respect for the law. His argument for upholding legality is four-fold.[64] First, he is the victim of men and not the law itself. The actions of the men who have condemned him may be challenged, but not the legal status of their verdict, for the decision of a court must be obeyed as if it were a regular law. Second, he has a filial duty to respect and uphold the laws as if they were parents who had raised, protected, and educated him. Third, by remaining in Athens when coming of age and enjoying all the benefits and advantages of citizenship he has entered into an implicit obligation to support and obey its laws. Finally, any deliberate violation of a specific instance of the law would serve to subvert the authority of law in general and to undermine the very foundation of the strength and unity of the polis.

It seems clear that Socrates never holds a natural law position in any conventional sense in respect to the problem of legal obligation.[65]

His life was an example of obedience to the law of the polis, and his pronouncements always give precedence to legality and obedience to the law on the grounds of utility. The fact that he never actually violates the law, his constant veneration of the law, and the sacrifice of his own life to the strict letter of the law—all outweigh any radical germ of natural law that may appear in his thinking about legal obligation in the *Apology*. He seems in general to have conformed to the standards of conduct expected by his ordinary Athenian contemporaries.[66] The good citizen of a democracy was expected to place the public interest above his private concerns. Verdicts and decisions in the name of the laws rather than the laws themselves might legitimately be criticized, but good citizens were expected to obey the laws regardless of deficiencies in their application. Violation of a law in the name of conscience or some higher principle of justice would not have been very meaningful to most ordinary Athenians of the time.

4. *Philosophic Recommendations: Definition, Knowledge, and Psyche*

An examination of Socrates' principal philosophic recommendations indicates in a rather striking fashion how they reflect the anti-democratic political ideology just outlined, together with his class position and affiliations. The very intellectual structure of the recommendations seems to have been shaped by his basic ideological position. Three of the primary philosophic recommendations—those dealing with definition, knowledge, and psyche will be discussed in turn.[67]

Socrates' procedure for arriving at the definition of anything is a lengthy and complex process of rigorous analysis and imaginative synthesis requiring a dispassionate mind.[68] His method assumes the duality of appearance and reality. Behind the world of becoming, a realm of ever-changing infinite particulars perceived by our senses, exists a changeless world of being or substance in some way accounting for or explaining the other. Socrates always begins with a question about the meaning of justice, or temperance, or courage, or virtue, or piety. Once he has chosen a specific subject for investigation, he proceeds to collect as many instances from the world of sensible existence of what, for example, are generally recognized as 'just' actions. These instances are then analyzed for common qualities that when discovered and isolated make up the definition or form (*eidos*) of the class of just actions. Socrates is interested in constructing real not nominal definitions. For him the definition of something comprises its essence or being or nature, outside and independent of the human mind. It is unvarying and distinct from other natures or forms, possessing a reality that the particular instances of it, manifested in the sensible world of existence, do not. Moreover, just as the essence of anything must be identified in terms of its function or purpose, so the essence of justice, a characteristic of human beings and human actions, must ultimately be referred to the purpose or function of man. Having arrived at the essence of something through postulating a real definition by focusing upon its function or purpose, Socrates can then make certain logical deductions from it. However, in the search for real definitions and essences he is much less concerned with epistemological problems and with the elaboration of a theory of knowledge than he is with the discovery of absolute moral ideals that will be of aid to men in conducting their practical affairs.

The most obvious trait of the Socratic mode of inductive reasoning, essential definition, and deductive inference is that it is open only to those who possess the leisure and intellect necessary for a life of continual questioning and analysis. Furthermore, whose definition of something in terms of purpose or function is to be accepted? Ultimately such a real definition rests upon intuition. Whose intuition is preferable? Socrates' answer would undoubtedly have been that it is the intuition of the contemplative man who has devoted his life to philosophic speculation, and whose insight must be accepted on faith because he is an expert, just as the architect is an expert on building. Hence, not only is the method available only to a few, but also the validity of its results are beyond the comprehension of the many—the common sense—and can only be judged by an elite. As guides to the practical moral life, Socratic real definitions are of doubtful value because of their intellectual exclusiveness. Of even great significance is that the whole Socratic procedure rests upon the premise that the world of particulars, the world of the many perceived by the common sense of the many, is to be distrusted and is inferior to the world of the few that can be perceived only by the few who have the leisure and requisite intellect. While the world of particulars—the many—is a necessary instrument for the perception of the world of forms, it has no real meaning apart from those forms, the world of the few perceived by the few. The dependence of the real upon the existential from the standpoint of ascertaining the real is curiously reversed once the goal has been achieved, so that the existential becomes subordinate to and dependent upon the immutable aristocracy of forms. The status of the essential definitions in relationship to the existential world of particulars, therefore, seems to mirror the Socratic notion of the well-ordered polis, divided between the vast majority of imperfect men enslaved by the impure desires of the flesh and subordinate to an elite. It is this elite that is ministered to by the many and for whose determination and direction the elite exists. The dualism of the world of socio-political actuality between rulers and ruled is transmuted into the Socratic worlds of sensible existence and metaphysical reality.

Socrates' famous paradox that 'knowledge is virtue',[69] again reflects his anti-democratic political ideology. The precise meaning of the dictum is none too clear. Certainly he rejects 'right opinion', the standard of morality for most Athenians. Virtue, he teaches, is comparable to a *technē*, an art or craft such as husbandry or carpentry dependent upon a mastery entailing practice and skill that can be acquired with patience and effort by the common man. But clearly there are important differences between virtue as *technē*, and every other *technē*. Virtue is superior in value to every other *technē*, and in contrast to others it is the necessary and sufficient condition of happiness. Furthermore, unlike another *technē* the end or purpose of virtue as *technē* takes priority over the means. The carpenter, since the end of his craft is clearly recognized and accepted, concentrates on the means, and the end takes care of itself, whereas with moral activity the end is everything. By 'knowledge is virtue' Socrates apparently means that knowing the virtuous is all that is necessary for acting virtuously. In other words, knowledge of the true moral ends—the real definitions of piety, temperance, courage, justice, etc.—implies the ability and the desire for moral action. Two corollaries follow from the principle that knowledge is virtue. First, virtue can be taught, not however as the rhetoricians might teach it. Second, one acts immorally only from ignorance—the lack of knowledge—and never voluntarily. The heart of the problem with the Socratic formulation evidently lies in his meaning of 'knowing'. Socrates' position seems to be that if one devotes himself to a philosophic life of questioning and self-examination, searching for the real essences of moral activity, he will discover the true moral ends of life and in the process, if successful, so purge and purify his soul, so acquire the attribute of self-control, that he cannot help acting morally. Philosophic enquiry, the very act of philosophizing as the search for truth, will produce a transformation in the individual that will supply the character and desire to act morally and render immoral action an impossibility. Virtue as knowing in this sense can be taught, and once virtue is philosophically comprehended, the actor can only act virtuously.

The knowledge so basic to virtue in Socrates' highly intellectualistic view, therefore, is beyond the attainment of the many. If the knowledge necessary for virtue depends upon leisure and constant enquiry and self-examination, it is quite outside the resources of the common man; and not only because he lacks leisure *time*, but because in a more fundamental sense he is bound in body and spirit to the world of material necessity by the need to earn his livelihood, while knowledge implies liberation from the world of appearances and necessity. So the attempt of the ordinary person—labourer, farmer, or craftsman—to lead a moral life must be on a far lower plane that the Socratic ideal. At best he can only follow the lead and imitate without any genuine moral understanding the example of those who do *know* in the Socratic sense. Moreover, it is only the self-denying few who can devote their lives to the philosophic enterprise. By contrast, the common people can never develop the self-control and dispassion necessary for acting rightly on the basis of 'knowing the right'. The privileged and leisured classes are in a position to be truly virtuous, and the masses are a sorry second who, if truth is to prevail, must remain the creatures, the animate tools of their social superiors.

By intimating that the chief end of the polis is a moral one in his special philosophic sense, Socrates has prepared the way for a select few to dominate the common people, a final step to be taken by Plato. A pragmatic politics of equality, common-sense, and consensus is replaced by philosophy. If the end of the polis is moral in this sense, and if politics becomes chiefly a moral-philosophic activity, then the exclusion of the many from rule is absolute and final. Once politics is equated with philosophy, then quite clearly the direction of the affairs of the polis can only be in the hands of the few, those most capable philosophically, and the many are reduced to the condition of minions. By definition the true politics must practically result in authoritarianism.

The Socratic identification of knowledge with virtue is also directly related to his idea that the good, i.e., the excellent or virtuous, is the useful.[70] In the *Memorabilia* and the early Platonic dialogues Socrates affirms that to ascribe virtue or excellence to anything is to say that it performs its function or purpose. A shield is good if it fulfills the purpose of defence, but not good if used for an end other than the one for which it was designed and constructed. Something cannot be good and useful for all purposes, only for a specific purpose. The good and the useful for one man or object cannot be the good and useful for all men and objects. In addition, the standard of the good is the same as that of the beautiful. The good and the beautiful are both defined in terms of whatever contributes to our pleasure and well-being, in turn characterized by functional excellence. Here is the link with the proposition that knowledge is virtue, for when a man genuinely knows or recognizes the good and the beautiful he can only choose them and act accordingly. Authentic knowledge and recognition imply wisdom and temperance. The man who knows but does not act accordingly, does not truly know because he lacks wisdom and temperance. What is good conduct or human excellence? It is that which is useful in regard to man, which occurs when man acts in keeping with his natural purpose or function. How is man's natural function or purpose to be determined?

Socrates' answer is that it is only ascertained by the few who can devote their lives to self-examination and philosophic questioning.

The problem with Socrates' conception of the good as the useful centres upon the notion of function or purpose, either by design or by nature. The idea of the useful would be appreciated by artisans and craftsmen, and undoubtedly Socrates derived it from his perception of *technē*. But he so transforms the idea of the useful that it bears little resemblance to what the common man might have in mind, at least, in specific cases. How does one decide the nature of the function of man, for instance? The function of man can only be postulated through essential definition by the philosopher who employs an inductive-deductive method of reasoning, something beyond the powers of the average individual. For Socrates both the purpose of man and the means of attaining his purpose can only be discovered by the expert and not by the ignorant. Such a view of man and human conduct transcends and contradicts the common sense and everyday experience of the vast majority of men, further serving to bolster Socrates' basic political ideal of the domination of the many by the few.

His third major philosophic recommendation has to do with the soul or psyche. He was not the originator of the idea of the psyche, but he was the first Greek to conceive of it in intellectual terms as the true self and to view the body as a tool to be used by the psyche. The psyche is that part of the divine in man that is immortal. According to the Socrates of the *Memorabilia* the psyche is the location of prudence.[71] It is 'man's most powerful part'[72] that perceives the existence of the gods, and 'shares in the divine....'[73] The function of the psyche is clearly to rule the body,[74] nevertheless men commonly love their bodies more than their psyches.[75] This is emphasized at some length in the *Apology* where Socrates exclaims that men think far more of their bodies and possessions than their psyches, of acquiring as much money, honour, and reputation as possible.[76] Another theme of the *Apology*, also appearing in the *Memorabilia*, is that the care of the psyche is the only path to goodness.[77] Not only is self-control the key to the health of the psyche,[78] but also in the *Crito*, Socrates stresses that the psyche can be benefited only by good action and harmed by evil action.[79] The first step in caring for the psyche is suggested in the *Apology* as critical self-examination, the Delphic 'Know Thyself'.[80] However, the individual cannot embark upon such a course of therapy unaided, for just as one calls in a doctor when one is troubled by a bodily ailment, so care of the psyche or soul is a matter for experts and not of the opinion of the many. As Socrates says in the *Crito*:

Ought we to be guided and intimidated by the opinion of the many

> or by that of the one—assuming that there is someone with expert knowledge? Is it true that we ought to respect and fear this person more than all the rest put together, and that if we do not follow his guidance we shall spoil and mutilate that part of us which, as we used to say, is improved by right conduct and destroyed by wrong? ... what we ought to consider is not so much what people in general will say about us but how we stand with the expert in right and wrong, the one authority, who represents the actual truth.[81]

Hence, it is only for the few with the leisure for critical self-examination under the guidance of a 'doctor of the soul' such as Socrates, who can improve their souls and truly master their bodies. But those engaged in the so-called illiberal arts—artisans, craftsmen, and labourers forced to spend long tedious hours working indoors—spoil their bodies, in turn ruining their psyches.[82] The notion that the common man has an inferior psyche brings to mind Socrates' view in the *Phaedo* that the natural relationship of psyche and body is one of domination and subordination, that of master and servant, craftsman and tool.[83] For most ordinary men the converse is true: the body usurps authority like a tyrant, weighing down and polluting the psyche. Only those who love knowledge and possess the leisure for study and freedom from material necessity, can liberate themselves from the tyranny of the body. The study of philosophy is a technique of purification. Just as death is the ultimate purgative of body from psyche, so philosophy considered in this light is fundamentally 'the practicing of death'. A proper civic order, therefore, on the basis of the correct relationship between body and psyche, would be one in which those weighed down by the body—the common people—submit to their natural masters—men of soul—and become so many animate tools at their disposal.

To stray even farther in time beyond the very early dialogues, Socrates in the *Phaedrus* categorizes people in a nine-tiered hierarchy in terms of the degree to which their psyches perceive the truth.[84] Those with the purest souls are the lovers of truth and beauty, the authentic philosophers; the impurest are the tyrants who are just below Sophists and demagogues. Immediately above the latter, ranking seventh from the top, are artisans and farmers. The poets and imitative artists in sixth place; prophets and priests in fifth place; and athletes, physical trainers, and physicians in fourth place. Occupying third place below law-abiding kings and warrior-rulers in second place and genuine philosophers at the top are *politikoi* (politicians), *oikonomikoi* (estate owners or managers), and *chrematiskoi* (men of business). Of some interest is the relative purity of soul, according to Socrates, of these three categories in the third rank, for no doubt they typify members of the aristocratic-oligarchic classes. *Politikoi* as legitimate politicians like Cimon and Pericles are far higher on the scale than demagogues, a Cleon or Anytus. *Oikonomikoi*, again stand well above mere farmers, for they are men of leisure who direct the labour of others rather than labouring themselves. And finally *chrematiskoi*, not to be confused with *kapeloi* or artisans and tradesmen, are members of the upper classes who have invested in lucrative ventures. So while all three assuredly cherish money and worldly goods more than most men, Socrates nonetheless gives them a high place in his hierarchy of souls; and their high ranking seems to suggest that class takes precedence over virtue in Socrates' scheme of things or at least that he tends to confuse class values with nobler values. From the aristocratic perspective these three groups in third place, despite their devotion to material advancement, were not tainted by the corrupting influence of agora and workshop. They clearly possessed superior psyches to shopkeepers, tradesmen, artisans, and farmers, all of whom existed by nature to obey their commands.

The political relevance of Socrates' conception of the psyche, therefore, can now be summarized. The natural relationship of psyche to body is that of master to slave, craftsman to tool. Body is qualitatively of lower value than soul. In the polis the vast majority of people minister to the body or perform strictly bodily functions, and a few perform the higher psyche or soul functions. These, in theory at any rate, are the experts whose psyches have fulfilled their natural function of ruling their bodies. The natural socio-political relationship between men of body—the common people—and men of soul—the ruling elite—is the same as the natural relationship between body and soul in the individual, that of obedience and command. Man is ultimately defined by wisdom, the highest end or function of the psyche, a characteristic of the few as against the many. So the majority of men in the polis who are incapable of being wise because of their arduous labours, their lack of leisure, and their bondage to material necessity, are something less than human and are the natural servants of those who are superior, at least by Socratic definition, in their qualities of psyche. There can be little doubt that the Socratic doctrine of the psyche favours the elite and is heavily weighted against the common people in general and democracy in particular.

From this brief survey the nature of the relationship between interest and knowledge, politics and philosophy in Socrates' thought should be fairly apparent. The interest of the few as against the many is built into the very substance of his philosophic doctrine. An anti-democratic political ideology seems to be at the root of his philosophic recommendations, giving them form and content. His claims of knowledge and truth appear to be permeated by very definite political values. Obviously he cannot be censured for believing that philosophy and a life of philosophic contemplation are beyond the powers of the ordinary citizen. But the charge against Socrates is more fundamental. There seems to be a correspondence between an elitest view of the polis, that is certainly in keeping with his own interests and social status and those of his associates, and the basic pattern of his philosophic thought. His very conception of reality appears to reflect his political prejudices. In fact one might claim that Socrates offers us a political interpretation of metaphysical reality.

The crux of the matter is his conception of the dualism of appearance and reality. He uses the dualism in two primary ways. The first is in his theory of definition. He erects, as it were, an aristocracy of forms or essential definitions arrived at through the existential realm of fluctuating particulars, but which in turn gives to that realm its only true meaning. This dualism reflects an essential aristocratic-oligarchic principle, the division of the polis between the few who rule by the nature of things and the many who are ruled. Just as access to the world of essences is through the sensible manifold of particulars, so in the well-ordered polis the leisured life of a few is possible only because of the ministrations of the many; but it is the few who give order and direction to the many and bind the whole into a functioning and functional organic duty.

The second way in which Socrates' use of the appearance-reality dualism seems to reflect his socio-political interests and values is in connection with his doctrine of the psyche. Not only does he discover the reality of the self in the invisible psyche buried behind the sensible appearances of the body, but he also defines their natural or ideal relationship in the political language of obedience and command, a vocabulary that is aristocratic-oligarchic. Moreover, he would extend the distinction by differentiating between the many with inferior souls who perform bodily functions in the polis and the few of purer soul who are the natural masters of the many.

Apart from these two ways in which his dualism tends to mirror socio-political interests and values, one cannot omit two other means by which his philosophy supports them. In restricting the life of true moral virtue to the few who can 'know' in the full philosophic sense he gives to that verb, he virtually relegates the common people to a life of moral inferiority. By definition the common man cannot live a life of genuine moral virtue. Finally, because he sees authentic politics essentially in terms of morality and the moral regeneration of the upper classes, his elitist exclusiveness comes to the fore. If politics is basically a matter of morality in the Socratic sense, then only the morally superior, whom at best he identifies with a select few from the noble, wealthy and cultured, and at worst with the group as a whole, are entitled to rule. Therefore, on the four counts mentioned Socratic philosophy tends to reflect and buttress his socio-political interests, attitudes, and values.

5. *The Case for Athens*

So much of the story of Socrates' trial and death has been shrouded with elements of subsequent legends enveloping his name, that the actual historical circumstances and the merits of the indictment have been distorted. Was he the victim of savage mob hysteria, the tyranny of the majority, and unscrupulous demagogy in a highly unstable, corrupt, and rapidly disintegrating society? Unfortunately, many of us judge his Athens almost entirely upon the basis of his persecution. In our own comfortable liberal atmosphere we are prone to castigate the people and the system for intolerance and bigotry in condemning such a saintly elder because of his outspoken views. But the event of 399, heinous as it may seem, must be viewed from some kind of balanced historical perspective with regard to the condition of Athens itself and the actual case against Socrates.

One important reason for the harsh judgment of Athens from the end of the fifth century to the Macedonian victory in the battle of Chaeronea in 338 is that too much reliance has been placed upon the testimony of the enemies of the new democratic politics (Thucydides, Aristophanes, Xenophon, Plato, Aristotle). Even today some scholars seem to take for granted the 'moral decline' of Athens in the fourth century. The emergent picture is one of social and moral disintegration, the growth of irresponsible and ignorant mob-rule and demagogy, the decline of civic spirit and religious belief, and the rise of corruption, idleness, self-seeking, and sensual gratification. As in the case of most caricatures some truth no doubt exists in this one. But Athens was still a remarkable polis, by no means so divided, unstable, decadent, and impotent as ancient critics and some modern commentators would lead us to believe. By 399 Athens had recovered from the final disastrous defeat and occupation by the Spartans. The revival was all the more remarkable when it is remembered that approximately one-third of the population had been lost during the plague years of 430–426, that about one-half of the armed forces had never returned from the catastrophic Sicilian venture of 415–413, that under the terrorism of the Spartan backed rule of the Thirty Tyrants, more lives had been lost, if we are to believe Xenophon, than in the previous ten years of struggle with Sparta, and that the war had ended with the loss of empire. Yet Athens, demonstrating remarkable resilience, recovered in the shortest possible time, admittedly never attaining her former position of preeminence, but with a marked restoration of morale that was maintained at a fairly high level throughout the century. The reinstituted democracy was not threatened internally until the final loss of independence in 322. In fact there was still a significant degree of civic participation, and social and political stability was unquestionably the greatest in the Greek world. From the middle of the century imperialism was renounced and the economy was beginning to prosper. A substantially broad base of support for democracy among both rich and poor existed, buttressed by an essentially wide distribution of wealth—factors helping to explain both the relative stability and moderation of the system. Democratic institutions and the democratic spirit in Athens were probably stronger than ever before. As Professor Pritchett has so brilliantly demonstrated,[85] contrary to the often accepted picture, the assembly did in fact maintain strict control over the conduct of the armed forces, citizens did actively participate in military campaigns, and office-holders were perhaps not as corrupt as sometimes portrayed. Moreover, he indicates, on the basis of many examples from the fifth and fourth centuries, that the numerous trials of generals, and probably of other public officials, were by no means confined to democratic Athens, but seem to have been a widespread feature of both Greek and non-Greek city-states throughout the ancient world. Of the thirty-one cases in the fourth century cited by Pritchett, nineteen were from Athens and the others from such poleis as Sparta and Thebes; and in the fifth century only sixteen of the thirty-nine trials he considers took place in Athens. Military leaders were tried for failure and incompetence. Justice was apparently meted out when legal procedures were followed, which seems to have been the rule. A notable exception was the mass trial and execution of the Athenian generals for deserting their men in 406 in Arginusae. While such extra-legal action cannot be condoned, it perhaps served as a salutary warning to Athenian commanders in the future, helping to save the lives of many courageous citizen-soldiers, or so George Grote, quoted by Pritchett, has observed. In sum, by no stretch of the imagination can the record of Athenian democracy in the fourth century be described accurately as one of the domination of politics by the military, of the shirking of civic obligations by the citizens, of universal corruption and mob violence. Finally, there is no evidence that the ordinary Athenian worked any less industriously during these times or lived a life of state-subsidized leisure on the labour of slaves. Athens, however, was apparently becoming more dependent upon a burgeoning slave force. The citizen population declined as a result of the ravages of the Peloponnesian War, and many citizens were forced by economic straits either to emigrate or to enlist in foreign military ventures that relied for financial support upon the capture of booty.[86]

Still other features of fourth-century Athenian society are far from suggesting any fundamental moral decline or decay. After the trial of Socrates freedom of thought and absence of persecution of intellectuals prevailed. While in the previous decades eminent cultural figures besides Socrates had been hounded and harried—the most notable among them being Phidias, Anaxagoras, Aspasia, probably Diagoras, possibly Protagoras and Euripides—no such black marks sullied the record of Athenian democracy in the fourth century. Nor should it be forgotten that the earlier witch-hunting was not solely the work of the democrats; for the first three, at least, were probably brought to trial by the aristocratic-oligarchic opponents of Pericles, evidently inspired in the cases of Phidias and Aspasia by Thucydides, son of Melesias, after his return from exile. The climate of freedom and extraordinary vigour of the still great city attracted a host of curious and creative visitors. With the flourishing of the Academy, the Lyceum, and the opening of similar centres of study, the polis became more of the 'school of Hellas' than ever before, drawing students and savants from near and far. Much of the ancient military spirit seems to have disappeared to be replaced by cultural concerns. Although Athens was never again such a major force in Greek politics, something of the old vitality was revealed in its spearheading the opposition to Macedonia, calling for the unity of the Greeks and generating ideas about the community of man. Now that the aristocrats were being pushed from the political arena and aristocratic values no longer dominated the social and political scene, life and politics may have appeared to be vulgar and uncouth to the scions of noble families such as Plato and Xenophon, but a more genuine democratic spirit seemed to prevail despite the division between rich and poor. And in the lively social and intellectual atmosphere of the new Athens, something of the old parochialism and narrow chauvinism had disappeared in a novel freedom and self-consciousness. In sum, Athens' defeat at Chaeronea probably cannot be blamed upon moral degeneration, decline of civic spirit, or social disintegration arising from arbitrary and immoderate mob-rule, but rather was due to the might of Macedonia.[87]

If this was the Athens beginning to emerge in 399, what of the accusations against Socrates? He was charged with disbelief in the gods of Athens, the introduction of new gods, and the corruption of the youth. Religion and politics were inextricably entwined in Athens, and, as we have just noted, heresy trials often serving political purposes had been common-place. In the tense and uncertain atmosphere following the restoration of democracy and the end of the Peloponnesian War, Athenians increasingly sought comfort in mystery sects and occultism. Anxious about the future and bearing the burden of past sorrows and tribulations, the average Athenian was quite possibly fearful that his gods would be enraged by the outspoken barefoot eccentric of Alopeke who relied for guidance on his inner divinely inspired voice or 'daimon' rather than upon the traditional deities of the polis. Moreover, his example and teaching could turn the youth from conventional religious belief at a time when strict piety might be most prudent. Of course, the question arises to what extent the trial was in fact a political one, an act of political vengeance. Socrates had been closely associated in the minds of the Athenian democratic leaders, if not the people, with both Alcibiades and Critias who had betrayed the polis to Sparta, the latter having established a ruthless reign of terror over the citizenry. Was Socrates tried for being a threat to Athenian democracy? The question is probably unanswerable. No doubt the religious indictment was genuinely motivated. One can only speculate that had Socrates not been politically suspect, the trial might never have occurred, or had it taken place he would have been acquitted. Without engaging in such conjectures, we do wish to comment briefly about some neglected aspects of the trial, and to indicate by way of summary why Athenian democratic leaders had every cause for alarm over Socrates' activities and views.

The reason why political charges could not be brought against Socrates in 399 was that a general political amnesty—the first of its kind in Western history and one that was on the whole scrupulously honoured—had been declared in 403 after the overthrow of the Thirty Tyrants, and constituting part of the democratic party's policy of moderation and reconciliation. But if the democrats actually connected Socrates with the anti-democratic terrorism of 404–403 why did they not bring him to trial immediately? The reason was that a Commission had been appointed to revise and codify Attic law, and until it finished its task in 400 legal proceedings against him could not have commenced. Finally, it should not be forgotten that Anytus, the chief prosecutor of Socrates, was probably not the often portrayed demagogic leader of the Athenian rabble. Little is known about him, except that he was a wealthy owner of a tannery, who headed the democratic party and whose sensible, moderate, and liberal policy and leadership were at least in part responsible for the restoration of Athenian democracy and the remarkable recovery of the polis. As the principal architect of the rejuvenation of Athens, he probably had no desire to bring Socrates actually to trial, opening up old wounds and animosities, but only wished that the philosopher would go into exile. However, he had not reckoned with

Socrates' old age or his principled and not entirely reasonable stubbornness. Suffice it to say that Anytus possibly approved of the indictment because he saw the activities and teachings of Socrates as a distinct threat to all he and his colleagues had accomplished in such short order.

A political indictment would have been damning. Socrates, given the dubious nature of his associates, his apolitical stance and constant criticism of Athenian politics and statesmen, his belittlement of the common people, his admiration of Sparta, his anti-democratic political ideology in general, and the politically subversive nature of his philosophic recommendations, would seem to have constituted a definite threat to Athens. No wonder even Anytus and the moderate democrats should have had qualms about the wisdom of allowing him freedom to undermine the way of life they were attempting to salvage and reconstruct with such painstaking care and skill in the period immediately following the disastrous defeat by Sparta and the traumatic experience with the Thirty Tyrants. Although the severity of the penalty and the callousness of the treatment of Socrates cannot thus be easily excused or dismissed, nevertheless one should reflect upon the question of the trial from this perspective. Perhaps it is time that some of the saintly aura about the person and ideas of Socrates is dispelled. Philosopher he indisputably was, and political partisan to the end.

Notes to Chapter III

1. This listing and the next one beginning with the *Gorgias* follows the chronological suggestions of W. K. C. Guthrie, *A History of Greek Philosophy* (Cambridge: Cambridge University Press, 1969), IV (1975), 'Plato, The Man and his Dialogues: Earlier Period', pp. 72, 93, 101–2, 124–5, 134–5, 155, 177, 199, 213–14, 236, 266–7, 284–5, 312–13, 325, 365, 396–7, 437. Naturally the dating of the dialogues must be a speculative concern. So R. G. F. Robinson, 'Plato', *Oxford Classical Dictionary* (2nd ed.; Oxford: Clarendon Press, 1970), p. 842, puts the Socratic dialogues in the following order: *Hippias Minor*, *Laches*, *Charmides*, *Ion*, *Protagoras*, *Euthyphro*, *Apology*, *Crito*. At least we can be fairly certain that the Socratic Dialogues are separated from the later early works by Plato's first visit to Italy and Sicily in 387 BC.

2. On Aristophanes see below, pp. 87–8.

3. *Euthyphro*, 11b; *Alcibiades I*, 121a. Sculptors traced their ancestry back to Daedalus just as doctors did to Asclepius. On the authenticity of *Alcibiades I*, see below, p. 98 and n. 36.

4. *Laches*, 180e.

5. Plato, *Apology*, 22d; Xenophon, *Memorabilia*, III, x; IV, ii, 1–3. Xenophon, *Memorabilia*, I, ii, 60, claims that Socrates 'was a man of the people' and that 'he liked his fellow men'.

Unless otherwise specified translations of Plato are from those contained in Edith Hamilton and Huntington Cairns, eds., *The Collected Dialogues of Plato Including the Letters* (Princeton: Princeton University Press, 1963) [Bollingen Series LXXI]; and translations of Xenophon are those of Anna S. Benjamin, trans. and ed., Xenophon, *Recollections of Socrates and Socrates' Defense Before the Jury* (Indianapolis: Bobbs-Merrill, 1965) [Library of Liberal Arts].

6. *Apology*, 22d.

7. *Memorabilia*, III, x, 6–8; *Symposium*, 172–4. Apollodorus was noted for his stringent self-criticism.

8. *Memorabilia*, III, x, 1–5; 9–15; IV, ii, 1–2.

9. Plutarch, *Aristides*, I.

10. *Apology*, 36b.

11. Xenophon, *Memorabilia*, I, ii, 18; III, xiv.

12. A. W. H. Adkins, *Merit and Responsibility: A Study of Greek Values* (Oxford: Clarendon Press, 1960), p. 238.

13. Ernest Barker, *Greek Political Theory* (New York and London: Methuen University Paperbacks, 1960), p. 85.

14. Guthrie, *op. cit.*, III, p. 130.

15. E. A. Havelock, The Liberal Temper in Greek Politics (New Haven and London: Yale University Press, 1957), p. 157.

16. *Apology*, 31c–33b; *Gorgias*, 473e; *Memorabilia*, I, vi, 15.

17. *Gorgias*, 521a.

18. *Gorgias*, 521d.

19. *Laches*, 179a–e; *Apology*, 21b–22a, 31c–32e; *Protagoras*, 319a–320a; *Gorgias*, 515a–517e; *Meno*, 90a–95a.

20. *Memorabilia*, IV, ii, 2, 11; *Euthydemus*, 290a–292e.

21. *Memorabilia*, I, ii, 12–18; II, i; III, i, 4–5; iv, 1; vi; ix, 10–13; IV, ii.

22. *Memorabilia*, I, i, 16; vi, 15.

23. *Apology*, 33a–b.

24. *Apology*, 31c–d.

25. *Apology*, 36b–c.

26. *Apology*, 31e.

27. *Apology*, 30e–31a.

28. *Apology*, 36c.

29. W. Robert Connor, *The New Politicians of Fifth-Century Athens* (Princeton: Princeton University Press, 1971), chs. 3–4.

30. *Ibid.*, pp. 194–5.

31. *Ibid.*, pp. 196–7.

32. *Ibid.*, p. 197.
33. *Memorabilia*, III, vii, 5–9.
34. *Euthyphro*, 4a.
35. *Gorgias*, 474a.
36. Guthrie, *op. cit.*, III, p. 470.
37. *Alcibiades I*, 110d.
38. *Alcibiades I*, 120b (Jowett translation).
39. *Alcibiades I*, 131a. In *Hippias Major*, 284e, whose authenticity is also questioned, Socrates agrees that the multitude does not know truth.
40. *Laches*, 184e.
41. *Memorabilia*, III, ix, 10.
42. *Gorgias*, 515e.
43. *Laches*, 179a–e; *Protagoras*, 319a–320a; *Gorgias*, 515a–519e; *Meno*, 93a–94e.
44. *Gorgias*, 516e.
45. *Gorgias*, 518e–519a.
46. *Meno*, 94e.
47. *Gorgias*, 515e.
48. See the summary in Glenn R. Morrow, *Plato's Cretan City: A Historical Interpretation of the 'Laws'* (Princeton: Princeton University Press, 1960), pp. 42–3.
49. *Memorabilia*, III, v, 13–14.
50. *Memorabilia*, IV, vi, 15–17.
51. *Protagoras*, 342a–343b.
52. *Crito*, 52e.
53. *Memorabilia*, III, vii, 5–6.
54. *Memorabilia*, III, vii, 9.
55. *Memorabilia*, III, i, 1–5; iv; v, 21–4.
56. *Memorabilia*, IV, ii, 2.
57. *Memorabilia*, IV, ii, 6–7.
58. *Protagoras*, 319b–d. Cf. *Gorgias*, 455b–d.
59. *Apology*, 22d.
60. *Charmides*, 161a–164e.
61. For example, *Memorabilia*, IV, vi, 12.
62. *Memorabilia*, IV, iv, 14–18.
63. *Apology*, 29d.
64. *Crito*, 49–53.
65. On the question of Socrates' attitude to the law in the *Apology* and *Crito* in general, and in regard to his 'natural law position' in particular see A. D. Woozley, 'Socrates on Disobeying the Law', in Gregory Vlastos, ed., *The Philosophy of Socrates: A Collection of Critical Essays* (Garden City: Doubleday Anchor, 1971), pp. 299–318.
66. A conclusion based on the examination of K. J. Dover, *Greek*

Popular Morality In the Time of Plato and Aristotle (Oxford: Blackwell, 1974), pp. 273, 301–3, 306–9.

67. Throughout the subsequent discussion we are indebted to Norman Gulley, *The Philosophy of Socrates* (London, Melbourne: Macmillan, 1968) and Guthrie, *op. cit.*, III, Pt. II, 'Socrates', pp. 323–507 for the explication of Socrates' technical philosophic position, but the conclusions we draw in relating it to his political ideology are our own.

68. For Socrates on definition see: *Memorabilia*, I, i, 16; IV, i, 5; v, 11–12; vi, 1; *Laches*, 190c–d; *Charmides*, 159a; *Protagoras*, 361c; *Euthyphro*, 7c–d; *Gorgias*, 474 ff.; *Meno*, 72a ff.; *Phaedrus*, 263a ff.

69. See esp. *Memorabilia*, III, ix, 5; IV, vi, 6; *Laches*, 190b; *Protagoras*, 319a–320c, 349e–350a, 360a–361a; *Meno*, 71a, 87b ff.

70. *Memorabilia*, III, viii, 4–8; ix, 4–5; IV, vi, 8–9; *Protagoras*, 358b–d; *Gorgias*, 474d–475a; *Meno*, 87d–e.

71. *Memorabilia*, I, ii, 53.

72. *Memorabilia*, I, iv, 13.

73. *Memorabilia*, IV, iii, 14.

74. *Memorabilia*, I, iv, 9; IV, iii, 14.

75. *Memorabilia*, I, ii, 54.

76. *Apology*, 29d–30b.

77. *Apology*, 29e–30a; *Memorabilia*, I, ii, 2.

78. *Memorabilia*, I, ii, 1–4.

79. *Crito*, 47e–48a.

80. *Apology*, 38a; cf. *Alcibiades I*, 129a.

81. *Crito*, 47d–48a.

82. Xenophon, *Oeconomicus*, IV, 2–3. Cf. *Republic*, 495a–b with the words of Creon's herald in Euripides, *Suppliants*, 420.

83. *Phaedo*, 80a–82d; cf. *Alcibiades I*, 129e–130a.

84. *Phaedrus*, 248c–e.

85. W. Kendrick Pritchett, *The Greek State at War* (Berkeley, Los Angeles, London: University of California Press, 1974), esp. Pt. II, pp. 5–10, 18, 20, 24–5, 31, 34, 55, 59, 84–5, 97, 101–4, 109–10, 115–16, 131–2, 288.

86. *Ibid.*, Pt. I, chs. III–V, for a discussion of booty.

87. *Ibid.*, Pt. II, p. 116: 'We should look not so much to the moral decline of Athens but the military power of Makedonia to explain Chaironeia'.

IV

Plato: Architect of the Anti-Polis

Perhaps the greatest beneficiary of the perverse judgment that history has rendered on the Athenian polis has been Plato. It is no doubt in keeping with the ironies of history that the citizen of Athens who showed the greatest contempt for the principles of the democratic polis should have come to be regarded as the greatest product of the democracy; that the weapon he so skillfully forged to attack the democracy should have survived as the most honoured legacy of the democracy, the tradition of Western systematic philosophy; in short, that our judgment of the Athenian polis should be so often derived from a man who rejected the very principles on which that polis was based.

The concept of the *polis* lies, needless to say, at the very heart of the Western political tradition and its intellectual apparatus. It is, therefore, a fact of no small significance that our conception of what the polis was and what it meant to the Greeks is largely based on a concept of the Athenian polis that deliberately rejects the reality of Athens and makes its very principles appear as its corruption. A counter-historical redefinition of the polis has come to represent for us its essence, while its essential reality, that which was most vital and unique in it, has come to represent a departure, a degeneration.

The Socratic tradition—in the persons of Socrates, Plato, and Aristotle—has been the source of this redefinition; but it is above all Plato who turned the concept of the polis inside out, and the completeness of this reversal is perhaps the greatest tribute to his inventiveness. The genius of Plato's thought lies as much in the originality of his political invention as it does in his elaboration of a unique mode of speculative thinking which launched the tradition of systematic philosophy in the West. Indeed, it can be argued that his political inventiveness is the source of his philosophical creation. The word 'invention' is being used here advisedly to describe Plato's political ideas, because there can be no doubt of their radical uniqueness when they are considered against the background of Greek political history as it actually evolved. To put it briefly, the revolutionary nature of Plato's political thought lies in his attempt to 'aristocratize' the polis, or 'politicize' aristocracy—that is, to synthezise what were in their very essence antithetical forces in the history of Athens, the *aristocratic* principle and the *political* principle.

As we have seen, the history of the rise of the polis and the gradual establishment of the *political* as a principle of association transcending, and up to a point replacing, the traditional 'private' principles of kinship, tribe, and *oikos*, is the history of a gradually declining aristocracy. By Plato's time, the aristocracy had reached its lowest ebb. 'It was', as Ehrenberg writes, 'a crisis from which there was no return.' He continues:

> For a long time the Athenian aristocracy had been politically, socially and intellectually, the ruling class, also in the democratic State. Gradually they lost their position and the upper classes changed in character. Much more fatal than the partial intrusion by the more wealthy among the middle classes was the change the nobility underwent in itself. This was even more devastating in its effect than the war casualties which had fallen most heavily on the upper classes. The nobles were rapidly moving towards self-destruction.[1]*

This decline became a favourite theme in 4th century Athenian literature, especially, as Ehrenberg has shown, in old Attic comedy, where aristocrats are often depicted as having either 'given way to the commons or ... become degenerate',[2] dissolute and effete. The same literature also testifies to the fact that, with the degeneration of the aristocracy, the anti-political character of that class had entered a new phase. It is significant that pro-aristocratic critics of the declining aristocracy viewed political participation by the aristocracy as a sign of its corruption. A recurring theme in comedy, as well as elsewhere in Athenian literature, is that in the democratic polis no decent, well-bred man succeeds. Politics is the province of the vulgar, and to remain an

*Notes for this chapter begin on p. 202.

aristocrat means to withdraw from the political arena.[3] 'In earlier times,' writes Ehrenberg, summarizing a view that appears more than once in Aristophanes, 'the young man went to the gymnasium or went hunting, now he frequents the agora and concerns himself with *psephismata*, the decrees accepted in the assembly of the people.'[4] Thus politics and dissoluteness are simply two different aspects of the same degeneration of the aristocracy, and to participate in politics is by definition to 'give way to the commons', to assimilate oneself to their vulgarity and to cease to be an aristocrat. Young aristocrats are exhorted to return to the ways of their fathers, which has now come to mean to withdraw from politics, to abandon the agora for the gymnasium.

In fact, in an increasingly hostile and distasteful environment, an environment in which they seemed no longer to be the dominant force politically or even culturally, it appears that many of the young aristocrats of Athens, those who had not 'capitulated' to the masses, did withdraw from politics. Their clans, friendship groups, and clubs, once the private sources of their public power, now revealed their essentially private character, their estrangement from the public sphere of the polis. The anti-political nature of the aristocracy, which had been kept in check as long as their archaic private associations were important sources of public power, now asserted itself more strongly than ever. Some aristocratic groups continued to have a political function—which can more accurately be called an anti-political function—as counter-revolutionary cabals dedicated to the destruction of the democracy. Many of them, however, became simply dining and drinking societies, expressing the complete alienation of their members from the life of the community.

1. *Life and Outlook*

Plato, as a product of the same declining and disaffected aristocratic culture, can best be understood in the context of this anti-political movement. He was born in 427 in Athens or Aegina. It is well-known that he belonged on poth parents' sides to the most distinguished of Athenian families, as notable as any in Athens for the nobility of their pedigrees, if not for their wealth—although that too was not inconsiderable. His father, Ariston, was supposedly a descendent of Codrus, last of the Athenian kings; while his mother, Perictione, granddaughter of Critias (III)—featured in Plato's *Timaeus* and its incomplete sequel *Critias*—traced her lineage back to Solon. Her brother, Charmides, after whom the Platonic dialogue is named, became one of the Thirty Tyrants, and a cousin Critias (IV), participant in the *Charmides* and *Protagoras*, was the wealthy man of letters who actually led that bloody counter-revolution. Both were friends and students of Socrates. Plato's elder brothers Adeimantus and Glaucon also appear in the dialogues and probably were members of the Socratic circle, the former listed by Plato in the *Apology* as being present at Socrates' trial. The nephew and pupil of Plato, Speusippus, succeeded him as head of the Academy. Ariston having died when Plato was quite young, his mother married Pyrilampes, probably her uncle, who had been an intimate of Pericles. Receiving a good education and joining the Socratic circle, Plato served in the cavalry, evidently on active duty during the last five years of the Peloponnesian War.

If we are to accept the testimony of the *Seventh Epistle*, Plato himself had political ambitions in his youth, ambitions which he felt were favoured by the oligarchic revolution, led by his aristocratic relations and friends in whom he placed all his hopes for the regeneration of Athens. To his credit, however, he could not accept the excesses of their reign of terror and did not join them, as he was expected to do. When soon afterwards the Thirty Tyrants were overthrown, his ambitions were briefly revived, though, not surprisingly, with less eagerness. As the democracy was restored, he again became disillusioned. Despite his praise for the 'great moderation' of the returning democrats, who, according to his own testimony treated their enemies with remarkable restraint, and despite the obvious contrast to the bloody excesses of the oligarchs in whom his hopes for Athens had been invested, Plato was repelled by what seemed to him the corruption of Athens, which 'was no longer ruled by the manners and institutions of our forefathers', and where 'the whole fabric of law and custom was going from bad to worse at an alarming rate'.[5] The new democracy's most serious offense, of course, was the prosecution of Socrates, although even that did not prevent Plato from praising the moderation of the democrats. Perhaps their reasons for prosecuting Socrates were understandable, even to Plato, who recognized the justice of their fears after the oligarchic reign of terror; and he was not surprised that some of them took vengeance against the Tyrants and their friends. Nevertheless, the 'great moderation' of the restored democracy, even when contrasted to the lawlessness of the oligarchs, did not dispel Plato's view that the 'fabric of law and custom' was disintegrating and that Athens was 'falling to pieces'—a view that is not surprising in an aristocrat who had seen his best hopes for an oligarchic revival shattered and watched the democracy reestablished more firmly than before. Plato despaired and withdrew from active politics. It is doubtful, in any case, that in the climate of the restored democracy, with its memories of the Thirty Tyrants, and especially in view of Plato's own connections with them, he could have hoped for a role in the political life of Athens.

The dozen years following 399 were spent in travel and literary pursuits. Immediately after Socrates' execution Plato and some other associates retired to Megara where his friend the philosopher Euclides had established a school. The *Apology* and *Crito* were probably written about this time or shortly afterwards. Subsequently, having possibly visited North Africa and Egypt and written several other dialogues ending with the *Protagoras*, Plato in 387 journeyed to Southern Italy to acquaint himself with the Pythagorean communities there, the best known being that of Tarentum, where he spent some time with Archytas, the illustrious philosopher-statesman. Plato also took advantage of the opportunity of viewing political power at first hand by going to the royal court of Syracuse as the guest of Dion who had married his own niece, the daughter of his sister and Dionysius I. Apparently falling out with the tyrant of Sicily, Plato returned to Athens to write the *Gorgias* and the *Republic*, and to found the Academy, about a mile beyond the city walls on the sacred ground of Academus. Something like a college and requiring the payment of high fees, the Academy legally was a cult-association dedicated to the Muses with common meals, 'seminars', lectures, and a library. The curriculum was perhaps similar to that expounded in the *Republic*. Subjects taught included mathematics, geometry, astronomy, harmonics, philosophy, political science, and natural science. Although Plato himself never entered Athenian politics, the Academy had a definite political goal and was far from being instituted simply for abstract speculation. Besides educating the sons of wealthy Athenian and foreign families in Platonic politics, the Academy sent forth its students and members as consultants to rulers and cities throughout the Mediterranean world. Academicians advised on state policy, devised law codes, drafted new constitutions, and reformed existing ones. Among these 'Platonic politicians' were Aristotle who reportedly framed laws for his native Stagira and became a trusted aide and friend of Hermias, tyrant of Atarneus; and Xenocrates, the third head of the Academy, who was consulted on kingship by Alexander the Great. Plato himself could not resist the temptation of such activity; and he made his two further ill-fated visits to Sicily as a would-be adviser to kings, in 367–365 and 361. The rest of his life until his death in 347 was devoted to writing, especially to composing the lengthy *Laws*. He seems to have spent much of his inheritance during his lifetime upon the Academy, for his final estate was probably worth little more than a talent, including two country properties, cash amounting to six hundred drachmae (six minae), furniture, personal possessions, and five servants.

Although Plato clearly never lost his interest in politics, then, and although his intellectual activities and in particular his famous Academy were far from non-political, he did, willingly or not, 'withdraw' from Athenian public affairs. Just as his own life provides the most famous example of the aristocratic withdrawal from politics, his work can perhaps be regarded as a new genre in the anti-political literature characteristic of his time and class, another exhortation to his peers to return to the ways of their fathers. Certainly his work is anti-political in the sense that it represents a negation of the polis in its historical meaning—that is, the polis as a principle of association expressing the power and the right of the rising classes to challenge aristocratic supremacy and the traditional principles that supported that supremacy. And certainly he is exhorting young aristocrats to live up to a dying aristocratic ideal. Plato, however, is doing more than restating in a new form the exhortations of others who are nostaglic for the days of aristocratic dominance. He is not satisfied to relinquish the polis to the commons and to withdraw to an aristocratic enclave, to abandon the agora for the gymnasium. His vision is much more revolutionary than that. He would transform the polis itself. If assimilation to the polis now meant corruption of the aristocracy, he would assimilate the polis to the aristocracy.

In one sense, then, Plato's political doctrine represents a denial of Athenian history, and far from constructing a philosophical idealization of the polis, it negates the very principle on which the Athenian polis was historically based. But if his polis does not, as some commentators appear to think, represent an epitome of the uncorrupted polis but rather a negation of the Athenian polis, neither, of course, does it involve a return to the aristocratic pre-political golden age of the Homeric hero-nobles. If Plato's ideal city is an aristocratic one, it is nonetheless a *city*; and his aristocracy is not the *oikos*-centered warrior-society of Homeric legend, but a modern cultivated and *urbane* aristocracy with values appropriate to its condition. The aristocratic values that Plato propounds are clearly not those of the feudal household and its warlord masters, but rather the values of a landed leisure class which is to occupy its rightful place *in the polis* as a modern ruling class. Plato sets himself the almost self-contradictory task of elaborating a polis-centred aristocratic morality, virtually free of the tribal, anti-political values that had persisted in the aristocratic code throughout the democratic age—a transformation of values that was conceivable only if the polis itself were transformed. The disaffected, anti-political aristocracy could be restored to the polis only if the polis were restored to the aristocracy.

It should be clearly understood that the term *aristocracy* is being used here not simply in the sense of 'rule of the best', irrespective of social class. It is quite explicitly intended to refer to a particular social class—a hereditary landed nobility with a code of behaviour and a quality of refinement and cultivation specific to it. The suggestion that Plato represents the interests of a particular class is one which disturbs many of his admirers. The following is a typical response to this suggestion, expressing a widespread attitude to Plato and to philosophy in general that obscures perhaps more than it illuminates (and perhaps reveals less about Plato than about the author's own aristocratic prejudices):

> In several senses Plato was an aristocrat, but not in the opprobrious sense of some of his critics. His family on both his father's and his mother's side was a distinguished one and had produced men sufficiently able to assume the obligations of leadership. Plato accepted the responsibility of his inherited position. His dominant aim was to prevent the further disintegration of Greece. Two courses were open to him, either the assumption of public office or the reestablishment of the clarity of the Greek intellect which had become corrupted by many influences. The fate of Socrates perhaps suggested to him that his special strength lay in the restoration of the Greek view of life. His position in the *Republic* is that good government can be conserved only by statesmen with knowledge in proportion to their task. In the *Laws* he attempted a more direct approach through the formulation of a specific legislative program. He was also aristocratic in the lifelong discipline with which he held himself to his task. His view that the final stage of the statesman's education should not be undertaken before the age of fifty would have little support today in conjunction with our desperate efforts at mass education. In Plato's hands aristocracy meant the rule of the best, from whatever class they came. The able were to receive special training for the responsibilities requiring great ability; the less able were to perform the tasks suitable to their ability. Plato's political theory is an implication of the system of nature, and to call this philosophy aristocratic is meaningful only in the sense that nature is itself aristocratic. But to call any philosophy aristocratic in the sense of class interest is meaningless; preoccupation with the interests of one class to the detriment of others is not philosophy. Philosophy is disinterested or it is not philosophy. When ideas are manipulated for personal ends, for class or group interests, the name for this in Plato's day was sophistry. It was against this that his dialogues were directed. To accuse Plato of being in league with the sophistic forces that undermined the classical world is an instance of the more subtle misrepresentation of his position. Plato's disinterested pursuit of knowledge has not only made the word

> *Platonism* synonymous with the word *philosophy*, it has marked him as the aristocrat of aristocrats, the paragon of excellence emulated by high-minded men for over two thousand years.[6]

There is no intention in our own argument of dismissing Plato as a mere apologist for the aristocratic-oligarchic party in Athens. The sincerity of his moral criticism is undoubtedly too genuine and the depth of his philosophical vision too great for that. But to deny that he is deliberately and solely 'preoccupied with the interests of one class to the detriment of others' is not to deny that his vision is that of an aristocrat, or that his conceptions of good and evil are, to say the least, coloured by the values of his class. There are two fundamental aspects of Plato's aristocratic perspective and its bearing on his philosophy which will be dealt with in what follows: first, his essentially aristocratic conception of moral virtue—and vice—and his skillful universalization of aristocratic values into absolute philosophical principles; and second—and perhaps even more interesting—his surprisingly materialistic account of the conditions necessary for the existence of such virtue, conditions which are those of a society based on the economic and political dominance of a hereditary landed aristocracy.

The basic premise of this chapter, then, is that the Platonic teaching can be illuminated by placing it in its proper context as the product of an aristocratic mentality distressed at the increasing 'vulgarization' of Athens, its loss of aristocratic character, and extremely conscious of the social conditions underlying this development. Plato's doctrine is being viewed as the creation of a mind trying to come to grips with the essentially anti-aristocratic nature of the polis and, secondarily, the anti-political nature of the aristocracy, which had reached a crisis in the withdrawal from politics—in effect the final, if inevitable, surrender to the forces of vulgarity. Many of Plato's fundamental ideas, even those that are not explicitly or obviously political, become clearer in this context.

F. M. Cornford, in the introduction to his celebrated edition of the *Republic* writes that for Plato the

> ... drifting apart of the men of thought and the men of action was a disastrous calamity, indeed the root of the social evils of his time. His problem, as presented in the *Gorgias*, was not to be solved merely by dropping out of public life to become absorbed in abstract speculation. Philosophy meant to him what it had meant to his master. The Socratic philosophy, analysed and formulated in the early dialogues, was not the study of nature or logic or metaphysics; it was the pursuit of wisdom, and to achieve wisdom would be to

achieve human perfection, well-being, happiness. This again meant not merely 'caring for one's own soul' as an isolated individual, saving himself and leaving society to its fate. Human excellence, as Plato and Aristotle after him always maintained, is the excellence of an essentially social creature, a citizen. To produce this experience and consequent well-being is the true end of the 'Royal Art' of statesmanship. Hence the life of philosophy and the life of the active statesman ought not to be, as they appeared to Callicles, alternative careers, but a single life in which all the highest powers of man would find full expression. Society could be saved only by reuniting the two elements which had been drifting apart.[7]

With certain important reservations, this passage helps us to place Plato's central philosophical problem in its political context. Stated in these terms, the central problem of the nature of knowledge and virtue and the relationship between the two can without much difficulty be recognized as an ultimately political problem. Seen against its actual historical background, Plato's statement on the separation of thought and action can be recognized as a comment on the increasing democratization of Athens and the withdrawal from politics which this development seemed to demand. And if Plato's comment assumes the character of a lofty moral judgment based on universal philosophical principles, rather than engaged social comment by an interested party, an aristocrat addressing himself to others of his kind, it is precisely because Plato sincerely identifies democratization—cultural as well as political—with moral corruption *by definition*. What makes it more difficult for us to restore concrete and specific content to Plato's philosophical formulations, to break out of an otherwise circular argument, is the fact that many commentators—not least Cornford himself—seem ready to share Plato's aristocratic judgments and thus perceive them as disinterested and transcendent. Cornford, although he is prepared to place Plato's philosophical concerns in some kind of political context, however abstract, seems unwilling to pursue the consequences of this position and contents himself, for example, with identifying the separation of thought and action as some kind of disembodied 'root' or cause of the social evils that Plato abhors. Fortunately, however, Plato himself, unlike his modern interpreters, never completely abandons the social context of his philosophical argument. He never leaves any doubt that the separation of thought and action—at least as he conceives of thought and action—is the *consequence* of certain social developments, which he identifies very specifically and in very concrete terms. By the same token, the reunification of thought and action can be accomplished, according to him, only by a kind of social revolution, a transformation of the social conditions which led to their separation. And if Plato sometimes appears ambivalent concerning whether virtue is active or contemplative—as, for example, in the cave allegory of the *Republic*—his ambivalence does not represent a philosophical confusion because it is not fundamentally a philosophical problem but a social one. The nature of virtue is not absolute in this respect because it is bound to its social conditions. The ambiguity is to be resolved not philosophically but politically. It would seem obvious enough that if virtue is identified with aristocratic quality, the man of virtue cannot act politically in the alien world of the polis, from which he and his values are being gradually excluded. In such a polis, the aristocrat can retain his virtue—that is, his aristocratic character—only by withdrawing from the political realm. To participate in the political realm under such circumstances would require assimilation to the commons, the assumption of their *style*—that is, a loss of virtue. Virtue as an active quality is possible only in a polis dominated by aristocratic values and by an aristocratic ruling class, and such a polis can be brought about only by fundamental social and economic transformations. It is in this sense that Plato's fundamental philosophical problem turns out to be a social problem.

In the following discussion of Plato's major political works, an attempt will be made to characterize more specifically the values that lie at the heart of Plato's doctrine, to point out their concrete social meaning, and above all to give an account of Plato's almost materialistic analysis of the social conditions underlying the corruption and possible restoration of these values. These works will be treated in a somewhat different manner than is usually the case: for example, the *Republic* appears here as a less abstractly philosophical and more concretely sociological and political work than usual; while the *Laws* is credited with more importance than it is generally granted, as a significant 'revolutionary' (or counter-revolutionary) work based on careful and detailed social analysis, but at the same time in a sense more *utopian* than the *Republic*.

2. *The 'Protagoras': A Preface to Plato's Political Doctrine*

It is possible to look upon the dialogue *Protagoras* as the point of departure for all Plato's subsequent political theory. In this work, the crucial political questions are raised, at least in a rudimentary form, and the groundwork for their answers laid. Above all, here is perhaps the only more or less coherent and explicit statement of the political theory which is arguably the ultimate target of all Plato's elaborate argumentation on the nature of politics. Protagoras' long speech, the so-called Myth and Apology, is the most systematic expression available to us of what might be called the political theory of Greek democracy. Whether or not it specifically reflects the views of Protagoras or any other single person, it clearly represents the view of man and society which Plato associates with the democratic outlook.[8] The speech represents the democratic doctrine that constitutes the framework of Plato's own anti-democratic argument in the sense that he appears always to be addressing himself to that doctrine implicitly—when he is not actually engaging in deliberate distortions of the democratic world-view. The *Protagoras* is, in fact, the only extant dialogue in which Plato allows his Socrates to encounter a serious democratic argument, despite the fact that assaults on democracy constitute a central and constant theme of Plato's political thought. Even in this dialogue, however, his method is not to meet the argument head-on. Neither here nor anywhere else does he actually come to grips with a democratic argument and systematically refute it. Instead, when he does not simply distort the democratic position by equating it with the amorality of a Callicles as in the *Gorgias* (a point to which we shall return), Plato often proceeds by simply borrowing democratic premises and ideals and manipulating them so that their meaning is magically transformed into its opposite. The most important element of this approach, the one which is the very cornerstone of Plato's anti-democratic polemic, is the argument from the arts. At a time when artisans and craftsmen formed the mainstay of the radical democracy, and were leaving their imprint on social values, Plato borrows the ethic of craftsmanship and technical skill; he does this, however, not in order to enhance the dignity and status of the ordinary artisans and craftsmen who possess such skills, but on the contrary, by defining politics as a specialized art, to exclude these very people—and indeed all who labour for their livelihood—from the 'craft' of politics and the right to participate in self-rule.

The question that preoccupies Plato not only in the *Protagoras* but throughout his political investigations is set by Socrates at the beginning of his argument with Protagoras:

> Now when we meet in the Assembly, then if the State is faced with some building project, I observe that the architects are sent for and consulted about the proposed structure, and when it is a matter of shipbuilding, the naval designers, and so on with everything which the Assembly regards as a subject for learning and teaching. If anyone else tries to give advice, whom they do not consider an expert, however handsome or wealthy or nobly-born he may be, it makes

> no difference: the members reject him noisily and with contempt, until either he is shouted down and desists, or else he is dragged off or ejected by the police on the orders of the presiding magistrates. That is how they behave over subjects they consider technical. But when it is something to do with the government of the country that is to be debated, the man who gets up to advise them may be a builder or equally well a blacksmith or a shoemaker, merchant or shipowner, rich or poor, of good family or none. No one brings it up against any of these, as against those I have just mentioned, that here is a man who without any technical qualifications, unable to point to anybody as his teacher, is yet trying to give advice. The reason must be that they do not think this is a subject that can be taught.[9]

We shall return in a moment to what is—or at least appears to be—the central question of the dialogue: can virtue be taught? What must be noted at the outset is the framework established by Socrates for the pursuit of the argument. The issue turns on the Athenian democratic practice of permitting any citizen—'a blacksmith or a shoemaker, a merchant or a shipowner, of good family or none'—to make political judgments. Protagoras, too, takes up the argument on this basis, setting out to demonstrate that this practice is justified, that the Athenians are right because political virtue is necessarily a universal quality of which all citizens can and must partake if cities are to exist. Thus, the argument about the teachability of virtue is from the very outset a political dispute about the merits of democracy. Socrates has cast the question in the form of a debate about the democratic practice of granting political rights to even the most ordinary artisan or craftsman, and Protagoras responds by seeking to demonstrate that '... your countrymen act reasonably in accepting the advice of smith and shoemaker on political matters'.[10] This debate sets the direction of Plato's political thought; and his definition of politics as a specialized art on the model of crafts and technical skills such as those practiced by shoemaker, smith, or weaver—a definition which forms the basis of systematic political works like the *Republic* and the *Statesman*—can be understood as a response to the view expressed by Protagoras on the qualifications of 'smith and shoemaker' to make political judgments.

A great deal has been written about Plato's use of the argument from the arts and the function of *technē* in his philosophy. One rather curious suggestion has been made by Eric Havelock in *The Liberal Temper in Greek Politics*.[11] Havelock does not argue simply that Plato's argument from the arts turns the concept of *technē* to a deliberately anti-democratic purpose; he contends that the very notion of technique as specialized is itself a specifically Platonic idea opposed to the views of an 'anthropologist' and democrat like Protagoras. Indeed, Havelock seems to regard the appearance of this notion in Protagoras' speech as an indication of its doubtful authenticity as a representation of Protagoras' teachings. Someone like Protagoras, suggests Havelock, would insist on the universality of technical skill and the nature of the technical arts as the common creations of mankind, a point which Protagoras does, in fact, seem to be making at the beginning of his speech.

Havelock's view does not seem particularly helpful. First, there is no contradiction between, on the one hand, a view of the arts and techniques as common creations, or even a conviction that the *capacity* for technical skills is universal, and, on the other hand, the idea that arts and techniques are specialized activities requiring special knowledge and training, or indeed that they are unevenly distributed in a useful division of labour. Plato's analogy requires no more than the latter ideas. It does not, for example, require a belief in the inequality of innate capacity among human beings, even if Plato himself may hold such a view. Moreover, the Athenians—among whom crafts often passed from father to son surrounded by family secrets, craft traditions, and pride of craftsmanship, and who acquired the technical skills of their arts by means of training in the workshop as pupils learning from masters—hardly needed to be told by a leisured aristocrat like Plato about the expertise involved in crafts and technical skills. Nor would an astute observer like Protagoras be likely to dispute this rather commonplace point, whatever he may have thought about the common origins of the arts or the universal distribution of technical capacity among human beings. It is not surprising that, as Havelock remarks, this 'Platonic commitment', this view of technique and skill, is '... nowhere argued or defended, but always assumed....'[12] Indeed, the argument from the arts would be virtually useless if Plato could not assume agreement on this basic, almost trivial point. It seems rather unlikely that a man of Plato's genius would try to construct an argument based entirely on two fundamental premises—that the technical arts are specialized activities and that politics is such a specialized art—both completely unacceptable to his opponent. His argument makes a great deal more sense if Protagoras' speech, which assumes that the technical arts are specialized or expert activities, is an authentic expression of the democratic view that Plato is opposing. Plato thus would have a common and uncontroversial premise on which to build an argument that rests on the analogical identification of politics as an art sharing certain commonly recognized attributes of other specialized arts and technical skills. He is then able to harness the values and the pride of craftsmanship to a political doctrine inimical to craftsmen.

Another perhaps more common view of the argument from the arts, and one that is even more misleading, represents Plato's argument as an expression of his—or at least Socrates'—*respect* for the ideal of craftsmanship. Sometimes this view is accompanied by the equally misleading suggestion that such respect for *technē* was untypical in Athenian society amidst a general contempt for manual labour. Here is one such argument:

> Socrates did not come of a noble family: his father seems to have been a respectable skilled artisan, a statuary. Probably his earliest enquiries were not made of leading politicians and distinguished visitors to Athens, but among fellow-craftsmen in the market-place. At any rate we can be sure that his approach to politics was by way of the analogy of the skilled crafts—the argument we usually term the 'Argument from the Arts'. This may be put in its simplest form, 'There is an art of shoemaking. Only shoemakers know how to make shoes and only they are entitled to make them. It is absurd for an unskilled crowd to seek to be an authority on shoemaking. How much more absurd it is for an unskilled crowd to seek to be an authority on the art of ruling.'
>
> It was in fact normal at Athens for particular skills to be hereditary—as, indeed, we find it to have been throughout Greece, for the Asclepiadae and the Homeridae are more famous instances of the handing down of a mystery from one generation to the next. . . .The argument that the skilled craftsman has an authority, a prerogative and tradition was therefore a convincing one at Athens, however unwelcome its political implications might be. Yet it came from a mean source, for the 'arts' that illustrated it were generally as [sic] mean and beneath the notice of the free-born citizen who aspired to active public life. . . .
>
> Plato shows us in the *Symposium* and in the *Gorgias* something of the contempt which the ordinary Athenian felt—but was usually polite enough to conceal—for Socrates' constant discussion of the ways of butchers, cooks and shoemakers.[13]

The author then goes on to cite the speeches of Alcibiades and Callicles as illustrations of this contempt felt by 'ordinary Athenians', and to suggest that the argument with Callicles in the *Gorgias* may reflect the 'inner wrestling' of Plato himself, who, as an aristocrat, would find it even harder to accept Socrates' argument from the arts, but who eventually does accept it and makes it a 'permanent element in his thought'.[14]

Quite apart from any doubts that may be raised—as we have already suggested—about this account of Socrates' class associations and his attitude to craftsmen, this argument is somewhat perverse and illogical. Not only does it quite absurdly treat the wealthy Callicles and the aristocratic Alcibiades as typical representatives of 'ordinary Athenians', it also attributes a contempt for crafts to precisely the 'ordinary Athenians' who practiced them, while ascribing to anti-democrats like Socrates and Plato an exceptional appreciation of the merits of craftsmen, a respect for their 'authority, prerogative and tradition'—an appreciation and respect that are rather perversely expressed in a desire to exclude such men from the rights of full citizenship. There is also the peculiar logic according to which the author has Socrates and Plato attempting to strengthen their argument by constructing it on the basis of an analogy resting on an unpopular image which elicits only contempt from all their listeners, common or noble, rich or poor.

A much more likely explanation of Socrates'—or Plato's—procedure is, again, that he is adopting popular values and using them to buttress a case that would be far less popular among the adherents of those values. Plato chooses this procedure precisely *because*, as Skemp concedes, 'The argument that the skilled craftsman has an authority, a prerogative and tradition was . . . a convincing one at Athens'.[15] We shall have more to say in what follows about Plato's attitude to labour, but it should already be clear that he certainly does not choose to adopt and elaborate Socrates' argument from the arts because of his or his mentor's respect for the arts and their practitioners. His—and probably Socrates' —attitude to craftsmen in a non-metaphorical sense is sufficiently revealed by the hierarchy of souls outlined in the *Phaedrus*, where craftsmen and farmers are placed seventh in a list of nine, superior only to sophists, demagogues, and tyrants. In fact, Plato's own hardly disguised contempt is itself one of the chief sources of the view that Athenians generally regarded the 'base' arts with disdain, as gratuitous as it is to universalize the views of an aristocrat so at odds with the mass of his compatriots. It seems more reasonable to suppose that Plato adopted the argument from the arts, not out of any personal respect, but simply because in a democracy where 'ordinary' craftsmen and artisans had achieved a unique social and political status, respect for *technē* was more in keeping with common values than was Plato's own aristocratic disdain. Plato simply adapted to his own purposes values quite contrary to his own, using the status acquired by craftsmen to attack the democracy on which that status rested. It is not unlikely that as he did so, Plato had always in mind Protagoras' argument about the political qualifications of shoemaker and smith, a democratic argument more in keeping with the ethic of *technē*, insofar as that ethic reflected the status of craftsmen in democratic Athens, than was Plato's effort to turn the values of craftsmanship against their real adherents.

There is also another way in which Plato elaborates his political theory by turning Protagoras on his head. In the myth at the beginning of his long speech, Protagoras suggests that civilization was based on the technical arts and skills which are the original attributes of mankind; but, he argues, it became necessary to acquire the political virtues, justice and respect for others (*aidos*), which create a bond of friendship among men, to allow men to act together and indeed to render their technical skills useful. To establish the bonds of cooperation that would enable them to benefit from the various arts, *all* men had to share in the political virtues. Protagoras expresses this view by means of a myth in which, although he is a self-proclaimed agnostic, he makes use of the gods to symbolize what he clearly regards as very earthly anthropological facts. When in the story Zeus is asked by Hermes how justice and respect for others are to be distributed among men, whether they are to be distributed like the arts according to a specialized division of labour or to all alike, Zeus replies: 'Let all have their share. There could never be cities if only a few shared in these virtues, as in the arts.'[16] The suggestion seems to be that precisely because the arts, which are the foundation of society, are unevenly distributed in a division of labour, political unity and the bonds created by evenly distributed political virtues and equality are needed to permit men to join their various arts into a cooperative unity without which the arts are useless.

In the *Republic*, Plato's argument seems designed precisely to turn Protagoras' view of the arts as the foundation of society against itself. Here, too, the argument begins with an imaginary construction of society on the basis of the 'arts' and technology; but the consequence is, of course, the reverse of political equality. Plato's foundation of society on the arts becomes an argument, not for a community of equals joined in a cooperative exercise of their arts, but for a hierarchical social division of labour in which politics, like other arts, is a specialized and exclusive skill, so that there is a rigid division between rulers and ruled instead of a self-ruling community of citizens. Paradoxically, the very proposition that the polis is founded on the arts—a proposition that might easily be cited by shoemaker and smith in support of their political claims—becomes the basis for excluding their practitioners from politics.

It is in the context of this argument about democracy and the political qualifications of shoemaker and smith that Socrates' most essential doctrines—indeed the only ones that can be attributed to him with any degree of certainty—are introduced into the debate: his view concerning the unity of virtue and the proposition that virtue is knowledge. This mode of introducing these ideas may itself suggest something about the ideological motivations underlying the most basic elements of Socratic philosophy. Socrates begins by suggesting that, since the Athenians permit anyone, regardless of special qualifications or training, to advise them on political matters, they must believe that political virtue is something that cannot be taught. The implication is that it cannot be believed consistently that virtue is both universal and teachable; and, insofar as Protagoras claims to be able to teach virtue, he appears to be contradicting the democratic view that political virtue is a universal quality, common to all men.

Protagoras then sets out to show that political virtue can be regarded as both universal and teachable, that it is acquired by learning without being an exclusive, specialized art. Having begun with his suggestion that all men must share in the political virtues and that they all have the capacity to do so, he goes on to suggest that they actually *acquire* those virtues—which are not innate—in the process of growing up in a civilized community, amidst its customs and laws, the praise and admonitions of their compatriots. The polis itself is the teacher of political virtue through its laws and customs, its *nomoi*, and its citizens. Thus, the members of a polis *learn* virtue without having a specific teacher, just as they learn their mother-tongue. This explains, too, why especially virtuous fathers often do not have especially virtuous sons: since all people receive the education provided by life in a civilized community, no one has a special advantage beyond his natural talents; and while there are some differences of natural ability, all citizens can share in virtue to a degree sufficient to qualify them for political participation. The differences among citizens of a civilized community are minimal compared to the differences between them and those who do not live in a community instructed by *nomos*; even the least virtuous members of the former are better than any member of the latter. All that a teacher of virtue, like Protagoras himself, can do is to aid or accelerate a little the teaching that the community itself provides.

These ideas on the acquisition of virtue are clearly in keeping with Protagoras' notion that moral principles exist 'by convention' rather than 'by nature', a view which, as Protagoras' myth hints despite its religious symbolism, implies that moral principles are generated by the living community, by men in the process of maintaining their existence and working out their social relations. These conventions grow organically out of communal life, much as *language* develops among men. Protagoras also clearly believes that, as social norms built into the very fabric of society, moral laws are not arbitrary simply because they are conventional, and they have a stability, a tenacity, and an authority that binds men to them even in the absence of some 'natural' or 'supernatural' foundation. For Protagoras, moral laws, as necessary conditions of civilized life, are morally binding even though—or precisely because—they are 'merely' conventions and even though they may change and evolve with the changing needs of the community. Moreover, the fact that they are changeable by men clearly does not imply for Protagoras that men will lightly alter or discard them once it is acknowledged that moral norms are simply conventions. These conventions, which the community 'teaches' to its children as they grow up in it, are far too deeply ingrained in social life to give way to amoral chaos.

Protagoras' argument concerning the nature of virtue, which is a mundane quality accessible to the many, and the sense in which it can be taught is clearly designed to support the democratic case. Socrates' response—which is only hinted at in this dialogue and remains to be elaborated elsewhere—is to redefine virtue so that it is identified with something more exalted and less accessible. Virtue for Socrates is one, a single unity which is philosophic *knowledge*; and virtue as knowledge is something that can, indeed must, be taught, but can be learned only by a select few. Given the context in which these philosophic principles are introduced, it is difficult to deny their essentially political meaning.

After this dialogue, though the ghost of Protagoras, or someone very like him, continues to stalk Plato's work (and though Protagoras reappears almost explicitly in the last dialogue, the *Laws*, where Plato asserts that god and not man is the measure of all things, in response to Protagoras' most famous dictum),[17] he never again directly confronts a serious democratic argument. Even in the *Protagoras*, Plato's Socrates evades the issues raised by his opponent. Thereafter, Plato becomes even more evasive. In later dialogues, Protagoras' view that moral principles are conventional appears only in the amoral form espoused by Callicles in the *Gorgias* and to some extent Thrasymachus in the *Republic*. In sharp contrast to Protagoras, Callicles argues that moral conventions are evil and should be disobeyed because they are merely conventions. Instead, natural law, the principle of natural justice which prescribes the rule of the strong over the weak should prevail. The rule of *nomos* is a bad thing because it establishes an artificial equality that gives the weak an unnatural advantage. Despite this vivid contrast between Callicles and Protagoras, Plato with great subtlety makes Callicles appear as representative of the democratic world-view: just as Socrates is in love with philosophy, he suggests, Callicles is in love with the democracy of Athens.[18] And this identification of Callicles with the democracy is made despite the explicitly anti-democratic and anti-egalitarian nature of his argument and despite the fact that he shares Plato's own view that rule and subordination are natural, that equality is merely conventional and therefore evil, and that the rule of law is bad insofar as it establishes equality. In the *Gorgias* and elsewhere, Plato constantly creates the impression that the sophistic view of morality as conventional is reducible to Callicles' amorality and that this amorality is an essential characteristic of the democratic world-view. (On the other hand, Plato's own commitment to the subordination of the many to the few, unlike Callicles', is the embodiment of the highest absolute morality.) This undifferentiated view of Sophism, in which Protagoras is at least implicitly lumped together with the amoral and unprincipled Callicles, has been very influential and tenacious; and yet, Plato's presentation of the Sophists is itself a supreme example of the argumentative trickery we have come to know as 'sophistry'. It is almost as if Plato dare not confront Protagoras face-to-face.

3. *The 'Republic': A Redefinition of the Polis*

It was suggested at the outset that Plato's genius lies in his attempt to 'aristocratize' the polis and politicize the aristocracy, to transform the notion of the polis in such a way as to synthesize two essentially and historically antithetical principles, the political and the aristocratic. The *Republic* should be considered in the light of this suggestion. In that work Plato systematically reconstructs the polis so that its very essence becomes the subordination of the community to a ruling class that personifies the values of the Athenian aristocracy. At the same time, he formulates the modern aristocratic code in such a way that it does not entail rejection of the polis. As extreme as his programme may appear, however, he does not go as far as he does in the *Laws*, a seemingly more moderate and practical work. In the *Republic* he does not yet outline a complete transformation of the economic and social infrastructure of the polis. Instead, he simply imagines the superimposition of a new aristocratic ruling class upon the existing social structure, and addresses himself primarily to the problem of philosophically justifying its rule. In the *Laws* he will follow up the clues provided in the *Republic* and actually propose the kind of total transformation of the social structure which would make the existence of an aristocratic ruling class possible. In the *Republic* he is not so much outlining a programme for the new polis as constructing a philosophical foundation for aristocratic rule, primarily by transforming the *idea* of the polis, but in part also by reformulating the code of the aristocracy so that it might contribute to its own justification by proving its truly 'political' nature.

The theme of the *Republic*, then, is the adaptation of the polis to the aristocracy and, to some extent, the aristocracy to the polis. The former task is clearly the more essential one from Plato's point of view, and it takes up most of the work. The latter involves an updating of the aristocratic code, or rather a philosophic systematization of current aristocratic values appropriate to the current realities of the polis. The new code was to replace in theory the old Homeric code—that relic of by-gone aristocratic supremacy—which had long since been replaced in practice. Homer was still regarded by many as the greatest of moral teachers at a time when few of the principles embodied in Homeric poetry could be realistically applied. The point now was not so much to invent a new set of values, since historical circumstances had for the most part done that, but systematically to codify a system of values that reflected more accurately the actual position and values of the contemporary aristocracy, while modifying those principles somewhat to further the rather unrealistic, largely nostalgic, hope of reinstating that aristocracy as an unchallenged ruling class. A new *form* for the new code was needed, too. Epic poetry, recounting the exploits of aristocratic heroes, may have been an appropriate form for the moral education of a dominant warrior-noble class. It had little to offer an urbane polis-dwelling leisure class no longer supreme in war or council. The form of the poetic ethic may be explained by the fact that in a society completely dominated by hero-nobles and their values, object lessons in the form of model hero-nobles might in themselves carry sufficient absoluteness and universality to serve as absolute and universal moral principles. In a society where they no longer reigned supreme such models must have appeared much too particular and relative. One could no longer take for granted that the values of the noble class were regarded as universal or that the audience being addressed shared them. If the values of that class were to be universalized, they had to be embodied in a more unassailably absolute form. The individual hero-models of Homer had to be transformed into universal philosophical moral principles. Thus, as Plato replaced Homer, philosophy replaced poetry as the great moral teacher of the upper class.[19]

Werner Jaeger has even argued that the Platonic doctrine of Ideas is 'directly descended' in its form from the old aristocratic ethic of hero-models:

> The poet [Homer] considers that the appeal to the example of famous heroes and traditional instances is an integral part of all aristocratic ethics and education....But the later Greeks also held to

> the *paradeigma*, the *example for imitation*, as a fundamental category in life and thought.... It is part of the very essence of old aristocratic ethics.... And if we remember that Plato's whole philosophy is built on the conception of pattern, and that he describes the Ideas as 'patterns established in the realm of Being' [*Theaetetus*, 176e], we can easily see the origin of the category. The Idea of the 'Good' (or more correctly the Idea of the ἀγαθόν), that universally applicable pattern, is directly descended from the models of heroic areté which were part of the old aristocratic code.[20]

If the *Republic* is considered in this light, Plato's opening arguments assume a new significance. The first substantive discussions on the nature of justice occur between Socrates and Polemarchus and then Thrasymachus. The conceptions of justice with which Socrates takes particular issue are, first, a traditional notion of justice as 'helping your friends and harming your enemies', suggested by Polemarchus; and second, Thrasymachus' proposition that justice is 'the interest of the stronger'. The choice of these two principles as a point of departure is noteworthy. It is curious that Plato does not begin by engaging Socrates with proponents of a typically democratic conception of justice—such as the kind that might be proposed by a disciple of Protagoras, for example—although the purpose of virtually the entire subsequent argument of the *Republic* is to oppose precisely such a democratic view.[21] Instead, he launches his argument against Athenian democracy with an attack on two principles that are fundamental to the old aristocratic ethic. Moreover, although the burden of the *Republic*'s argument is opposition to the democratic conception of justice as entailing equality, Plato introduces his argument with an attack on a conception of justice based on a principle he shares—the principle of rule and subordination. As democracy evolved, *diké* had increasingly acquired the implication of *equality*. To quote A. D. Winspear, '... at one point it seemed in danger of becoming equated with equality (*to ison*) or, at least, the moderate form of the same idea, "equality before the law" (*isonomia*)'.[22] Although not democratic in its origins, the concept of *isonomia* gradually became the slogan of the democracy. 'Against tyranny and against the oligarchic rule of the rich families,' writes Ehrenberg, 'was raised the plain demand for Isonomia which—whether as "equality of distribution" or "equality before the law"—became the expressive symbol of a democratic constitution. Inside democracy the principle of equality could imply a variety of different contents ...' (equal right to vote, equal freedom of speech, equality of honour and privilege, etc.).[23] Plato's concept of justice deliberately rejects the identity of justice and equality, even equality in its moderate form of *isonomia*. It does so, however, not by attacking the democratic concept directly, but rather by essentially ignoring it and allowing his Socrates to debate only those conceptions of justice which, like his own, have nothing to do with equality or explicitly reject it. In fact, throughout the *Republic* Plato never directly confronts any reasoned statement of a democratic position, unless one interprets the argument of Cephalus—which is hardly taken seriously and is quickly dismissed—as a rather naive version of the Protagorean doctrine of *nomos* and 'respect'. This contributes to the air of absoluteness and universality with which Plato invests his new aristocratic code, since, while it is never directly confronted by anything essentially antithetical to itself, it appears to evolve out of a true dialectic, rising from the particular and relative to the universal and absolute.

It would seem that at this point in the *Republic* Plato is attacking not so much moral relativism in general—the moral relativism of Sophistic doctrine and the democratic culture that spawned it—as the 'relativity' of particular forms of the aristocratic ethic, to which he is opposing an aristocratic ethic in a more absolute and universal form. The values of a dominant class, like the aristocracy in Homeric times, have their own, as it were, practical absoluteness and universality; the values of a no longer dominant class become practically relative and particular. For example, the proposition that justice is the interest of the stronger, for all its inherent relativity, would serve the unchallenged Homeric nobility very well as an 'absolute' justification for their rule. In Plato's time, however, the relativity of that old aristocratic principle becomes much more apparent, for, as Thrasymachus concedes, in a democratic city the democratic faction is the stronger and the principle can be used to justify democratic rule. The universality and absoluteness that aristocratic values had lost in practice with the nobility's loss of political and even cultural dominance was to be regained philosophically, and this was the task of the *Republic*. In the *Laws*, Plato would show how it might be regained in practice.

To universalize the aristocratic ethic meant to *politicize* it, in other words to ground it in the polis. The traditional Homeric code was grounded in the *oikos*. The principal ties, rights, loyalties, and obligations were those of the noble household, based on the relationships of master-servant, head of the household and family, lord and retainer; the ties between households were the bonds of kinship and guest-friendship, which also constituted the class ties of the ruling society. The line of command within the household was clear, and the head of the household was lord and master, while whatever hierarchy existed among the largely self-sufficient households depended above all on power. The code of power and friendship enunciated in the *Republic* by Thrasymachus and Polemarchus, then, was eminently well-suited to an *oikos*-centered society. In the urban community of Plato's time, when the polis and not the *oikos* was the principal economic and political unit and the aristocracy no longer dominated, social bonds, rights, and obligations transcended kinship- or friendship-group and household, and the line of command embodied in the rigid household relationships no longer applied. If the aristocracy was now to claim a place as the rightful ruling class of the polis, it had to claim the polis as its own as the *oikos* had been. It had to translate the principle of household hierarchy into a principle of subordination that encompassed the entire comprehensive community of the polis, to transform the ruling *society* of household-lords, each undisputed master of his own household, into a ruling *class*, the corporate master of an urban community.

Just as the realities of the contemporary polis, then, had made the doctrine of Thrasymachus unsuitable as an aristocratic principle—both because the aristocracy was not, in fact, the 'stronger' and, of course, because the virtues of a warrior-class are ill-suited to an urban community—the doctrine of Polemarchus had also been rendered inappropriate. Any tribal principle which implied the fragmentation of the community into particularistic associations like household, clan, or friendship group could no longer serve the purposes of the aristocracy. This is not, of course, to say that these associations play no role in Plato's thought. It is simply that in order to fit the position of the aristocracy to the realities of the polis and to establish the claim of the aristocracy as the rightful ruling class, with absolute authority over other classes, he had to emphasize that all classes are united in a comprehensive whole that transcends the more particular associations of kinship and friendship, a whole in which some parts are by definition subordinate to others. The polis must be recognized as a unity with ties and obligations as compelling as those of the old *oikos*; the aristocracy must be as much a part of the polis as the lord was of the *oikos*; and the community as a whole must be bound to the aristocratic ruling class as the household was bound to its lord. The tribal principle of Polemarchus, moreover, is unsatisfactory even if all members of the polis are identified as 'friends', because in this form the principle implies equality among members of the polis and does not inherently contain the principle of hierarchy and subordination that Plato requires.

The doctrine of justice that Plato goes on so painstakingly to construct in his well-known argument embodies precisely the principle of organic unity and hierarchy that is needed. The polis becomes by definition an organic whole in its very essence composed of parts that are related to each other according to a natural and hierarchical social division of labour based on fundamental differences and inequalities among men; and justice is nothing more than the principle of proper and natural subordination of the lower parts to the higher. Plato with great subtlety transforms the traditional notion of justice, *diké*, as 'to each man his due', which as the democracy progressed had increasingly acquired an implication of equality or *isonomia*, into the dictum 'to each man his proper function and no other', in accordance with Plato's hierarchical conception of the social division of labour. Thus, the principle that historically has tended toward equality is transformed into a principle the essence of which is inequality and subordination. More particularly, this new concept of justice, firmly based as it is on a clearly defined social division of labour, does not simply establish the principle of hierarchy and subordination in general, but also specifies precisely the necessary position in the hierarchy of each existing social class.

For all its abstraction and the highly fanciful nature of the *Republic*'s ruling class, there is no mistaking the practical consequences of Plato's argument and its imaginary hierarchy. If one extracts the *principles* contained in Plato's imaginary ruling class, isolating them from their fictional personification, it is not so difficult to identify the one class in the concrete world of historical Athens which most nearly embodies those principles. Above all, Plato's rulers must belong to a leisure class not corrupted by labour, trade, or profession, a class which, in its freedom from labour and its ability to command the labour of others, rises above the realm of necessity. In the historical reality of Greece, one class satisfies those conditions: a landed hereditary aristocracy which gains its livelihood from inalienable property acquired without effort according to strict rules of inheritance, not by its own labour but by the labour of others to which that property entitles it, and not by the free disposal and exchange of property.

One should not be deceived by the seemingly antithetical differences between a propertyless ruling class and a landed aristocracy that is the hereditary and virtually exclusive possessor of all property. Both represent the same fundamental principles, as Plato makes very clear in the *Laws*. In that work, where Plato outlines a 'second-best' substitute for the fanciful city of the *Republic*, he argues quite explicitly that a system of hereditary and exclusive private ownership will come as close as possible to achieving the same effect as the 'communism' he proposes for the ruling class in the *Republic*.[24] For Plato, as apparently for others of his class and perhaps for Greeks in general, the abolition of private property (in a particular sense) was not the diametrical opposite of hereditary private ownership; and it is quite understandable, in the historical context, that this should be the case. Both the propertylessness of the *Republic*'s ruling class and the hereditary landed property of the *Laws* are opposed to private property in a narrower sense: what we might call bourgeois property, the more strictly private and individual, alienable, and more freely disposable property that is the basis of a commercial society, as distinct from the entailed, ideally inalienable and exclusive, family or clan property that is the basis of an agrarian feudal order and the source of aristocratic power. The guardians of the *Republic* and the citizens of the *Laws* represent, at different levels of abstraction, the same aristocratic ruling class and embody the same fundamentally aristocratic values.

4. *The Social Conditions of Virtue and the 'Philosophic Nature'*

Plato's aristocratic perspective is revealed both in the nature of the specific virtues he demands of his ruling class and even more strongly in his account of the *conditions* of virtue, the particular social and existential circumstances that alone permit the existence of virtue. To put it another way, it can be argued that what is most aristocratic about Plato's moral philosophy is its synthesis of moral quality and social position—the kind of synthesis suggested by the English word 'nobility', which implies both a moral attribute and a social status, the one inherent in the other. A similar synthesis is contained in the Homeric concept of *hero* and in the *aretē* which characterizes the true hero. Homer's heroes are not simply men who display the qualities of courage and honour; they are equally, inseparably, and by definition landowners, heads of household, warlords, or their kinsmen. And, certainly, such a synthesis is a factor in the Greek concept of *kalokagathia*, as in its English counterpart, the virtues of the 'gentleman'.[25] At any rate, in Plato's ethic, as at least by implication in other aristocratic codes, virtue is an attribute of a life-situation or social condition. Each class has virtues peculiar and appropriate to it; but the important point is that *true* virtue—that which is not simply relative—is the specific virtue which is peculiar to the upper class, the nobility, and which only the life-situation of members of that class can make possible. Only that life-situation is not inevitably bound to the world of material necessity, the world of 'multiplicity', which is the enemy of philosophy; and only that life-situation permits the fulfillment of the 'philosophic' nature which is the embodiment of the highest virtue. By the same token, true moral inferiority is the special vice of the lower classes, the 'vulgar' mob of labourers, craftsmen, and traders, those who of necessity are tied to the world of appearances, the material world, those who because they earn their living necessarily live 'among the multiplicity of things'

—in short, those 'stunted natures, whose souls a life of drudgery has warped and maimed'.[26] It is their condition that in its very essence represents the diametrical opposite of the philosophic nature, the essence of true corruption. An aristocrat may lack virtue, may even be guilty of the greatest evil, but he can never—as long as he continues to live in the conditions of an aristocrat—be corrupt in this essential and absolute way. Just as there are different kinds of virtue, relative or absolute, so are there different kinds of evil and corruption. In effect, Plato's most basic *moral* distinction is not so much between virtue and vice in general as between the *aristocratic* and the *common* or *vulgar*.

Before we pursue in greater detail these suggestions about the nature of virtue and corruption in Plato's doctrine, an important question must be raised concerning the correspondence of moral distinctions with class distinctions in that doctrine. It is well-known that in the *Republic* Plato proposes that all talented children, irrespective of their class origins, be selected for training to the ruling class. It is often contended that this is enough to invalidate any argument that *class* is the crux of Plato's moral philosophy, since what Plato wants is a meritocracy which raises up the best from all classes, and not the rule of a particular class. One could, of course, simply respond that, if one chooses to emphasize that aspect of Plato's argument which stresses innate differences among men, one must still deal with the fact that he is justifying class differentials by arguing that they are based on profound natural inequalities and with the fact that, in any case, his utopia is based on the assumption that with rare exceptions 'gold' will breed 'gold' and 'brass' will breed 'brass'. The advocates of Platonic meritocracy must still deal with the awkward implications of a theory which grounds class inequalities in natural inequalities and which, perhaps not as logically as they would like to think, draws political implications from these inequalities concerning the right to rule. Nevertheless, this is not the central issue here. The problem with which the present argument is concerned, and which the proponents of this view of Plato tend to overlook, is the tremendous importance he attaches to the social conditions of virtue, or, at least, his ambiguity concerning the relative importance of natural talent and social status as the determining factor in the production of virtue.

Let us look again at Cornford, who subscribes to the meritocratic version of Plato. Here is his account of Plato's argument:

> In the *Republic* his fundamental thesis is that the inborn disposition which can develop the highest qualities of intellect and character required to make a good ruler, is very rarely found and very

> easily corrupted. The human race will not see the end of trouble until society is effectively controlled by the few men and women in whom those qualities have been developed to the full by an arduous moral and intellectual training and by experience in practical life. Plato was an oligarch and an aristocrat in the sense that he thought mankind can be well governed only by a few, and those few the wisest and best. He also believed that the capacities required are normally inherited, but may appear in any stratum of society. They can be discovered and brought to the front only as they emerge in childhood and youth. Accordingly, all children of all the citizens in the ideal state are to receive the same elementary education, during which their behaviour, under tests of every sort, will be carefully watched. The most promising will be sifted out without any regard to their parentage....[27]

Plato's position according to this account, then, is that the qualities of soul that characterize the 'philosophic' nature are inborn, generally but not always hereditary, and that they are properly developed or else corrupted, but in no way produced, by the particular conditions of upbringing and education. Nothing, apparently, is at issue but the natural talents, the innate intelligence and character of any individual and the training he receives to develop that natural and innate talent; and to counter any argument that Plato is proposing a hereditary ruling class of landed aristocrats, it seems sufficient to remind us that in the *Republic*, children of natural talent from any stratum of society will be selected for the special training of the ruling class, that 'the most promising will be sifted out without any regard to their parentage'.

This, however, is not enough to lay to rest the suggestion that Plato is arguing a philosophical brief for the Athenian aristocracy. Again, we may leave aside the implications of the assumption that, since for the most part like breeds like, fitness to rule is for all practical purposes hereditary. Far more important from our point of view is the fact that Plato identifies very specifically the social circumstances, the position in the social division of labour, the role in the productive process which a man must occupy in order to fulfill the conditions of the philosophic nature. The very least that can be said is that, whatever the natural talents of any individual, an absolutely essential condition for the development of those talents is that he occupy the proper position in the social division of labour; and that if he is improperly situated in the productive process, his soul will be warped and his natural talents will wither and die. So much is perhaps compatible with Cornford's account, although he seems to be thinking more in terms of the consequences of education as such than of the social division of labour. What is usually overlooked, however, is that Plato is far from unequivocal about the importance of natural differences. It is possible to argue that for Plato, in the final analysis, the significance of natural talents and natural inequalities pales before the consequences of the social division of labour.[28] If this is so and Plato is some kind of 'environmentalist', his doctrine may in one sense be less reactionary than a theory that stresses natural inequalities. On the other hand, given the historical realities of ancient Greece, such an emphasis on the social conditions of virtue must be reactionary and anti-democratic if it is associated with Plato's preference for a particular kind of 'virtue' and life-style. If one takes for granted the inevitability of the traditional social division of labour and if one shares Plato's aristocratic values, 'environmentalism' is very likely to lead to the conclusion that in the real world, a hereditary landed aristocracy—a class which inherits not so much the appropriate natural talents as the necessary social conditions—is the only rightful, indeed natural, ruling class, a conviction which is clearly reflected in the *Laws*.

Let us examine Plato's 'environmentalism', then. What precisely goes into the make-up of the philosophic nature? Plato speaks of several necessary qualities, notably, of course, the love of truth, combined with quickness to learn, good memory, high-mindedness, grace, justice, courage, and temperance. The impression left by interpretations like Conford's is that all these qualities—the qualities of the 'wisest and best' who alone can govern well—are innate and natural qualities of soul, which are simply activated and developed by rigorous training. In the course of Plato's own account, however, it often appears that these qualities must be divided into primary and secondary qualities—that is, those that are in fact innate, and those that are dependent on the conditions of life and training, not simply for their activation, but even for their creation. The primary qualities consist of what might be called instrumental qualities or skills; to these may perhaps be added certain inborn personality traits that constitute capacities for specific virtues, although Plato is rather ambiguous on this score. The secondary qualities are the substantive virtues themselves; and these are not innate, but dependent on education and condition in life. The primary skills are no more than neutral implements; the primary personality traits no more than open-ended possibilities. The innate or natural skills that go to make up the 'philosophic' nature appear to reduce themselves to quickness to learn and good memory.

The better the tools, the more effectively they will perform the tasks to which they are set; but the nature of the task to which they will be set is not predetermined. The higher the degree of skill, no doubt, the more quickly and easily can the other virtues be learned; but natural skills can just as easily—even more easily—become the instruments of injustice, wickedness, and falsehood, as of justice, temperance, and truth. As for any inborn personality traits that may be essential to the philosophic nature, the only one that appears to have anything like the status of the innate instrumental skills of intelligence is the quality of *spiritedness*. This quality may be something more specific than the general instrumental quality of intelligence; it may be something more akin to a specific capacity for particular virtues, like courage or highmindedness. But even this quality, insofar as it is innate, is never more for Plato than a neutral capacity which in the absence of correct upbringing will produce qualities very different from the philosophic virtues. If innate spiritedness is the basis of courage, or any of the other philosophic traits, it is equally true that, in the absence of proper training, the spirited nature will be 'unmanly and boorish'. In other words, Plato is, at the very most, speaking of *capacities*, not *dispositions*, for the philosophic virtues; and the capacities are equally capacities for very unphilosophic qualities: spiritedness is a 'capacity' not only for courage, but for boorishness; just as 'quickness to learn' and 'good memory', the skills of intelligence, can be used at least as easily and naturally in the interests of falsehood as of truth.

Although Plato is, again, sometimes ambiguous—or ambivalent—and not entirely consistent on this score, on the whole his theory of education, his account of the corruption of the philosophic nature and of the decline of the state all confirm the view that the virtues—courage, temperance, justice, grace, highmindedness, and love of truth (and consequently the truly essential differences of quality among human beings) are *created*, not simply activated, by painstaking education and an upbringing in the proper conditions, a constant exposure to the 'beautiful' and 'harmonious', a careful avoidance of the 'vulgar' and 'base'. After all, the entire system of education is obviously predicated on the assumption that the desired qualities must be laboriously inculcated. 'Grace of body and mind . . . is only to be found in one who is brought up in the right way';[29] 'courage and steadfastness may [i.e., by proper training] be united in a soul that would otherwise be either unmanly or boorish';[30] and so on. If, however, upbringing and education are the decisive factors, it must be understood that the upbringing and education are the decisive factors, it must be understood that the upbringing and education which Plato has in mind are not simply a kind of schooling, but a total social condition. The ultimate dividing line between the 'educated' and 'uneducated' is the line between those who work, especially with their hands, and those who have had a 'liberal upbringing'. The education that makes the difference between virtue and vice is clearly an aristocratic one, unmistakably based on the traditional education received by the upper-class youths of Athens, before the 'new education' of the Sophists. It is clearly an education for those who have been 'set free from all manual crafts to be the artificers of their country's freedom, with the perfect mastery which comes of working only at what conduces to that end....'[31] Just as clearly, it is an education which is possible only for a very few, quite irrespective of the distribution of talent in the population, given the existing conditions of the division of labour and the necessity for the majority to be engaged in 'base and menial' (banausic) occupations. A life prepared for such 'banausic' occupations, moreover, is the diametrical and essential opposite of a 'liberal' upbringing. Indeed, it would appear that a liberal education, even when combined with great natural talent, is more likely to be nullified by over-exposure to the 'banausic', which may come about if one is forced by circumstances to work for a living, or even if one lives in a democracy surrounded and ruled by the 'banausic' masses. Again, Plato's stance is revealed by this typically aristocratic opposition between the 'liberal' and the 'banausic' which for him clearly represent both moral qualities and social conditions. In short, the 'philosophic nature' is the shape given to natural talent by aristocratic upbringing.

The very least that can be said, then, is that Plato is not unequivocal in attributing the 'philosophic nature' to inborn qualities which are the exclusive property of a few select souls. A careful consideration of his argument reveals that, although he speaks of the inborn qualities necessary to the creation of a noble character (*kalos kagathos*) and appears to assume profound natural inequalities among men, much if not most of the time he is saying no more than could be accepted by many modern environmentalists who would be the last to think in terms of 'philosophic natures' or 'golden souls': namely, that there are varying degrees of natural intelligence among men and, perhaps, that there are varying degrees of constitutional energy or vigour among them. It must be noted, too, that differences in intelligence and 'spiritedness' are gradual, continuous, not dichotomous. There may be differences of degree among various qualities of soul, but there can be no clear dividing line between those who can learn and those who cannot. If, therefore, the dramatically antithetical and dichotomous opposition of 'philosophic' to 'unphilosophic' or 'gold and silver' to 'iron and brass'—an opposition so sharp that it must be reflected in a permanent division between rulers and ruled—has any meaning, it must refer to something other than the differences among innate qualities of soul. It is, of course, clear that when Plato differentiates among natures of different quality, between 'gold and silver' on the one hand and 'iron and brass' on the other, or between philosophic and unphilosophic, he does intend a far more fundamental and dichotomous distinction, a much more sharply defined dividing line, than is suggested by subtle gradations along the continuum of natural intelligence quotients and innate capacities, and that the category of superior natures is meant to be far more exclusive than such vague distinctions would allow.[32] The vastness of the difference between the virtuous few who are by nature qualified to rule (both 'gold' and 'silver') and the vulgar many who are not ('iron' and 'brass') cannot be accounted for simply by the natural inequalities among men, by their degrees of 'quickness to learn' and 'good memory' or their degrees of 'spiritedness'. The unbridgeable chasm between those who are fit for rule and those who are not is less a consequence of natural inequalities than of the vastly different conditions of life imposed by the social division of labour. The principal dividing line in that division of labour is between those who must engage in labour or trade for their livelihood, and those that need not and do not do so. That dividing line is the essential one not simply for the obvious reason that leisure time is required for the kind of education Plato proposes (indeed, members of the trading classes may have leisure time) but above all because work for a livelihood—and in this respect labourers, craftsmen, merchants, and farmers[33] are all tied to the material world, the 'multiplicity of things'—is by nature and necessarily corrupting.

Plato confirms the impression that corruption is relative to social conditions in his account of the decline of the ideal state. The watershed in the decline is the fall from timocracy, a kind of warrior-state like Sparta dominated by the love of honour, to oligarchy, the rule of the wealthy—or more precisely, the possessors of alienable property and hence men of money.[34] This transition must be regarded as the watershed because oligarchy marks the beginning of rule by the lowest part of the soul, the sensual appetites, although the love of money is the best of the appetites because it still keeps the baser appetites in check. Apart from the importance Plato attaches here to the effect on the soul of changes in the nature of property, it is significant that, again, he regards as essential to his typology the question of whether or not those who govern belong to a class that 'works for a living'. The timocracy will resemble the ideal state in several essential respects, notably that 'authority will be respected' and 'the fighting [i.e., ruling] class will abstain from any form of business, farming, or handicrafts'.[35] On the other hand, here is how Plato describes the transition from the timocratic man to the oligarchic man and the circumstances in which the sensual appetites capture the soul: The son of a timocratic type whose fortunes have suddenly been ruined is terror-stricken at the sight of his father's ruin:

> At once that spirit of eager ambition which hitherto ruled in his heart is thrust headlong from the throne. Humbled by poverty, he turns to earning his living and, little by little, through hard work and petty savings, scrapes together a fortune. And now he will instal another spirit on the vacant throne, the money-loving spirit of sensual appetite, like an eastern monarch with diadem and golden chain and scimitar girt at his side.[36]

However schematic or metaphorical Plato's account of the state's decline may be, it is clear that he is doing more than simply classifying states according to the 'pyschological types' that dominate them.[37] He is saying that psychological types change according to social circumstances, and he is telling us something about the effects on the soul of certain social conditions. Despite his poetic remarks about the 'breed of iron and brass', on the one hand, and the 'breed of silver and gold', on the other, pulling the state in different directions and determining the quality of the state by their struggle, he goes on to show, if anything, not how the 'breed' of man makes the state, but how social conditions and the social circumstances of the individual create the 'breed'. The quality of the state apparently depends to a great extent on the nature of property and the position in the social division of labour occupied by members of the ruling class; the quality of the individual soul depends to a great extent on the individual's relation to property and the division of labour.

This brings us back to the suggestion that there are two types of corruption: the 'absolute' corruption of the lower classes and the 'relative' corruption of the aristocracy. If absolute corruption is a quality inherent in and exclusive to the 'productive' classes, what kind of corruption is possible among the non-productive classes? Again, no one whose life has been free from the necessity of labour, no one who has 'abstained from any form of business, farming, or handicrafts', no one who has had an aristocratic upbringing, can ever be totally corrupt in the way of someone whose soul has been 'warped and maimed' by earning his livelihood. He can, of course, like anyone else be a man of indifferent talents and hence be incapable of either great good or great harm; but in such a case, he will at least, as long as he lives in the condition of an aristocrat, be free of the fundamental sins of vulgarity and baseness inherent in the condition of the lower classes and associated with a life that is unavoidably tied to the realm of matter and necessity. At worst, such an aristocratic mediocrity will be uncorrupted without being truly virtuous. What is more intriguing, however, is what Plato has to say about the corruption of a truly superior nature, one which is talented enough to be capable of great evil. Plato readily concedes—even stresses—that a superior nature, with the makings of a philosopher, may be guilty of great evil, greater evil than that of lesser natures. Nevertheless, his corruption is very different from the basic corruption of the vulgar. The vice of the superior nature is not so much vice as it is, so to speak, an inversion of moral virtue; and in Plato's hands it even becomes a kind of proof of the inherent superiority of the aristocratic few and their fitness to rule over the vulgar many. The whole tone of the argument suggests that Plato is not concerned simply with the corruption of the naturally gifted, irrespective of class, but with the corruption of a nature that has already been distinguished from the mass by upbringing and social position. While his gifted counterpart among the lower classes will, by means of his upbringing, have been able to do little more than develop his gifts in the form of mere 'mechanical cleverness' and, perhaps, a 'spirited' boorishness, the potential philosopher's gifts have already been given an aristocratic shape; his education and social position have already developed in him many of the qualities that identify the philosophic nature. Plato's model of the corrupted philosophic nature is clearly, as many commentators have pointed out, the talented, handsome, and refined, even courageous, young aristocrat like Alcibiades, led astray by the vulgar mob. In short, just as the philosophic nature is, as it were, the shape given to natural gifts by an aristocratic upbringing, the corruption of the philosophic nature is the corruption of a gifted individual whose gifts have already taken an aristocratic shape; it is corruption by 'all the good things of life, as they are called...: beauty, wealth, strength, powerful connexions, and so forth',[38] when misdirected by the mob, as distinct from the kind of corruption by poverty, drudgery, and baseness that comes with a lowly position.

It would appear that the corrupted philosophic nature proves its superiority even in its pursuit of evil: 'Great crimes and unalloyed wickedness are the outcome of a nature full of generous promise, ruined by bad upbringing.'[39] By the same token, the lesser or 'counterfeit' natures prove their inferiority in the very pursuit of the good, giving philosophy and the philosophic nature a bad name because they 'take to a pursuit too high and too good for them....'[40] Again, there is more than a suggestion that these 'counterfeit' natures who illegitimately strive to become philosophic are to be identified with a particular class. It is natural, says Plato, that philosophy is dishonoured

> ... when any poor creature who has proved his cleverness in some mechanical craft, sees here an opening for a pretentious display of high-sounding words and is glad to break out of the prison of his paltry trade and take sanctuary in the shrine of philosophy. For as

> compared with other occupations, philosophy, even in its present case, still enjoys a higher prestige, enough to attract a multitude of stunted natures, whose souls a life of drudgery has warped and maimed no less surely than their sedentary crafts have disfigured their bodies.[41]

Furthermore, it soon becomes clear that the 'bad upbringing' which Plato blames for the corruption of the 'promising' natures does not refer to their home-life—which, if it is aristocratic, will presumably be the source of their virtues, not their vices—or even to their education, but rather to the influence of the mob: 'Or do you hold the popular belief that, here and there, certain young men are demoralized by the private instructions of some individual sophist?' asks Plato. 'Does that sort of influence amount to much? Is not the public itself the greatest of all sophists, training up young and old, men and women alike, into the most accomplished specimens of the character it desires to produce?'[42] This is precisely the danger of life in a democracy, where the vulgar masses rule. Thus, while the corruption of the aristocracy is different from that of the masses, the source of both kinds of corruption is to be found in the masses. In this sense, too, the masses are 'absolutely' corrupt: the condition of the aristocracy is the source of all virtue; the condition of the masses is the source of all corruption.

Let us sum up, then, some of the apparent implications of Plato's account of corruption: Not only is the essential vice of the vulgar responsible for the conditional vice (or inverted virtue) of the nobles, and the democracy for the sins of the aristocracy; the vices of one class reflect its insurmountable unsuitability for politics, while the vices of the other, paradoxically, prove its capacity to rule. On the basis of Plato's moral standard, the worst excesses of the aristocracy—such as the rule of the Thirty Tyrants, whose regime even Plato (if the *Seventh Epistle* is to be believed) regards as the worst that Athens has ever known, worse than even the democracy of his day—far from proving that the aristocracy is no more fit to rule than the mob, could, on the contrary, conceivably be used to justify aristocratic rule. It is the democracy itself which corrupts the aristocracy, and the superior quality of that aristocracy is proved by the very magnitude of its crimes. In any case, there are two kinds of 'corruption', only one of which represents a truly fundamental moral inferiority: one is the corruption of an aristocrat led astray by the mob, the other is that of the mob itself. The one is conditional, the other absolute. While the particular virtues of the lower classes, the 'stunted natures', can never be more than relative, their vice is absolute; indeed, since their position in life has 'warped and maimed' their souls, making it impossible ever to achieve true virtue, and since the lesser virtue relative to their class is the highest they can attain, they are 'bad' even when they are 'good'. In short, Plato's most basic moral distinction is not so much between virtue and vice, or morality and immorality, as between the *aristocratic* and the *common* or *vulgar*; in fact, as we shall see when we look more closely into the precise nature of the 'philosophic' qualities of the virtuous man, it is often difficult to draw the line between moral virtue and aristocratic refinement, or between vice and 'commonness' or vulgarity.

It is difficult, then, to avoid the conclusion that the essential condition for the existence of the virtuous or philosophic few is the ensured existence of a class of men whose livelihood does not depend on their own labour or trade and who can command the labour of others to supply their needs and wants. In the *Republic* that condition is met rather fancifully by the existence of the gentleman-Guardians, who are the non-labouring, though propertyless, servant-rulers of the community and whose basic needs are supplied by the labour of the community, the 'productive' classes. In the *Laws*, the condition is met in the more obvious—though, given the historical realities, no less utopian—form of a ruling hereditary aristocracy of landowners (of varying degrees of wealth in movable property) possessed of land acquired not by purchase or exchange, but only by inheritance according to the strictest rules, and commanding the labour of a non-citizen community of slaves, artisans, craftsmen, and traders. Despite the differences between the ruling classes of the two works, the fundamental conditions are present in both, and in this sense, the ruling class of the *Laws* can be seen as the concrete form of the principles idealized in the ruling class of the *Republic*. If in the *Republic* Plato remains ambiguous about the most crucial factor determining the quality of souls, in the *Laws* he has apparently concluded that, whatever the likelihood of gold breeding brass or brass breeding gold, there is far greater certainty that labour will breed corruption; and he appears to have decided that if virtue is to survive in the world, it must be ensured that the social conditions, if not the natural qualities, for virtue be preserved and inherited. The *Republic*, however, for all its ambiguity, already points in the direction of the *Laws* in this respect, too. A central theme of the *Republic* is the doctrine that the health of a man's soul depends, first, on the total social context which surrounds him—that is, the nature of the society in which he lives—and, second, on the particular position he occupies in that social context. It is clear that, barring the rarest of accidents, even the noblest natures—like Alcibiades or Critias—possessed of native intelligence, distinguished by birth, bred in an aristocratic household, and even educated by Socrates himself, will be unable to withstand corruption by life in a democracy—that is, life in a society dominated by vulgar natures.[43] It is equally clear that whatever the nature of the society, democratic or aristocratic, the man who occupies a lowly position, the man who earns his livelihood, will possess a warped and stunted soul. A well-governed society, then, *must* be one that is ruled by men who are not subject to either form of corruption—the inherent corruption of the mob itself, or the corruption of an aristocrat led astray by the mob; it must, therefore, be a society governed by an exclusive ruling class composed of men whose livelihood does not depend on their own labour or trade, who can command the labour of others, and who, of course, share a common and exclusive kind of cultivation and refinement. A more effective philosophical basis for arguing the case of the traditional Athenian landed aristocracy can hardly be imagined than the principles established in the *Republic* and implemented in the *Laws*.

It is worth noting, in this connection, that by drawing the fundamental social dividing line where he does—that is, between those who engage in labour or trade for their livelihood and those who do not—and in his conception of the ruling class, Plato is returning to the principles of the old Homeric lords and an era when the landowning aristocracy was unquestionably the dominant class. In modern democratic Athens, in which free labourers were citizens, the fundamental divisions—the ones which distinguished citizen from non-citizen—were above all the division between free man and slave, and the division between Athenian and non-Athenian. In the Homeric world-view, as we have seen, the fundamental distinction is between aristocrat and commoner, appropriator and producer, and the difference between free man and slave is blurred, as all labourers are servants. Plato's adoption of this Homeric viewpoint which was undoubtedly shared by many of his aristocratic contemporaries, is further testimony to the aristocratic perspective from which he approaches social and moral problems and to his deliberate departure from the realities and principles of the Athenian polis.

5. *An Idealized Aristocratic Code*

Plato's ethic is aristocratic not only in the sense that the conditions for virtue—which are not so much conditions for as essential aspects of virtue—are peculiar to the life-situation of an aristocracy, but also in the sense that the virtues he extols are reminiscent of the more conventional aristocratic codes of his own and other times.[44] They are, of course, not the archaic heroic virtues of power and individual prowess extolled by Homer and perhaps surviving, if in a degenerate form, in Thrasymachus and Callicles. These qualities had served their purpose in the warrior society of ancient Greece, but had outlived their usefulness in the modern urban community of Athens, which required more orderly virtues. As M. I. Finley writes, commenting on the conflict between the virtues of the Homeric hero and the needs of a *community* like the polis:

> In the following generations, when the community began to move from the wings to the center of the Greek stage, the hero quickly died out, for the honor of the hero was purely individual, something he lived and fought for only for its sake and his own sake. (Family attachment was permissible, but that was because one's kin were indistinguishable from oneself.) The honor of a community was a totally different quality, requiring another order of skills and virtues; in fact, the community could grow only by taming the hero and blunting the free exercise of his prowess, and a domesticated hero was a contradiction in terms.[45]

Plato's virtues are, in idealized form, those of the 'domesticated' aristocracy of the advanced polis, albeit with a degree of community-consciousness that was hardly typical of the Athenian aristocracy. What is most striking about Plato's ethic is its similarity not only to the conventional values of his aristocratic contemporaries, as far as they can be determined, but also to the codes of more modern aristocracies which have left behind them a violent era of primarily military virtues and entered a calmer period when aristocratic culture and refinement combine with, and to some extent overtake, military valour and skill as the hallmarks of nobility. For all its philosophical complexity, Plato's is at bottom the ethic of an urbane leisure class whose fundamental moral distinctions correspond to the contrast between aristocratic style and common vulgarity. Like so many of his aristocratic contemporaries and successors, Plato tends to a remarkable degree to identify moral virtue with gentility, grace, refinement, cultivation, and so on, and vice with vulgarity, 'commonness', coarseness, 'insolence', and 'presumption'—to the point that it becomes difficult to distinguish moral judgment from class propaganda.[46]

A consideration of the specific moral qualities that constitute true goodness for Plato is again complicated by a certain inconsistency. The difficulty here is that Plato constantly shifts his ground and moves freely and almost imperceptibly from one conceptual level to another in his discussion of virtue. At one moment, he appears to be using conventional moral terms—temperance, justice, etc.—in more or less their conventional meaning, in much the same sense his less philosophical contemporaries may have understood the 'cardinal virtues'. At other times, the same terms are infused with an idiosyncratic philosophical significance. Then, too, there are certain complications associated with the difference between what we have called 'absolute' and 'relative' virtues, according to which a man can be virtuous and unvirtuous in two different senses at the same time. Nevertheless, if Plato's argument lacks complete philosophical or conceptual consistency and clarity, it is precisely because there is a fundamental logic of another kind, which takes precedence over purely philosophical consistency. Each concept of virtue tends in its own way toward the same goal: the identification of the aristocracy as the only rightful ruling class.

As a framework for discussing the various forms assumed by the concept of virtue in the *Republic* and the common thread that links them, it might be useful to make a brief comment on the relation of virtue in the individual to virtue in the polis in that work. It is sometimes said that the *Republic* is not a political work at all, that is, not a treatise on justice in the state but rather a treatise on justice in the individual in which the just state is nothing more than an extended metaphor used to clarify the nature of the just soul. A less extreme position suggests that, while the *Republic* certainly has political significance, its central theme is the moral doctrine of individual virtue, that the theory of the state serves as a useful analogy to introduce the main theme, and that, in any case, while the two are clearly related, the problem of individual virtue takes precedence over virtue in the state, since the latter depends on the quality of the souls—the 'psychological' types—that dominate it. It is, of course, true that Plato introduces his argument as if his primary intention were to elucidate the nature of the just soul and at first even leaves us in some doubt as to how seriously we are to take his political doctrine. The structure of the argument as a whole, however, suggests a different purpose. While it is doubtful that Plato expected his political prescriptions to be taken literally (we have already suggested that the *Republic* simply establishes idealized *principles*, which the *Laws* implements), it is still an eminently —even primarily—political work. What is most striking about the logic of the *Republic* is the degree to which everything is subordinated to the principle of justice in the state as Plato defines it: the principle that justice is the rigid ordering of the state according to a hierarchical social division of labour in which each man performs the function proper to his class, and only that function, and in which the ruling class is a non-producing, non-labouring class that commands the labour of others. This principle is far more clear and consistent than the doctrine of individual virtue; and everything Plato has to say about the latter, whatever conceptual shifts and changes it undergoes, always serves to support the former.

A brief consideration of the three principal forms that the concept of individual virtue takes in the *Republic* should suffice to illustrate this point. Let us consider first Plato's concept of virtue as it seems to reflect conventional contemporary usage—for example, in his account of the Guardians' temperament, the effects of poetry and music, and much of the discussion of the attributes essential to the philosophic nature. His enumeration of desirable qualities in these passages turns out to be little more than a catalogue of the qualities held in esteem by the aristocrats and anti-democrats of his time and just as typically contrasted by them, as by Plato, to the vulgarities of the 'multitude'. The most pervasive characteristic of this catalogue is the identification of a particular style and bearing with moral character. 'Good form' seems to be the essence of all the cardinal virtues at this conventional level. There are numerous examples in the literature of Athens which testify to this identification in the conventional aristocratic culture. Ehrenberg, who stresses 'the importance which form and style in living had for the *kaloi kagathoi*',[47] makes the following comment on the aristocratic code of fourth-century Athens, turning to Aristophanes as a prime witness:

> In general, the nobles paid much attention to their manners and bearing. It could be regarded as the duty of a nobleman to save his face and not to show his feelings in front of the people. In the *Birds* Poseidon, the special god of the knights, adopted a very distinguished manner, and was horrified at the barbarian god because he wore his coat in the wrong way.[48]

Aristotle serves as a good example of how thin was the line in this world-view between unseemly dress and bearing, and thorough moral depravity. In the *Athenian Constitution*, his only comment on Cleon, the archetype of villains to the critics of Athenian democracy, is as follows:

> This man, more than anybody else, appears to have corrupted the people by his violent methods. He was the first who shouted on the public platform, who used abusive language and who spoke with his cloak girt up about him, while all the others used to speak in proper dress and manner.[49]

Nor is the importance Aristotle attaches to style and bearing as essential moral qualities less clear in his most systematic and detailed account of virtues and vices in the *Nicomachean Ethics*.

A similar outlook is expressed by Plato, who constantly emphasizes that outward bearing and manner of speech reflect the quality of the soul. 'Grace and seemliness of form' are the expressions of moral excellence and self-mastery; unseemliness and vulgarity express baseness of character. There are simply two different styles in all things—talking, singing, walking, acting—'one which will always be used by a man of fine character and breeding, the other by one whose nature and upbringing are of a very different sort'.[50] The characteristics cited by Plato to explain the nature of the principal virtues, like courage or temperance, are typically 'grace and seemliness of form', measure, rhythm, harmony, delicacy, the meaning of which becomes clearer in their contrast to crudity, awkwardness, vulgarity, insolence, impudence, and so on. This is not, of course, to suggest that only Athenians of aristocratic-oligarchic persuasion respected qualities such as grace and 'measure'. What is important here is the aristocratic stress on style and bearing as essential to virtue, and the identification of 'commonness' with moral and political incapacity. This aristocratic view is clearly incompatible with the ideas of a Protagoras, or even a Pericles, in spite of his own aristocratic credentials, since their political principles are based on the assumption that even the 'common' or 'vulgar' partake of political virtue and need not submit themselves entirely to the mastery of others in order to approximate the qualities of 'temperance' and moderation. Not only does Plato regard the qualities associated with aristocratic style as essential to moral virtue, but his terms of moral condemnation again are reminiscent of conventional aristocratic characterizations of the *poneroi*, the middle and lower classes, or 'bad men' (as opposed to the *kaloi kagathoi*, the gentlemen), the ' "common" man not only in a social, but also in a moral sense.'[51]

Plato's terms of moral praise and contempt, then, like those of other conservative critics of the democracy, are notable for their identification of virtue with aristocratic ideals and vice with the attributes of the common man. We have already noted the degree to which this fundamental moral contrast corresponds to the differentiation of roles in the social division of labour. Often it is impossible to distinguish the characterization of an occupation—as 'banausic', 'menial' or 'base and mechanical'—from a judgment of the moral character of its practitioner—e.g., the 'banausos', whose 'base and mechanical' trade is his very essence. By such a standard, there is nothing illogical or asymmetrical about contrasting the 'menial', 'vulgar', or 'base and mechanical', on the one hand, to the morally virtuous, on the other.

This aristocratic logic certainly informs Plato's identification of the philosophic nature with *kalokagathia*.[52] And in his opposition of the philosophic and unphilosophic natures can be seen an idealization of the more mundane and openly class-conscious opposition of the 'banausic' to the 'gentlemanly' which occurs, for example, in the works of Plato's eminently '*kalos kagathos*' contemporary, Xenophon. This antithesis between *banausia* and *kalokagathia* is the most revealing expression of the aristocratic ethical code and may be the key to Plato's own moral system.[53] For Xenophon (or *his* Socrates) it is simply a question of what arts are suitable to the gentleman, the *aner kalos kagathos*; but as unphilosophic as his concerns may be, his rejection of the 'banausic' arts is strikingly reminiscent of Plato's contrast between the qualities of his 'philosophic' rulers and the 'stunted' natures, warped by a life of drudgery and unfit for philosophy, over whom they must rule:

> . . . the illiberal arts [*banausikai*], as they are called, are spoken against, and are, naturally enough, held in utter disdain in our states. For they spoil the bodies of the workmen and the foremen, forcing them to sit still and live indoors, and in some cases to spend the day at the fire. The softening of the body involves a serious weakening of the mind. Moreover, these so-called illiberal arts leave no spare time for attention to one's friends and city, so that those who follow them are reputed bad at dealing with friends and bad defenders of their country. In fact, in some of the states, and especially in those reputed warlike, it is not even lawful for any of the citizens to work at illiberal arts.[54]

For Plato, too, the banausic, or 'menial' and 'vulgar' is antithetical to *kalokagathia*; but when, in his hands, the *kalos kagathos* becomes the 'philosophic nature', the contrast between the 'gentleman' and the 'vulgar' banausic becomes the very essence of the contrast between moral goodness and evil, much more unequivocally than it is for Xenophon.

The same tendency to identify virtue with the qualities of the gentlemanly class and vice with the attributes of the multitude is apparent in Aristophanes. What is most significant about the following passage from the *Frogs* is the clear appropriation to the gentleman, the noble and well-born, of the cardinal moral virtues—notably justice and temperance, and, of course, *kalokagathia*—and the virtually definitional opposition of these qualities to the 'brazenness' of the 'base-born':

> It has often seemed to us that the city is similarily circumstanced with regard to good and bad citizens as to the old coin and the new gold. For neither do we employ the unadulterated and apparently most excellent of all coins, those which alone are correctly struck and proved by ringing everywhere, both among the Greeks and the barbarians, but rather these base [πονηροῖς] copper (brazen) [χαλκίόις] coins struck but yesterday and lately with the vilest stamp; and we insult

> those citizens whom we know to be well-born [εὐγενεῖς], and temperate [σώφρονας], and just [δικαιους], and good and noble [καλους καγαθούς], and who have been trained in palaestras and choruses, and in music; while we use for every purpose the brazen [χαλκοις], foreigners, and slaves, the base and base-born (rogues and sons of rogues), [πονηροῖς κἀκ πονηρῶν], who are the latest come. . . .[55]

Here again the 'just' (*dikaious*) and 'temperate' (*sophronas*) are the 'well-born' (*eugeneis*), who are 'trained in the palaestra' and have a 'liberal education'—that is, unmistakably, the aristocrats. Again moral quality and social class are inseparable. One cannot help but be struck by the appearance in this context of *temperance* (*sophrosyné*) and *justice* (*dikaiosyné*), two of Plato's favorite virtues, not to mention *kalokagathia*, the sum of all virtues; and by the similarity in tone and even in detail of Aristophanes' comic antithesis between the noble and good *kaloikagathoi* and the brazen and base-born *poneroi* to Plato's primary moral distinction between the philosophic and anti-philosophic natures, the noble and good and the common and vulgar. For Aristophanes, too, it is temperance and justice vs. vulgarity and brazenness; and his allegory of the coins is just another version of Plato's allegory of the metals, in which 'brass' or 'brazenness' (which in Greek as in English signifies a metal as well as a moral attribute) identifies the quality of the lower class.

Plato's more or less conventional account of virtue, then, makes a significant contribution toward his goal of identifying the aristocracy as the rightful ruling class. He has virtually named the rightful ruling class by identifying as the necessary qualities of his rulers the very attributes which the Athenian aristocracy claimed as its own, a list of qualities which seems to have been practically a convention for describing the aristocracy; and by defining as vice and the essential qualities of a naturally subject class precisely those attributes which the anti-democrats conventionally ascribed to the common multitude.

It is not enough, however, to spell out the attributes of a ruling class if the very idea of a ruling class is not accepted. Plato must characterize not only the classes themselves, but also the necessary relations among them. In other words, he must locate virtue not simply within the men who compose his classes, but also in the relations between them. The concept of virtue in the individual must be made to contain within it the principle of virtue in the state, the hierarchical social division of labour. This does not mean simply that justice in the state will serve as an analogy for the hierarchical structure of the soul, in which reason should rule the appetites: on the contrary, the concept of virtue in the individual will be used to reinforce the principle of hierarchy in the state.

Needless to say, if individual virtue is to 'contain' the principle of social hierarchy, it cannot do so in the same way for all classes. In the case of virtue as an attribute of the ruled, it is a simple enough matter. Their particular and sole virtue is *temperance*, but not in the same sense, of course, as it applies to the rulers. Here temperance above all means acquiescence in the rule of their superiors: 'for the mass of mankind [self-control] chiefly means obeying their governors. . . .'[56] The virtue of the 'common' man lies less within him than in the virtue of the polis in which he lives and in his submission to its hierarchical structure. He can be 'virtuous' lacking all true virtue, if his polis is hierarchically structured; indeed it is the only sense in which he can be virtuous. In this sense, the principle of virtue in the state—the principle of hierarchy—is the essence of 'vulgar' virtue.

In the case of the rulers, of course, virtue must lie within themselves as well as in the polis of which they are a part. Plato proceeds, then, to reformulate the traditional virtues so that they help to reinforce the principle of organic hierarchy in the just state. Although he never abandons the conventional virtues, he tries to attach to them something more than their conventional meaning by embodying in them his basic principle of justice in the state. The culmination of his argument concerning virtue is, of course, his discussion of the highest virtue, wisdom, knowledge of the Good. Here he departs most noticeably from conventional ethics, adding a philosophical perspective more distinctively his own. At this point all the other virtues seem to be simply conditions for this prime virtue; so it is not surprising that Plato's conception of knowledge of the Good should be the ultimate and perfect expression of his basic principle, his supreme justification for the hierarchical polis.

Much is made of the fact that Plato never reveals the meaning of the Good or what knowledge of the Good precisely entails. It can be argued, however, that this is true only in a very limited sense and that there is nothing really very mysterious about Plato's meaning. Certainly he never explicitly defines the Good, as he does justice or temperance, but one would hardly expect him to do so. Plato is, of course, at pains to point out that the Good is not a specific quality, like the particular virtues, but rather the universal principle that underlies them all; and that therefore knowledge of the Good cannot be imparted directly by a teacher to a pupil, but takes the form of a direct perception or recognition of that universal principle by the pupil himself after a painstaking journey through its particular expressions under the guidance of the teacher. The absence of an explicit definition

—of something which is necessarily indefinable—does not, however, preclude us from understanding what Plato's notion of the Good implies. His account of the particular qualities that reflect the universal principle and his description of the path to knowledge of the Good and the specific course of study most conducive to its acquisition should be sufficient to give us a very good idea of what he has in mind. We can know what Plato means by knowledge of the Good without ourselves knowing the Good, that is, without ourselves having experienced a direct perception of the Good.

Many readers of Plato have been struck by the similarity between his prescriptions for the path to knowledge and those of the Pythagoreans. One need only refer to the central position of music and mathematics in Plato's curriculum of study in the *Republic*. In the *Laws* astronomy takes its place beside mathematics as a necessary subject for all citizens, to be studied in detail by the select few. In any case, it can hardly be denied that *harmony* and *proportion* are the dominant and constant themes in Plato's educational programme. The object of all study for Plato is the recognition of harmony and the attunement or assimilation of the soul to the harmony, balance, and proportion of the objects of study, of the Cosmos itself. Now, as Cornford has pointed out in a lecture on Pythagoras,

> . . . in Greek the word *harmonia* does not mean 'harmony', if 'harmony' conveys to us the concord of several sounds. The Greeks called that *symphonia*. *Harmonia* meant originally the orderly adjustment of parts in a complex fabric; then, in particular, the tuning of a musical instrument; and finally the musical scale, composed of several notes yielded by the tuned strings.[57]

Harmony, then, is the 'orderly adjustment of parts in a complex fabric', and the order suggested by the musical scale, according to Pythagoras' discovery of the ratios composing an octave, is an order of proportion, a geometric order, an order of unequal parts. This principle of order in inequality is expressed also in Pythagorean mathematics. Winspear quotes an extremely illuminating passage that he attributes to Aristoxenus in which this conception of order is clearly expressed, and in such a way as to make the relationship between Pythagoras and Plato strikingly evident:

> Pythagoras, wishing to demonstrate that, in the midst of the unequal, the asymmetrical, and the indefinite, justice was present as a principle of limit of equality and symmetry, and at the same time, wishing to teach men how to practice justice, said that it [justice] was like

> that figure which alone of geometrical diagrams, though it has an infinity of shapes and is formed of sides unequal in their mutual relations, always preserves the demonstration of the right angle.[58]

It is difficult to avoid Winspear's conclusion that much of Pythagorean teaching was intended to establish the principle that order is not equality but proportion or 'harmony', or perhaps, to put it another way, to redefine equality as not arithmetic, but geometric, proportional, or harmonic.[59] The passage from Aristoxenus is particularly revealing in that it explicitly defines *justice* in terms of this notion of harmony, this order of inequality, and thus clearly establishes the connection between harmony and order in the Cosmos and the soul, and harmony and order in the state. Justice lies not in *isonomia* but *harmonia*. This would be a rather important idea at a time when the concept of justice as the ordering principle in society was increasingly coming to be associated with *isonomia*. This concept of justice as *harmonia* is certainly reminiscent of Plato, and the connection between Plato and Pythagoreanism continues to be apparent when one compares Plato's conception of virtue to the Pythagorean principle of harmony in the soul, about which Cornford writes:

> First, in the microcosm of the individual, not only are strength and beauty dependent on proportions and rhythms of form, of which the Greek sculptors might determine the canon, but health—the virtue of the body—was interpreted as a proportion or equipoise of contending elements, which any excess might derange or finally destroy. And virtue—the health of the soul—likewise lay in the golden mean, imposing measure on the turbulence of passion, a temperance which excludes both excess and deficiency. In virtue the soul achieves moral order and beauty; its *harmonia* is in tune.[60]

And for Pythagoras as for Plato, 'the soul must reproduce the *harmonia* of the Cosmos'.

What the principle of harmony meant to Plato and his disciples is perhaps best summed up by Aristotle: 'In *all* cases where there is a compound, constituted of more than one part but forming one common entity ... a ruling element and a ruled can always be traced. This characteristic is present in animate beings by virtue of the whole constitution of nature, inanimate as well as animate; for even in things which are inanimate there is a sort of ruling principle, such as is to be found, for example, in a musical harmony.'[61] Thus *harmonia* expresses the principle of natural division into ruling and ruled. In this respect, *harmonia* as a political principle may in a sense be considered the opposite of *isonomia* insofar as *isonomia* had become 'the expressive symbol of a democratic constitution'.[62]

It does not seem unreasonable to conclude, then, that knowledge of the Good for Plato is akin to the Pythagorean perception of the harmony of the Cosmos and the application of the principle of harmony to all lesser forms of order—'the orderly adjustment of parts in the complex fabric' of the soul and of the state. And keeping in mind the meaning of *harmonia*, we can perhaps conclude that Plato's wise man is one who recognizes that the proper 'orderly adjustment of parts', the cosmic principle of order, the highest and best order is geometric or harmonic, not arithmetic, implying hierarchy and inequality, not equality, and based on the principle of division into ruling and ruled, and who knows how to apply this principle to the ordering, not only of his own soul, but of men in society. In this sense, again, the principle of justice in the state is an integral part of the highest individual virtue.

6. *The Priority of Political Doctrine in the Theory of the Soul*

To return, then, to the proposition that 'justice' in the polis takes priority over individual virtue and is Plato's primary concern: we have seen how Plato's conception of individual virtue tends toward a hierarchical conception of the state and a particular placement of each class in the hierarchy. We may well ask ourselves if Plato is being quite honest with us when he claims to be using an analogy between virtue in the state and virtue in the individual soul to elucidate the latter. In fact, even without examining the consequences of his theory of individual virtue, we might be led by a simple formal consideration of the analogy to conclude that the reverse is the case—that the analogy with 'justice' in the individual, if anything, is meant to buttress his conception of justice in the state.

If an analogy is to have explanatory value, we must begin with some prior knowledge, some accepted premise, about one of the terms in the analogy, which we can then use to establish something about the parallel term. If, then, we want to know whether it is the state or the individual that Plato is above all trying to explain, we might start by seeking out the assumptions with which he begins the analogy. Plato begins, of course, with a discussion of the division of labour and only later takes up the discussion of the virtuous soul, suggesting that he is first establishing certain premises about society in order later to explain, by analogy, the nature of the soul. It is worth noting, however, that the discussion of the division of labour itself is already shot through with assumptions about the soul; and the *hierarchical* nature of the social division of labour is justified at the very outset by referring to the qualities of soul which are characteristic of each occupation and class. It is only by a sleight of hand that Plato makes it appear that he is seeking to define justice in the soul by the analogy of justice in the state, rather than the reverse. He appears to begin with certain premises about the state, which his interlocutors have no difficulty in accepting, and then to proceed by analogy to certain less self-evident propositions concerning the soul. His procedure is, in fact, not quite so straight-forward. It is very likely that he might easily gain acceptance, even from democratic adversaries, for his original premise that society is necessarily characterized by a division of labour; but he is claiming more than that as his basic premise. His argument shifts from the simple proposition that society is based on a division of labour to the rather more problematic proposition that the polis is based on the principle of natural rule and subordination; and this shift, which is, of course, absolutely essential to his argument, requires the insinuation of certain prior assumptions about the soul, as well as, of course, an acceptance of the correspondence of parts of the soul to classes in the social division of labour.

It must be stressed that Plato's primary object is not simply to establish that society is based on a division of labour, but to 'prove' that the social division of labour must be hierarchical and that there must be a special class whose exclusive occupation is to *rule*. The latter claims do not quite so easily stand on their own. It is, of course, in support of these claims that he takes such pains to establish that ruling is a specialized art, to which the same rules of specialization apply as to other skills or crafts; and it is to sustain the essential principle of natural rule and subordination from a different angle that Plato brings to bear certain prior assumptions about the soul. The crucial assumption about the soul is that it is 'hierarchically' structured and that the healthy soul is one in which reason moderates and guides the appetites, or to put it in Plato's terms, the 'better' part rules the 'worse'. Although the virtues of 'temperance' and 'moderation' which are expressed in this notion of the soul are associated with the Greek aristocratic ethic, and though Plato is not alone in associating the 'temperate' with the aristocratic, this conception of the healthy soul would not by itself be particularly alarming to a democrat. At any rate, it would, on its own, be far less controversial in Athens than Plato's radical theory of politics with its essential principle of rule and subordination and its attack on the fundamental principles of Athenian democracy; and it is clear that Plato relies on this assumption to support his more controversial propositions about rule and subordination in the state—always assuming, of course, that we accept the association between elements of society and parts of the soul. (It should perhaps be added that it is not here primarily a question of which is cause and which is effect—the division of labour or differences in qualities of soul; Plato's argument in support of an exclusive ruling class requires only that we accept that, for one reason or another, certain qualities of soul are associated with certain roles in the social division of labour.)

It is, then, the principle of rule and subordination in the state that, above all, requires proof, and Plato's objective in proposing his analogy is to prove something about the state by the analogy of the soul. To sum up, the structure of his argument, insofar as it rests on the analogy between the state and the individual soul, is as follows: It begins with the—at first unstated—premise that virtue in the individual has to do with self-control and moderation, or control of the appetites by reason and right belief. This premise, grafted on to the premise that society is founded on the social division of labour, is used to establish, by analogy and by the association of certain qualities with certain occupations, that the polis must be based on the subordination of the productive classes, which correspond to the appetitive elements of the soul (because they are dominated by their appetites), to a non-productive ruling class which corresponds to the ruling part of the soul.

It is worth noting that at this initial stage of the argument, although Plato makes references to the quality of 'spiritedness', he appears to require only that we accept a *bipartite* soul, a soul consisting of *two* parts, a 'better' and a 'worse'—something like reason and appetites—in which the superior should rule the inferior. The bipartite soul suffices to establish the principle of rule and subordination which is Plato's primary concern. How, then, does the theory of the *tripartite* soul fit into the argument? Since this theory is thought to be Plato's particular modification of Socratic doctrine, it may seem that he is using his analogy primarily in order to establish his special doctrine of the soul. A consideration of the function of the tripartite soul in Plato's doctrine, however, yields some particularly striking results and only serves to confirm our contention that for Plato the concept of justice in the polis takes precedence over everything else, and politics takes precedence over 'pure' philosophy. It is very likely that Plato adopted the rather awkward concept of the tripartite soul to support a particular conception of the state. It may be that the distinctively Platonic doctrine of the soul, that which represents Plato's most obvious innovation on his mentor's teachings, was not occasioned by any purely philosophical considerations, or even by any peculiarly Platonic insight into human psychology, but was rather the consequence of Plato's commitment to a particular form of social organization.

In his so-called Socratic dialogues, Plato adopts what was probably Socrates' conception of the soul as a bipartite entity, composed of rational and appetitive elements, or even as a unitary entity, the division between the appetitive and the rational expressing itself in the distinction between body and soul. It is in his first major 'Platonic' work that the tripartite soul is introduced—significantly, his first major political work—and thereafter it reappears only in perhaps two other works. In the *Republic*, where the idea of the tripartite soul receives its first and only complete and systematic development, it is associated with a tripartite social organization. The tripartite soul recurs clearly only in the *Timeaus*, where it accompanies a recapitulation of the plan for an ideal state outlined in the *Republic*. If the tripartite soul appears anywhere else, it is only in the imprecise and unsystematic imagery of the *Phaedrus* (now generally regarded as having been written sometime after the *Republic*), in which Plato speaks of the charioteer, reason, and his two horses, one good and one bad. Whether or not this allegory represents a tripartite concept of the soul comparable to that of the *Republic* has been a matter of some dispute. In any case, the tripartite notion is clearly visible only in the two works in which it is associated with a particular conception of the state, and one is left with a strong impression that the latter is prior to the former.

Cornford has also argued that a model of the state precedes the tripartite notion of the soul. In his view, Sparta is Plato's model; and the three divisions of the state and their respective virtues correspond to the three main age-grades into which many primitive societies, including early Greek societies and Sparta in Plato's day, are divided. He argues, too, that three of the 'cardinal virtues'—wisdom, courage, and temperance—were popularly associated with the three ages of human life. He concludes 'that it is therefore probable that Plato started with the three divisions of his State and their several virtues, and then, proceeding on the assumption that the "natural" state must reflect on a large scale the constitution of the individual "nature", arranged the structure of the soul to correspond with his polity'.[63]

The difficulty with Cornford's analysis is that it fails to point out that Plato's principle of organization has to do with a social division of labour, and that his divisions explicitly correspond to functions in the social division of labour, even to *classes*, more than to age-grades. In a sense, Sparta also exhibits a kind of tripartite social division of labour, if the helots are included in the model.

In such a case, Sparta might present a kind of tripartite model in which there is a fundamental division between a leisured ruling class and a subject producing class; and the division between the two essential functions of the ruling class, deliberative and military, is to some extent institutionally expressed in the division between the *gerousia*, the council of elders which has significant political powers, and the *apella*, the assembly of warrior-citizens, whose political functions are rather limited.

Another social model for Plato's tripartite soul suggests itself, however. Egypt seems to have held a certain interest for Athenians who concerned themselves with the structure of society, however imprecise their conceptions of Egyptian social organization may have been. Herodotus, who was probably the source of most Athenian notions about it, cited Egypt until the reign of Rhampsinitus as an example of *eunomia*.[64] Indeed, according to Martin Ostwald, this is the first application of the noun, *eunomia*, to a non-Greek state.[65] Plato too refers to Egypt at several strategic points in his political argument. In the *Laws*, he gives high praise to the unchanging nature of Egyptian art; and, as we shall see in our discussion of that dialogue, his comments have clear political implications. More significantly, in the *Timaeus* he explicitly establishes a connection between the social organization of Egypt and the *Republic*—again, in a work in which the tripartite soul appears.

It is perhaps worth noting that, while Plato draws a clear connection between Egypt and the *Republic*, he is often at pains to dissociate Sparta from his ideal. In the *Laws*, he openly criticizes Sparta. In the *Republic*, the type of state which Sparta represents, timocracy, is identified as the first step in the decline from the ideal. There is no need to make too much of Plato's admiration for Egypt; but whatever his reasons may have been for thus singling it out, there is one aspect of Egyptian society—at least as he appears to have understood it—which would particularly appeal to him. If Egypt is his model in any sense, it is probably because of one particular principle which the Greeks thought—perhaps not altogether accurately—it embodied: the principle of a rigid social hierarchy, a caste system (which strictly speaking it was not) in which the social division of labour and the specialization of function were fixed in statutory law. This is a principle which, needless to say, Plato would have strongly approved, given the essential role that the social division of labour, specialization, and particularly the division between ruling and productive classes have in his political theory.[66]

It is worth noting, too, that Aristotle cites Egypt to illustrate that the division of society into classes, and particularly the separation of the fighting from the farming (*not* landowning) class, has long been recognized as necessary.[67] He was probably mistaken about the clear separation of military and farming classes in Egypt, since the warriors, although they constituted a distinct and clearly privileged class, may have been drawn from a section of the peasantry. The important point, however, is that Aristotle, like Plato, appears to have regarded Egypt as a model, even as the origin, of a strict division of society into classes, and that he stressed the antiquity of Egyptian social and political organization as support for the principle of such class division and particularly for the principle of separating ruling from producing classes.

Apart from the general principle embodied in the Egyptian state as the Greeks seem to have perceived it, there may have been certain more specific features that attracted Plato. Perhaps he appreciated the strongly centralized, authoritarian, and monarchical character of Egypt. Perhaps he preferred a model devoid even of the 'democratic' element attributed to Sparta by some of its admirers, who spoke of her 'mixed' constitution in which monarchy was represented by the kings, oligarchy by the *gerousia*, democracy by the *apella* (with the ephors). The Egyptian model is one in which there is no democratic element, no 'popular' assembly—even as restricted as the Spartiate *apella*. The state is clearly ruled by an autocratic king, with his officials, and a class of priests, aided by the powerful instrument of a warrior class. In any case, its tripartite structure, in which the essential ruling functions—the military and the more spiritual (including educational)—are more clearly divided than in Sparta between the warrior and the priestly 'castes' which share the functions of rule with the king, may have contributed to the tripartite soul which supports the tripartition of society in the *Republic*.

It is, of course, possible that Plato's Egypt is as much an imaginary construct as his Atlantis. On the other hand, his picture not only resembles the image which Greeks generally seem to have had of Egypt, based to a large extent on Herodotus, but actually bears some relationship to reality.[68] During long periods of its history Egypt was in effect divided into two major groups for administrative purposes concerned with the imposition of various taxes, tributes, and labour services: a privileged group exempt from the charges imposed on the rest of the population; and the mass of the people, consisting essentially of peasants and craftsmen. The privileged group included, above all, the priests and warriors, together with various officials, scribes, and vassals of the king and the priests. Within this group, warrior and priestly classes obviously had a distinct and special status, especially since they were the 'classes' entitled to large land-holdings and labour services. The Greeks seem to have believed—no doubt mistakenly, thanks to Herodotus—that land was equally divided between the king, the priests, and the warriors. Though these 'classes' were not strictly speaking castes, the Greeks were not entirely unjustified in thinking of Egypt as characterized by a clear-cut, even statutory, social division of labour with a ruling class of warriors and priests and a subject class of producers.

There is, however, no need to seek specific social models for Plato's concept of the tripartite soul. It is enough that the kind of state Plato most admired embodied in one form or another the basic principle of a sharp division between a leisured ruling class and a subject producing class, while the ruling class had two essential functions: the 'deliberative' (including the spiritual) and the military. Indeed, the tripartite soul with its 'spirited' element may simply reflect Plato's recognition of the importance of the military function as an essential element of rule, perhaps even the element on which the possibility of the political function rests. He makes very clear his conception of the role of military power in sustaining political authority, and the importance he attaches to a complete monopoly of military power by the aristocratic ruling class, when in the *Laws* he gives as one of his reasons for founding his city away from the sea the fact that a maritime state must give too much 'honour' to the 'inferior elements' who necessarily form the basis of the navy.[69] He is well aware of the role played by the evolution of the hoplite army and then the navy in the development of Athenian democracy. Thus, the necessity of joining military to 'deliberative' functions may by itself provide the social 'model' for the tripartite soul. In that case, the tripartite principle is simply a blueprint for any rigidly aristocratic society in which the power of the ruling class rests on a monopoly of political, spiritual, and military power, which sustains the economic power of the aristocracy to extract surplus labour from the subject producers. One need only consider the striking similarity between Plato's tripartition and, for example, the traditional three Estates of France: the clergy, the nobility, and the Third Estate, which were originally based on the medieval divisions among those who pray and those who fight—who together constitute the privileged Estates—and those who labour to support the other two.

It must be stressed, however, that even where the tripartite model prevails, the essential division for Plato is still only bipartite. The 'spirited' element is the instrument, the 'auxiliary', of the 'rational'. Plato eventually finds it easier to return to a conception of the soul which simply expresses this basic division. In so doing, he may be stressing the same principle which Aristotle later embodies in the ideal state outlined at the end of the *Politics*, a state remarkably similar to that of Plato's *Laws*. Aristotle makes it clear that it is vital to unite in the same landed ruling class two essential functions, the deliberative and the military, and he divides them only according to age. If Plato's tripartition is designed to emphasize the importance of the military function to the exercise of rule, his return to bipartition stresses the more fundamental principle dividing ruler and ruled.

Whether or not Plato had in mind any specific model of the state, then, his conception of the soul appears to be secondary. The impression that the tripartite soul, if not derivative from is at least secondary to the tripartition of society is strengthened by the often strained quality of Plato's conception of the soul's three parts and the difficulty with which he keeps the intermediate element—the 'spirited'—distinct. His tendency seems to be to think in bipartite terms. It is as if, having first used the analogy of individual self-mastery to support his doctrine of the hierarchical anti-democratic polis, he went on to introduce a modification into the Socratic notion of self-mastery in order to support either a specific kind of hierarchy, perhaps Egyptian, which at that moment seemed most attractive to him, or at least a specific political principle which he felt needed to be stressed. It has been suggested that the tripartite soul was a Pythagorean notion;[70] but Plato's debt to the Pythagoreans need not alter the impression that the concept of the soul is secondary to his political doctrine. Whatever the Pythagoreans may have had in mind if and when they invented the tripartite soul, Plato may, when he encountered it, have been struck by its suitability to his political theory.

That Plato had no deep commitment to the tripartite soul is further demonstrated by the fact that he abandoned it in his last work—having apparently made only limited and intermittent use of it—and returned to the Socratic bipartition of his earlier works. In the *Laws*, where Plato's social ideas are worked out more specifically and concretely than in the *Republic*, it appears that the tripartite soul has lost its usefulness. Although the example of Egypt is still very much in evidence, as we shall see, it is simply the *principle*—the rigidity and immobility—of Egyptian society rather than its specific institutions which informs the *Laws*. Here Plato invents a new, specifically Greek, class system, utilizing specifically Athenian institutions. The essential division between the non-labouring and labouring class (the division which is at the heart of the *Republic*, too, despite the complications of tripartition, and which is expressed, for example, in his tendency always to pair 'gold and silver' against 'iron and brass') comes more clearly to the fore as the most fundamental social division. Is it accidental, then, that this essential social bipartition is duplicated in the concept of the soul that appears in the *Laws*, that the tripartite soul is simply dropped without comment, and the simpler Socratic bipartition casually reinstated as if no significant modification had ever been made?

7. *The 'Statesman': A Bridge between the 'Republic' and the 'Laws'*

The *Statesman* is often represented simply as the mid-point in a declining scale of ideality between the *Republic* and the *Laws*, corresponding to Plato's declining hopes in the possibility of an ideal state ruled by philosophy. This interpretation stresses too much the changes in Plato's political theory from the *Republic* to the *Laws* when, in fact, the *Statesman* if anything emphasizes the fundamental unity of his thought on the state throughout his creative life. This work does not, like the other two major political dialogues, outline a specific political programme, utopian or otherwise. Instead, it painstakingly elaborates a definition of the art of rule or statesmanship, the art which, in one form or another, is embodied in the programmes of the other two dialogues. Although the statesman is not explicitly identified with the philosopher-king—and many commentators regard the statesman as something distinctly less exalted than the philosophic ruler—he like his predecessor nonetheless possesses a highly specialized and exclusive knowledge, so far above that of his fellow men that he ought not be constrained by laws but must be permitted to follow only the dictates of his special knowledge, his art. At the same time, while Plato is at pains to demonstrate that the rule of law is antithetical to the true art of statesmanship, he nevertheless proposes a 'second-best' case in which a rigid system of law can 'imitate' the ideal system governed by the art of statesmanship. The *Statesman* thus looks back to the *Republic* and its absolute ruler pursuing his special knowledge above the law, and forward to the *Laws* with its second-best embodiment of the political art in a code of laws fixing and regulating the relations among people which the statesman would have skillfully 'woven' together by means of his art. Even in the *Republic*, Plato suggests that the ideal may be unattainable on earth and may serve only as a heavenly pattern upon which men must fix their eyes as they fashion their 'second-bests'. In the *Statesman*, an assault on the rule of law as antithetical to the true political art paradoxically lays the foundation for a redefinition of law, a new conception of the rule of law, in which law may be not the antithesis, but the second-best embodiment, of the political art, the nearest approximation to the heavenly pattern. This redefinition of the rule of law is the foundation for the programme of the *Laws*.

In the *Statesman* the 'argument from the arts', on which so much of Plato's political theory depends, is given full play as he searches out and elaborates in detail the most exact analogy from the technical arts in order to define the art of statesmanship. The familiar analogy between politics and the technical arts, introduced in the *Protagoras*, was given a central role in the *Republic*, where it supported the anti-democratic principle of a hierarchical social division of labour based on a conception of politics as an exclusive activity to which the majority, and particularly the banausic classes, cannot be admitted. In the *Statesman*, this theme is elaborated by a more precise analogy and by a detailed differentiation of the various arts on which the life of the community depends, a careful separation of the conventional arts from the 'art' of politics, stressing their mutual incompatability. Another dimension, too, is added to the argument which makes it particularly significant for Plato's subsequent political thinking in the *Laws*. This is the opposition of *art* and *law*, the rule of law and the practice of art. The predetermined rigidity of law by its very nature precludes the practice of art when it binds the hands of the artist himself. The *Statesman* stresses this antithesis and yet goes on to suggest that the 'second-best' constitution must be one that is strictly governed by law. The reconciliation of these apparently contradictory ideas depends upon a transformation of the concept of law, which bridges the gap between the city governed by a philosophic ruler, who is above the law and guided only by his art, and the city in which all citizens are alike subjected to a rigid system of laws.

Plato begins, then, by working out his definition of the art of statesmanship. Significantly, his very first point is that the art of statesmanship is essentially one with the arts of household management and the mastery of slaves, that the polis is the *oikos* writ large. The implications of the identification of polis and *oikos* and its violation of the principles on which the Athenian polis was based have already been discussed. Here, the implications are made unequivocally clear and explicit in the identification of the statesman with the household-lord and the slave-master, the *despotēs*.

To characterize the art practised by king or statesman, household-lord and slave-master, Plato begins by tentatively proposing what was probably a conventional metaphor, the ruler as shepherd of his people; but this metaphor does not satisfy him. He expresses his dissatisfaction first by recounting a myth about the Age of Kronos and the cycles through which the universe has passed, sometimes guided by the Divine Shepherd and his assistant, sometimes left to run itself and to degenerate slowly but inevitably into chaos from which only a renewal of the divine rule can rescue it. The myth ends with a modified version of the story told by Protagoras in the dialogue bearing his name, concerning the origin of the arts and politics. Here in the *Statesman*, the story represents the Age of Zeus in which Plato and his fellow-men live, an age bereft of divine guidance, the bottom of the cosmic cycle. In the Age of Kronos, the herd of men was governed and physically nurtured by their herdsman. The earth needed no cultivation, but gave of its fruits freely and spontaneously. Men needed little if any clothing or shelter.[71] In short, there were no crafts and no labour. When men were deprived of this divine tendance and the earth ceased to supply their sustenance spontaneously, they had to labour for their subsistence and came to need tools and crafts,[72] as well as earthly government. Thus, labour and the arts, like earthly politics, are associated with the cyclical fall of men and the universe.

The general significance of this fable can perhaps be assessed by comparing it to Protagoras' story on the same theme. It will be remembered that Protagoras uses the myth as a means of asserting the universality of political virtue and hence justifying Athenian democracy. In Protagoras' doctrine society is founded on the arts, and the universal political wisdom that allows men to benefit from them clearly reaches its highest development in democracy, which acknowledges the universality of political virtue. For Protagoras, then, whose perspective is completely earthly (despite symbolic reference to the gods which clearly have no profound meaning for this self-proclaimed agnostic), the development of the arts and of democracy are closely related and together represent progress and the betterment of the human condition. In Plato's hands, the same myth, which here becomes the story of the Age of Zeus, represents only one point—indeed the lowest—in a great cosmic cycle; while the technological progress as well as the democracy, which for Protagoras are the high point of human development, suddenly become aspects of cosmic degeneration, signs that mankind and the universe generally have been left temporarily to the chaos and misery of a godless condition.[73] This degradation of the technical arts, of the city and the politics associated with them, establishes the framework within which Plato develops his subsequent discussion of the art of statesmanship and its relation to the conventional technical arts.

A more specific purpose served by the myth is revealed when Plato sums up the difference between the herdsman, mortal or divine, and the king or statesman in the Age of Zeus. It should be noted, first, that the analogy of the shepherd is not completely rejected, and that Plato probably wants to retain the principle that the cosmic ideal is monarchical rule and perhaps to suggest that in the Age of Zeus men can best slow down the descent into chaos by imitating whenever possible the cosmic principle in their earthly politics—politics that are necessary precisely and *only* because the universe has been temporarily deprived of divine guidance. Nevertheless, the analogy between the shepherd, human or divine, and the statesman is imperfect. To begin with, the earthly statesman is more akin to his subjects than is either the Divine Shepherd to his human flock or the human shepherd to his animal charges. This point of difference may have many implications; but the one which Plato singles out is that the statesman is unlike other herdsmen, including the Divine Shepherd, in that the statesman '... is not charged with the bodily nurture of his herd'.[74] Plato stresses that, while men in the Age of Zeus must labour and make use of arts in order to provide their own sustenance, their earthly ruler unlike other herdsmen or their divine ruler in the Age of Kronos, is not, or should not be, involved in the bodily nurture of his charges.

This point appears to be an introduction to Plato's subsequent argument—which we shall consider below—excluding from participation in government all practitioners of the 'subordinate' and 'contributory' arts, arts concerned with ministering to the needs of the community. That the myth is intended to lay the foundation for this exclusion is confirmed by the fact that the fable is introduced explicitly in order to set aside the claims advanced by the practitioners of arts who rival the statesman and claim a share in the tendance of mankind. 'Do we find,' asks Plato, 'any other herdsman challenged by a rival who practices another art and yet claims that he shares with the herdsman the duty of feeding the herd?'[75] Plato then introduces the myth in order to separate the statesman from all these 'rivals' whose claims are based on their contribution to the feeding and nurturing of mankind. In the light of what precedes and follows it, the objective of the myth can be understood as a general degradation of the 'banausic' arts and, specifically, as a foundation for the exclusion of these arts and their practitioners from a share in government.

The shepherd metaphor, apart from its role in the myth, is set aside not because it is essentially incorrect—it does at least stress that the political art concerns *rule* rather than citizenship—but because it is incomplete. It does not convey with sufficient refinement the task of the ruler. Moreover, Plato wants the focus to be placed on the art and its object, rather than on the person of the ruler, not only because this allows him to suggest that the art of statesmanship may sometimes be practised by an *adviser* to a ruler rather than by the ruler himself (as Plato hoped would be the case in his own relationship with Dionysius of Syracuse), but probably and more importantly, because it must be possible to judge constitutions other than the monarchical in terms of the principle of the political art. The analogy of the shepherd and his art is too narrow in this respect.

Plato goes on, therefore, to redefine the art of statesmanship in terms of another art which suggests more exactly and circumstantially the object of the political art. He now proposes the analogy of *weaving* to replace the tending of sheep. The art of weaving has several advantages as a model for the political art. First, what distinguishes the art of weaving is that it deals with the joining together—the interweaving—of different strands into a variegated but unified fabric, a process that also presupposes selection of the proper strands and discarding of useless or inappropriate materials. This analogy expresses neatly Plato's conception of the political art's primary function: the creation of a social *fabric* by means of the selection and interweaving of varied human strands, the careful regulation of social relations. The metaphor of the shepherd, who tends a *herd* of more or less undifferentiated animals, does not adequately convey the complexity of an art which does not simply tend an undifferentiated human herd but creates and maintains a complex social fabric.

Plato argues that the function of the statesman is to interweave different *types of character*, drawing them together into the 'web of state', forging links between the good strands and separating the good from the bad.[76] In particular, Plato proposes that gentle characters be joined to brave, not only by bonds of conviction but by intermarriage, so that these two virtues can be united in the web of state, like warp and woof; but he obviously has in mind more than this union of virtues. It is clear, for example, that the fate of those who are unable to attain either of these virtues is as much a concern of political weaving as is the handling of those who can. In his supervision of the educators who will produce his materials, '... the type of character fitted for his own task of weaving the web of state',[77] the statesman must see that the inferior strands are rejected or caught and held in their proper place by the web of state:

> This is the way I see the true Statesman dealing with those who rear and educate children according to the educational laws. He keeps the power of direction to himself. The only form of training he will permit is the one by which the educator produces the type of character fitted for his own task of weaving the web of state. He bids the educator encourage the young in these activites and in no others. Some pupils cannot be taught to be courageous and moderate and to acquire the other virtuous tendencies, but are impelled to godlessness and to vaunting pride and injustice by the drive of an evil nature. These the king expels from the community. He puts them to death or banishes them or else he chastises them by the severest public disgrace.... Furthermore, he makes those who prove incapable of rising above ignorance and grovelling subservience slaves to the rest of the community.[78]

The weaving metaphor is extended to include not only the good strands that are actually woven into it, but also the servile elements, those that are made to serve the rest of the community: they are not woven into the web of state but *enveloped* by it:

> Now we have reached the appointed end of the weaving of the web of state. It is fashioned by the Statesman's weaving; the strands run true, and these strands are the gentle and the brave. Here these

> strands are woven together into a unified character. For this unity is won where the kingly art draws the life of both types into a true fellowship by mutual concord and by ties of friendship. It is the finest and best of all fabrics. It enfolds all who dwell in the city, bond or free, in its firm contexture. Its kingly weaver maintains his control and oversight over it, and it lacks nothing that makes for happiness so far as happiness is obtainable in a human community.[79]

The purpose of the statesman's art, then, is to supervise the selection and rejection of materials, to create the web of state out of the warp and woof of mankind, and to control and oversee the 'enfolding' in the web of state of the remaining elements necessary to its maintenance. In short, the various stages of his art are concerned with the establishment and regulation of the social relations, the supremacy and the subordination of certain varied human types.

The weaving analogy proves useful in yet another way. In the process of defining the art of weaving, Plato carefully divides and distinguishes it from other arts related but subordinate to it, either in the sense that they are subordinate aspects of the productive process itself—as carding and spinning are subordinate aspects of the weaving process—or in the sense that they produce the tools used in the weaving process and are thus 'contributory' arts—such as the production of shuttles. The political implications of this laborious process of division and distinction are soon made clear. Drawing an explicit analogy with the 'contributory' arts that provide the tools for weaving, Plato groups all the productive functions of a community under the heading of 'contributory' arts, separate from and subordinate to the political art:

> Every art which fashions any object, large or small, which ministers to the needs of an organized human community must be classed as 'contributory'. For without the things provided by these arts there could be no community and so no art of rule; and yet we can hardly regard it as the duty of the kingly art to produce any of these things.[80]

He goes on to enumerate these 'contributory' arts. They include all the arts that produce the community's physical requirements, its food, tools, and implements, clothing, shelter, conveyances, and other materials used to maintain existence and health, provide amusement, or give protection. It must be stressed, furthermore, that Plato makes it unequivocally clear that the separation of these arts from the 'kingly' art means the exclusion of their practitioners from any share in ruling. Such people, he points out, 'since they pursue what we have described as "contributory" arts, have been disposed of along with their occupations which we have enumerated just now and they have all been severed from any share in the kingly art of ruling the state'.[81] Here, Plato uses the weaving metaphor to draw a distinction similar to the one later proposed by Aristotle between the conditions and the 'parts' of the polis, the latter alone exercising the functions of citizenship as a leisured ruling class while the former, the productive classes, merely provide the conditions for their rulers' existence, well-being, and freedom.

Plato goes on to deal similarly with 'slaves and personal servants of all kinds' on the analogy of the subordinate arts, like carding and spinning, which 'dispute the fashioning of clothes with the weavers'.[82] Under this heading Plato includes not only slaves and servants in the conventional sense, but *all* labourers, as well as retailers or merchants who distribute agricultural and manufactured goods for those who produce them, since all these categories of people equally *serve* others. 'You can be sure,' asserts Plato, 'that such men who can be hired for pay, who work for a daily wage and who are always ready to work for any employer, will never be found daring to claim any share in the art of ruling.'[83]

Plato has thus very neatly excluded from a share in rule all classes that labour for a livelihood, all the 'banausic' classes and more; and, paradoxically, he has again used the metaphor of the arts specifically to exclude the practitioners of non-metaphorical arts from the 'art' of politics, thereby attacking the foundations of Athenian democracy.

The argument from the arts has a more general significance, too, since Plato uses it in this dialogue to attack the rule of law, at least as he understands its conventional meaning in Athens. *Nomos* and *technē* are opposed to each other. The true Statesman, argues Plato, cannot be bound by law any more than the doctor can follow a pre-determined course of action in dealing with a patient, whose condition will differ from that of any other individual and may change from one moment to the next. Regulation of action by rigid pre-established rules is by definition antithetical to the practice of art; but what makes matters worse is that *nomos* as it is commonly understood in Athens implies rules established and supervised by people who are not themselves practitioners of the art. It is as if, argues Plato, a body of non-experts were to dictate to doctors and sea-captains by pre-established rules how they are to act, and then to control the practice of their art by constantly monitoring their observance of those rules. This would be fatal to the arts of medicine and navigation.

This latter aspect of law is crucial to Plato's conception of the rule of law as it is normally understood. In other words, as he perceives it, law in the conventional sense necessarily implies at least a degree of democracy. A consideration of the meaning of the Greek word *nomos* may reveal the nature of Plato's concern and explain his reasons for attacking the concept so vigorously. Martin Ostwald, in *Nomos and the Beginnings of the Athenian Democracy*, discussing the emergence of the word *nomos* to describe statutory law in addition to its earlier non-legal meanings, and its apparently sudden replacement of the word *thesmos*, sums up the difference between these two concepts as follows:

> The basic idea of θεσμός is ... that of something imposed by an external agency, conceived as standing apart and on a higher plane than the ordinary, upon those for whom it constitutes an obligation. The sense of obligation is also inherent in νόμος, but it is motivated less by the authority of the agent who imposed it than by the fact that it is regarded and accepted as valid by those who live under it. And when we apply these basic concepts to the connotation of 'statute', which both θεσμός and νόμος assumed at different periods in Athenian history, we see that the two terms approach the notion of a statute from opposite directions. θεσμός envisages it as being imposed upon a people by a lawgiver legislating for it, while νόμος looks upon a statute as the expression of what the people as a whole regard as a valid and binding norm.[84]

Ostwald suggests that the replacement of *thesmos* by *nomos* probably occurred at the time of the establishment of the democracy by Cleisthenes, and that it may even have been deliberately instituted by Cleisthenes himself at the same time as he applied the word *isonomia*, the principle of political equality, to the new democratic constitution of which his *nomoi* were a part. In any case, it is significant that, as Ostwald writes, '... in preference to other possible terms for "statute", the Athenians adopted νόμος, the most democratic word for "law" in any language'.[85]

It is, then, this 'democratic word' which Plato is combatting. Law in this sense implies rules requiring acceptance by the community, even imposed by the community on itself, not simply by a kingly 'weaver'. It suggests the imposition of constraints on governors and even the right of a popular assembly to supervise those who may hold office on their behalf by monitoring their observance of the law. If, then, the rule of law is to be made acceptable to Plato—and he goes on to suggest that in the almost inevitable absence of the ideal, a rigid rule of law is not only acceptable but necessary—it must be dissociated from any implication of democracy. To put it another way, the object of the rule of law must be differently conceived, the focus shifted away from the concept of *nomos* as an expression of the people's role in determining the course of their own communal life, away from the notion of law as a constraint placed by the demos on its leaders, to a rule of law that approximates the purposes ascribed by Plato to the art of statesmanship. The meaning of law must lose the connotation of *commonness* implied by *nomos* and acquire a new meaning which would reinforce rather than oppose the specialization and exclusiveness of *technē*, perhaps recovering some of the meaning attached to *thesmos*. More specifically, it is clear that for Plato, the rule of law, if it is to imitate the political art, must be conceived as a means of creating and maintaining a certain kind of social fabric, certain kinds of social relationships, which, in the absence of on-going supervision by an ideal statesman, must be rigidly fixed in law. The purpose of the rule of law for Plato is not to establish a form of equality, but on the contrary, to create and maintain a well-defined inequality. For a democrat like Protagoras the function of the political community is to overcome the separation inherent in the division of labour, and law is a means of forging bonds of equality. For Plato, the political sphere institutionalizes, reinforces, and renders rigidly hierarchical the social division of labour; and law is the chief instrument of this political objective. As we shall see, the function of the rule of law outlined in Plato's last dialogue, the *Laws*, is precisely this kind of social engineering. In that work, the separation of social types or classes and the regulation of their relations by law in a fixed and permanent structure replaces the philosophic regime of the *Republic*, where the creation and maintenance of the social hierarchy is more a matter of philosophic discretion and discrimination exercised continually by rulers expert in the political art. In the *Laws*, where the founding constitution has apparently been established under the guidance of a philosopher, the state may not have the advantage of a constant supervision by a single true statesman who is free to respond inventively to immediate needs and circumstances, to exercise his art of selection, rejection, and 'weaving' as circumstances demand, unfettered by fixed rules and guided only by his art; nevertheless, the city of the *Laws* does the next best thing by fixing in law the basic form of essential social relations, instituting certain basic divisions of the population, to approximate as closely as possible—in gross, as it were—the effects of the weaver's art. In certain details the *Laws* departs from the proposals of the *Statesman*; but in its basic conception of the function of law, Plato's last work seems to be built on the foundation laid in the earlier dialogue.

The art of statesmanship becomes the criterion for judging all constitutions according to their degree of adherence to the principles and objects of that art. Plato thus places the traditional Greek debate about the major constitutional types into this context, first dividing the three conventional categories—monarchy, oligarchy, and democracy, which are classified according to the number of rulers—into their 'law-abiding' and 'lawless' forms: law-abiding rule by one man or monarchy; lawless monarchy or tyranny (not to be confused with rule by the ideal king who is above the law but guided by his art); law-abiding rule by a few or aristocracy; its lawless form, oligarchy; and the two forms of democracy. All these are, of course, 'imitative' constitutions, inferior to the *true* constitution which is a monarchy ruled by a true statesman (or perhaps a king advised by an expert in the political art) who follows only the dictates of his art and not the law. Plato has therefore somewhat refined the classification suggested in the *Republic*, where he speaks of timocratic, oligarchic, democratic, and tyrannical man and their corresponding constitutions, and where the distinction between law-abiding and lawless versions of each type is not clearly made. In the *Statesman*, he adds the category of 'imitative' monarchy, to be distinguished from the rule of the philosopher-king; and he divides oligarchy and democracy each into 'law-abiding' and 'lawless' versions, just as rule by one man is divided into monarchy and tyranny. With the introduction of these new categories, democracy in one sense attains a higher place in Plato's ranking of constitutions than it has elsewhere. In both the *Republic* and the *Statesman*, tyranny is the worst form of constitution; but in the latter the new category of lawless oligarchy ranks below lawless democracy. The 'imitative' constitutions are ranked as follows in descending order: first the law-abiding constitutions; monarchy, aristocracy, democracy; then the lawless constitutions: democracy, oligarchy, tyranny. Plato argues that of the lawless constitutions, democracy is easiest to live with, because democracy is weakest since sovereignty is diffused, and hence is less capable of great evil as well as of good than are other forms of constitution. This argument corresponds to the observation in the *Republic* that inferior men can do neither great good nor great evil, while superior men, if improperly trained, may do the greatest evil. Nevertheless, while the argument of the *Statesman* is not inconsistent with that of the *Republic*, it is true that in the former, by his somewhat back-handed praise, Plato appears to concede more to democracy than he does anywhere else. The concession is, however, a minor one. It involves nothing more than the admission that of evil constitutions, democracy is easiest to bear, that it is weaker rather than better.

The important point is that among the law-abiding constitutions, democracy is worst; and this is what one might expect from Plato's conception of the rule of law. No democracy, however strictly it adheres to its laws, can approximate the object of law as Plato conceives it, law as an embodiment or imitation of the political art. In its very essence, democracy violates the very idea of the social fabric which is the object of political 'weaving'. It is the antithesis of Plato's 'web of state' because it involves an indiscriminate and unselective mixture of human types and functions, especially an intrusion of subordinate and 'contributory' arts into the art of politics, instead of a careful selection of types, their assignment to their proper function, the severance from politics of practitioners of subordinate and contributory arts, and the regulation of relations among social types. In other words, again, Plato's conception of the rule of law is directly opposed to the conventional Athenian conception of *nomos*, in which law and democracy are closely intertwined; so that for Plato even the most law-abiding democracy is barely superior to lawless constitutions.

Aristocracy, which Plato here identifies with rule by the wealthy (it is worth noting that aristocracy and its lawless form, oligarchy, are here distinguished only according to their adherence to law or lack of it, not by any distinction between rule by the best and rule by the wealthy) at least embodies the principle of selection and approximates the 'web of state' in which only certain strands are woven into the ruling fabric while the rest of the community is enveloped by the web. Moreover, although this imitative constitution is not ruled by a true statesman, by reserving a share in ruling the state only to the wealthy and excluding from rule the lowly productive classes, it comes closer to the requirement that subordinate and 'contributory' arts and their practitioners be severed from the political art.

The claim of monarchy to the highest place among law-abiding constitutions appears to rest on its formal similarity to the ideal state ruled by the philosopher-king or the true statesman, and presumably on the greater ease with which an 'imitative' constitution could be transformed into a true constitution when only one man needs to be converted. In any case, the repeatedly stressed exclusiveness of the political art and Plato's principle that '. . . no large group of men is capable of acquiring any art, be it what you will',[86] may be enough to make oligarchy better than democracy and monarchy better than either.

Since monarchy is classified as the best law-abiding constitution, it is possible to argue that in the *Laws*, where Plato proposes something more akin to an aristocracy as the 'second-best' constitution, he is departing from the views expressed in the *Statesman*. In part, his choice of constitutions in the *Laws* may be dictated simply by the fact, established in the *Statesman*, that rule by a few (the wealthy) is the mid-point of both law-abiding and lawless constitutions, so that by establishing an aristocracy, though one falls short of the best imitation, one also lessens the risk of degenerating into the worst, tyranny. In the *Statesman*, too, he points out that

> We must take things as they are, however, and kings do not arise in cities in the natural course of things in the way the royal bee is born in a bee-hive—one individual obviously outstanding in body and mind and capable of taking charge of things at once.[87]

More fundamentally, however, the choice of constitution in the *Laws* may reflect the essential principle established in the *Statesman* that the primary concern of politics is not simply the superficial nature of political institutions, their numerical composition alone, but the fundamental social fabric that underlies them. The constitution of the *Laws* represents above all a particular social fabric, a particular structure of relations among types of men and social classes, a distinction of human types and a subordination of certain types and certain 'arts' to others. While the state is not itself ruled by a political weaver, or even by an imitative monarch, its *social fabric* approximates to the product of the weaver's art. Indeed, it *is* the product of a weaver's art, since its founding laws are created by the archetypal political weaver, the philosopher Plato, in the person of the mysterious Athenian in the dialogue, who has given the constitution its basic shape even if he does not remain to oversee the maintenance of the web of state.

8. *The 'Laws': Subversion of the Athenian Constitution*

In our discussion of the *Republic* and the *Statesman*, a number of remarks were made in passing concerning the *Laws* and the principles that inform it. Although this is not the place for a minute examination of the very detailed and specific programme proposed in that work, something can be said about the organizational framework of the polis in the *Laws* to illustrate the general points already made.

Plato's proposal in the *Laws* for a radical transformation of society in many ways reverses several centuries of Athenian history, while it seeks at the same time to retain the fruits of that history—that is, to retain the polis as the basic principle of association, together with its cultural legacy. The proposal in a sense involves a return to the agrarian aristocratic society of Homeric times, without a return to the *oikos*-centered primitivism of that society; and it provides an ingenious and perceptive, if utopian, account of the social and economic conditions necessary for the establishment of such an historical anomaly. The *Laws* represents a detailed programme for the establishment of a polis firmly grounded in the aristocratic division between non-labouring landowners and non-landowning labourers, a polis ruled by a hereditary landed nobility whose wealth is based on inheritance and the labour of others, which is at their command by virtue of their inheritance. The object of this social transformation is to breed a virtuous citizen body and to avoid 'the servile yoke of rule by the base' and a 'polity which will breed baser men'.[88]

The fundamental principle of the laws in the 'Magnesian' polis, then, is that there are certain occupations and conditions in life that are corrupting and others that are not; and that inasmuch as many will have to pursue a corrupting course in life if the society's work is to be done and if others are to be able to lead an untainted life, there must be a clear and fixed separation between the two kinds of life, and citizenship must be confined to the untainted. The citizens will be 'men whose necessities have been moderately provided for, their trades and crafts put into other hands, their lands let out to villeins who render from the produce such rent as is sufficient for sober livers'.[89] All those who supply the livelihood of these citizens, all those who engage in the necessary trades and crafts, all the 'villeins', slaves, and merchants, will be deprived of citizenship and the ownership of land on which it is based. To minimize the degree and effect of corruption in the city—and some corruption is, of course, necessary in order to supply the city's needs—'no native, and no servant of a native, is to practice a craft as his calling. A citizen has already a calling which will make full demands on him . . . in the preservation and enjoyment of the public social order. . . .'[90] As for trade, it is proposed that

> . . . the numbers of those employed in trade be kept as low as possible; next that such occupations be assigned to the sort of men whose corruption will do no great mischief to society; thirdly some means must be found to prevent the characters of those actually engaged in these callings from readily taking the contagion of complete abandonment and baseness.[91]

The law which will ensure that such corrupting occupations will be confined to 'the sort of men whose corruption will do no great mischief to society' is that 'no one of all the five thousand and forty landowners who are our householders shall follow a trade, by his own will or against it, nor even engage in merchandise. . . .'[92] And to keep to a minimum 'the contagion of complete abandonment and baseness' among those who must follow these corrupting occupations, there will be 'curators' to regulate their activities:

> . . . the Curators must not be regarded merely as guardians of the class whom it is easy to protect from falling into crime or vice, the favourably born and properly educated and trained; still more careful

guard must be kept over those who have not these advantages, and follow callings which have a marked tendency to predispose to vice.[93]

The basic principle underlying the organization of the polis is this division between the 'class whom it is easy to protect from falling into crime or vice', the class of non-labouring landowners, and the classes engaged in 'callings which have a marked tendency to predispose to vice', the non-landowning labouring classes who supply their rulers' needs. An examination of the structural framework of the city, through which this basic principle expresses itself, should suffice to reveal Plato's intentions, especially if we consider it in light of historical Athenian practice. It will be helpful as we proceed to keep in mind in particular the principles established by Solon and Cleisthenes and the milestones in Athenian social development their reforms represent.

In Book V of the *Laws*, Plato outlines three organizational principles according to which his city is to be structured. First and most important, the city is to be divided into a fixed number of land allotments divided and distributed according to the strictest rules and never to be altered. Second, the citizens to whom this land has been allotted will be divided into four classes according to their wealth in movable property. Thirdly, the citizen body will be further divided into twelve sections or tribes, all roughly equal with respect to the total property of their respective members. Each of these organizational divisions has its role in the implementation of the aristocratic principle, and each one illustrates Plato's ingenious synthesis of the archaic aristocratic and the modern political.

The crucial element in the construction of the ideal city is the system of land allotment and tenure. The polis will be divided into 5,040 land allotments, that is 5,040 households. The number of households will remain forever unchanged, and the land will be inalienable, to be passed on from father to son. A head of household with more than one son may choose his heir among his sons, and the remaining male offspring will be distributed among citizens who have no natural heirs or, failing that, sent out to colonies. As we have already noted, this system of hereditary and inalienable landownership is regarded by Plato as a practical substitute for the 'communism' of the ruling class in the *Republic*. This system of land tenure is 'the nearest approach to immobility',[94] and its purpose, like that of the *Republic*'s 'communism' is clear: '... 'tis a consequence of it that none [of the householders] has either need or licence to make [fortunes] in any sordid calling —as even the sound of the reproach "base mechanical" [banausic] repels the man of free soul—and none will ever stoop to amass wealth by such devices'.[95] The land tenure system is for Plato the very foundation for the eradication of commercialism and the reversal of the democratization of society—that is, its moral corruption—a more fundamental device than other provisions to the same end such as the city's distance from the sea and a convenient harbour.[96] Above all, the system of land allotment is the basis of the division of society into two rigidly permanent classes.

Historically, the power of the aristocracy had depended to a great extent on a land tenure system that preserved—probably more by tradition and custom than by law—the integrity of aristocratic property and the hereditary command of dependents that accompanied it; while the weakness of a peasantry impoverished by subdivision of already small and infertile farms would have served to strengthen the hold of the aristocracy over the community, even permitting the nobles to force the free peasantry into dependence. As the need for trade and commerce, as well as the opportunities afforded by them, grew, however, pressures for a freer disposal of land must have grown even among the aristocracy whose power the traditional system of land tenure had sustained. At any rate, property gradually became more freely disposable, and, of course, in a money economy, more often *sold* rather than alienated in other ways; so that Plato had reason to complain that in a democracy a man can sell everything he owns.[97]

By Plato's time, then, landed property was to a great extent alienable, and the buying and selling of land was a common practice; so that his proposed system of land tenure is consciously archaic, perhaps modelled on Sparta or possibly on traditions about aristocratic Athens, and clearly opposed to the system of property that existed in the Athens of his day. The fact that he proposes it and regards it as fundamental to his utopia demonstrates his understanding of the economic conditions that underlie the social, cultural, and moral developments he deplores and the weight he attaches to those economic conditions. In order to reverse the 'corruption' of democratic Athens, Plato proposes a reversion to a system of land tenure appropriate to a pre-political, almost feudal aristocracy, but now enforced by well-developed political institutions. His stated object in reverting to such a system of land tenure is, of course, to stave off commercialism and materialism; but it is not out of any concern about the possibilities of exploitation inherent in a system of free private property. On the contrary, his aim is to recreate an all-powerful aristocratic class with undisputed power based on hereditary inalienable and indivisible land with a command of labour even more complete than that of the early Attic aristocracy. He proposes to achieve this aim by rigidly fixing the positions of the classes and drawing more clearly than ever the line between landowning aristocracy and non-landowning commons, between appropriators and producers, eliminating the grey areas, freezing the position of each class as never before in explicit and enforceable statutory law, with the whole institutional apparatus of the polis to support it. His society is without qualification divided between a landowning citizenry and everyone else—slave, labourer, artisan, or metic-merchant—whose primary purpose is to serve the landowning citizenry; and, as never before, the institutions of the polis are available to enforce and perpetuate the very social structure that the historical polis had helped to undermine.

The citizen body created by the distribution of land is itself divided into four classes according to degrees of wealth in movable property. The citizens are expected to be equal with respect to land, since an allotment of lesser quality is to be compensated for by greater quantity; but inequalities of wealth will result from differences in the amount of property the citizens brought with them upon settlement of the colony and in the success with which they work their land. Certain honours, offices, and duties will be unequally distributed among the classes. It is curious to find Plato, who so often expresses his contempt for wealth, giving it such a role here, ranking it with 'personal and ancestral virtue' and 'bodily strength and comeliness'[98] as a qualification for position in the polis. Part of the explanation seems to be that, while Plato expects his citizenry to consist entirely of men who are free from menial labour (even suggesting that their land will be let out to villeins), men whose household tasks must be presumed to be of a general supervisory and managerial nature, he seems to assume that some will be freer than others, their wealth permitting them even more leisure for public affairs than their less successful colleagues.[99] What is most significant about Plato's four-class system, however, is its insignificance. The 'classes' are not classes at all. The members of all four categories belong to the same class of hereditary landowners whose essential characteristic is their separation from the 'banausic' masses. The differences in the conditions of the four groups are minimal, and even the differentials of privilege and duty are not profound. There is no comparison between the division of Plato's society into two fundamental social classes—a division which is radical and permanent—and the division into four groups of 'unequal census' (whose membership will change constantly as the 'census' reveals changes in the movable wealth of any citizen) within a citizen body of virtual equals who share the same basic social condition. A comparison of Plato's proposal with actual Athenian practice, however, suggests that this institution has a significance in Plato's argument that goes beyond its rather inconsequential effects on the social order he is designing. He reveals his fundamental purpose, as he does more than once in the *Laws*, by transforming a familiar Athenian institution into something superficially similar to, but essentially very different from, its original, ingeniously depriving it of its revolutionary significance and using it—sometimes only symbolically, perhaps—to negate the very principles which it represented in Athenian history.

It was Solon who first adopted the division of the Athenian citizenry into four economic classes for political purposes. Like Plato, Solon provided for unequal political functions on the basis of these classes. As we have seen, the important aspect of the Solonian class system, however, is that it marked the first time that purely economic qualifications rather than qualifications of birth or hereditary right became the politically relevant considerations, reflecting the rise of trade and commerce, together with new forms of wealth. Equally significant is the fact that Solon, having freed a large proportion of the population from servitude, also used the occasion to give the lowest class, the *thetes*, important powers by admitting them to the newly created people's court and, probably for the first time, to the assembly.[100] This reform is perhaps a logical extension of the principle underlying his class system, since according to the new standard the differences among Athenians were more quantitative, as it were, than qualitative. Solon's class system, unlike Plato's, while it still gave an advantage to the wealthy landed aristocrats, in certain respects replaced and in general undermined the fundamental social division which Plato is at such pains to preserve.

However exclusive the democracy continued to be, the basis of exclusion from the citizen body, at least after Solon, was not a man's labouring status.[101] It is very likely, as we have already suggested, that the Greek democratic polis is the first stratified society to give the labourer this kind of status. At any rate, Solon's four classes, while maintaining the requirement of free Athenian birth, included all classes from wealthy landowners to poor labourers; and eventually these very different categories of men, citizens in a polity where the effect of citizenship was not inconsequential, achieved a fair degree of political equality, no doubt much more than Solon would have wished and perhaps more than any other 'democratic' class-society has known to this day.

The blurring of the division between labouring and non-labouring classes as it concerned political and legal status and the power that accompanied it in Athens, and in general the dilution of qualitative distinctions among Athenians with respect to political life, represent a fundamental development in the decline of the Athenian aristocracy and the rise of the middle and lower classes. It need hardly be said that this was a development Plato could not countenance. His praise of Solon notwithstanding, Plato must have regarded Solon's reforms as the beginning of the end. Perhaps he praises Solon simply in order to attach to some of his own proposals, which are superficially Solonian, the prestige of that constitutional father and to lend his radical proposals the authority of the ancestral constitution. It may even be that his introduction of a four-class system is simply an artificial device, not really essential to his programme, but intended more to give the Solonian imprimatur and a deceptive similarity to actual Athenian practice to a programme that violates the very essence of that practice. In any case, if this is too extreme an interpretation, it is at least clear that in Plato's hands, the institution that in its Solonian form had democratic implications and consequences becomes an expression of the aristocratic principle and, if anything, reinforces the gulf between Plato's two principal social classes. Instead of combining all classes from wealthy landowners to poor common labourers into a single, albeit differentially privileged, citizen-body, Plato's four-class system simply ranks the members of the highest class itself—even emphasizing the aristocratic principle by classifying the members of the leisure class according to *degrees* of leisure—and dismissing the other classes altogether.[102] Far from undermining the aristocratic principle that divides society between non-labouring landowners and the non-landowning labourers who serve them, Plato's system accentuates it; and the Solonian system is turned almost into its opposite, having been deprived of the very quality that made it historically significant.

If Plato resented the reforms of Solon, he must have despised Cleisthenes, who more than completed the damage done by his great predecessor. It is certainly worth noting that Plato seems never to have mentioned Cleisthenes in his works (except perhaps obliquely, as we shall see), although many Athenians recognized Cleisthenes rather than Solon as the true father of the ancestral constitution.[103] Plato no doubt shared with many of his fellow aristocrats a preference for the more moderate Solon, who may after all have been acting on behalf of the aristocracy and whose reforms were probably the minimum necessary to maintain civil peace—and, for that matter, to preserve whatever aristocratic power could be salvaged in the new and threatening social circumstances. He did, after all, maintain some kind of hierarchy among types of citizens. From the perspective of Plato and his like, Solon was undoubtedly the lesser of two evils, if one had to choose one's constitutional founder; although like the more extreme oligarchs, Plato would probably haved liked to reject both Solon and Cleisthenes as founding fathers.

It is in light of Cleisthenes' reforms that we can best understand the significance of Plato's third and last organizational principle, the division of the citizen-body into twelve sections or tribes. It will be remembered that Cleisthenes devised the new system of Attic tribes or *phylai*, *trittyes*, and demes which became the organizational basis of Athenian democratic politics. Plato's modification of that system is noteworthy, and it is curious that its significance is so often overlooked. The most comprehensive commentary on the *Laws* available in the English language, for example, describes the system of tribes in that work as a point of basic similarity between Plato and Cleisthenes, apparently dismissing the differences between them as relatively unimportant.[104] It appears, however, to be another case of superficial similarity and the adaptation of familiar Athenian institutions to ends quite contrary to the spirit of those institutions.

Cleisthenes, as we have noted in an earlier chapter, dealt a severe blow to the Athenian aristocracy by attacking the institutional source of its political power—the old tribal system and the religious institutions that supported it. Now Cleisthenes, while not destroying the traditional tribal and religious institutions, simply established a new set of institutions for political purposes—a system of 'tribes' based on locality and arranged so that the mixture of population in each political unit would give predominance to the non-aristocratic classes. In chapter II, we noted H. T. Wade-Gery's suggestion that Cleisthenes' mode of procedure was to create a parallel institution to each important religious institution, simply transferring political relevance from the old to the new rather than eliminating the old. Wage-Gery might have added that the decline in the political significance of religious structures was part of a general weakening of the tribal structure that had sustained the hereditary authority of the aristocracy. It is also worth recalling Ehrenberg's argument that Cleisthenes' use of the decimal instead of the duodecimal system for political purposes (ten tribes, ten months in the new political year, instead of the twelve sections—four tribes each divided into three trittyes—in the traditional system) represents the conscious application of a rationalistic, humanistic principle of social organization to replace the 'natural' order of the traditional tribal principle. Thus, the number as well as the nature of the new tribes may have reflected the decline of the tribal source of aristocratic authority.

Plato's revision of Cleisthenes' tribes is particularly ingenious. Plato does not, in fact, return to the ancient system of tribes that was so favourable to the aristocracy, but instead retains certain similarities to the system of Cleisthenes. As Morrow points out, Plato's tribes and those of Cleisthenes share certain characteristics, such as their large number compared to the traditional four, and the fact that they do not represent, even in principle, any kinship relations. Nevertheless, the differences are more significant. Plato's return to the duodecimal basis, substituting twelve tribes for the tripartite four tribes of ancient Attica, has at least symbolic meaning. More important, however, is a point that Morrow mentions, though he makes surprisingly little of it in his comparison of Cleisthenes and Plato: that is, the fact that Plato's tribes are politically insignificant, in contrast to the actual phylae of Attica.

Since the tribes and the demes of which they consisted played such an important role in the political life of Athens, their unimportance in the politics of the *Laws* is probably significant. A possible explanation lies in the fact that the reforms of Cleisthenes had firmly established the system of tribes as a democratic institution; the new tribes and demes were the institutional source of democratic power, having overtaken the political role of the old tribes that had served the aristocracy so well. It could not suffice for Plato simply to return to the old system, since the system of tribes was by now too closely associated with democracy and since, as we have noted several times before, Plato was anxious to replace the old tribal principle, based on the particularistic ties of kinship, with a new aristocratic communal or *political* principle. So Plato simply disarms the new system of tribes by rendering it politically insignificant, just as Cleisthenes had done to the old, leaving it with primarily religious functions.[105] The four-class division of the citizen body assumes some of the organizational functions of Cleisthenes' tribal divisions: for example, Plato's Council will consist of four groups of ninety councillors, each group representing one of the four property classes, while in Athens it was the various tribal groups and subdivisions—phylae and demes—that usually constituted the relevant categories to be represented in various political bodies. More fundamentally, the crucial political division between citizen and non-citizen in Plato's city corresponds to the basic class division between landowning aristocrats and labouring commons, which provides a much more secure and well-defined institutional basis for aristocratic privilege than had ever existed in Athens. By tying citizenship directly to landownership—and very exclusive landownership with no possibility of extension—Plato avoids any suggestion of the flexibility associated with Cleisthenes' system of citizenship by inscription in a deme, a classification based on territorial boundaries rather than class. Plato's principle of citizenship has the advantage over the pre-Cleisthenean tribal system, even dominated as it was by the aristocracy, that it draws the class line much more clearly and reserves the exclusive right of citizenship to the landowning aristocracy more explicitly, definitively, and rigorously than the indirect and often nebulous requirements of the old system, which too easily admitted of manipulation and extension to the lower classes.

Plato's purpose in the *Laws*, as suggested by the organizational framework he proposes for his city, seems to be deliberately, if indirectly, to attack the fundamental constitutional principles of the

Athenian polis. The attack takes a subtle form: it is not an outright rejection of those principles or an open critique of the reformers who instituted them. Indeed, as some commentators have pointed out, for all his admiration of Sparta and his claims to be following the examples of Sparta and Crete, it is Athens that provides Plato with the models for most of his political institutions.[106] It is precisely by adopting these institutions, however, that Plato seeks to destroy them. It is not the *form* he attacks, but the very *essence*, the ends which these institutions served and particularly the social realities underlying them. The city of the *Laws* is founded on a transformation of Athenian social realities and class relations; and Athenian institutions are perverted to serve this transformed reality. It should, at any rate, be clear that Plato is not simply bemoaning the corruption of modern Athens, the perversion of its basic principles, or its departure from the ancestral constitution. He is attacking the very principles themselves, the ancestral constitution itself, as a perversion of the aristocratic ideals he holds most dear. Indeed, he may be attacking the very essence of the polis itself, and in his ingenious if unrealistic synthesis perverting the idea of the polis by using its institutions and law to buttress the rigidly hierarchical social structure which the historical polis, with the rule of law and the idea of *citizenship*, had helped to undermine.

9. *The Meaning of the Rule of Law*

In retrospect and against the background of his institutional proposals, the rather obscure and apparently light-hearted arguments with which Plato introduces these proposals seem less like digressions and more like an oblique statement of his basic and recurring theme. He begins by demonstrating, quite seriously and at some length, that the essential problem with which the political order must deal is not external war but *internal* strife, by which he appears to mean above all class conflict. Three possible approaches to the containment of civil strife are suggested: the extermination of the 'worse' elements and self-government of the good; the voluntary submission of the worse to government by the good; a reconciliation of the warring elements by means of regulations.[107] The first solution is clearly unfeasible. In the second, we can easily recognize the solution of the *Republic*. The third seems to be the solution chosen for the city of the *Laws*: the *regulation* of internal strife, the careful structuring of class relations by means of law. His subsequent discussions of drinking and music appear to be somewhat tangential, and perhaps only half-serious; but they may be intended at least in part as metaphorical explanations of this solution to civil strife by regulation.

Drinking, argues Plato, which brings out the worst in men and can be very destructive may have quite the opposite effects if properly organized and regulated—as, for example, in a well-organized drinking party:

> Then if wine and merriment were used in such fashion, would not the members of such a party be the better for it, and part, not as they do today, on terms of enmity, but with an increase of friendship, seeing their intercourse would have been regulated throughout by laws, and they would have followed the path marked out by the sober for the unsober?[108]

At one level Plato no doubt means this literally as a comment on the educative value of drinking parties or any other carefully regulated exposure to temptation as a means of developing self-command. But the very language of his description of the drinking party cries out to be understood as metaphor, a comment on the curing of 'enmity' in society by means of law and the careful regulation of social relations. Certainly Plato has given us licence to read it as metaphor by establishing an analogy between order in society and order in the soul, an analogy he reiterates in the *Laws*:

> It is this dissonance between pleasure and pain and reasoned judgment that I call the worst folly, and also the 'greatest', since its seat is the commonalty of the soul; for pain and pleasure are in the soul what the populace or commonalty is in a community. Accordingly, when the soul sets itself at variance with knowledge, judgment, discourse, its natural sovereigns, you have what I describe as unwisdom, alike in a community where the commons rebel against magistrates and laws, and in one individual man when fair discourse is present in the soul, but produces no effect, but rather the very contrary. These are the types of folly I would pronounce the gravest dissonances in community or individual citizen. . . .[109]

If, as Plato tells us, the object of education—the establishment of order in the soul—is 'the rightly disciplined state of pleasures and pains',[110] and order in the polis has to do with 'the rightly disciplined state' of the commonalty, and if Plato's account of the drinking party tells us something about the proper ordering of pleasures and pains, presumably it also tells us something about the proper ordering of the populace, the maintenance of 'consonance' instead of 'dissonance' in the community.

Perhaps, then, the point of the metaphor may be understood as follows: In an imperfect society composed of imperfect men, the very imperfections that lead to the worst evils—notably civil strife—can be the source of great good if properly organized and regulated. A society composed of 'good' elements and 'bad', *kaloi kagathoi* and *poneri*, the gentlemen and the common multitude, whose relations are the source of civil strife, can be healthy, peaceful, and good if the relations between these classes are carefully orchestrated, as the well-regulated drinking party or any educational device helps to harmonize the relations between the passions, pleasure and pains, and reason, the 'natural sovereign'. Indeed, given the realities of an imperfect world, a world of material necessity, a society composed of both noble and base elements is necessary to the existence of the 'good'; because a division of labour that frees the 'good' is necessary for true virtue, and the service of the *poneroi* is essential to the true goodness of the *kaloi kagathoi*. The point is to find the right regulatory principle.

Another elaborate metaphor provides a key to the nature of the required regulation and orchestration of class relations. Plato's description of order in society and the soul in terms of 'consonance' and dissonance' suggests how we are to understand his discussions of *music*, which is a persistent theme especially in the earlier sections of the book. Music supplies the model for civil order. Rhythm and melody can give order and purpose to otherwise chaotic movement and noise, and man's inherent sense of rhythm and melody is the basis for his earliest education, the beginning of the right ordering and discipline of his pleasures and pains:

> no young creature whatsoever, as we may fairly assert, can keep its body or its voice still; all are perpetually trying to make movements and noises. They leap and bound, they dance and frolic, as it were with glee, and again, they utter cries of all sorts. Now animals at large have no perception of the order or disorder in these motions, no sense of what we call rhythm or melody. But in our own case, the gods of whom we spoke as given us for companions in our revels have likewise given us the power to perceive and enjoy rhythm and melody.[111]

Thus, music is the basis of education; and if we 'understand what is good in song and dancing, we likewise know who has been rightly educated', whereas if we cannot judge the good and the bad in music, we can have no standard of right education.[112]

If we recall the Pythagorean element, the role of *harmony*, in Plato's thought as it appears in the *Republic*, we should not be surprised to find him attributing such a fundamental role to music; nor should we be surprised to find him using musical order as a model for social order, a means of putting right the chaos of our social relations. Not unexpectedly, the Pythagorean motifs of harmony, proportion, consonance recur constantly in the *Laws* as principles of order, both in the soul and in society. There is another recurring theme, however, a new and intriguing elaboration of Plato's familiar arguments concerning music—and interestingly enough, it is here that Egypt reappears.

Having established the importance of music in education and suggested that judgment of the good and bad in music is the standard of right education—'this rightly disciplined state of pleasures and pains'—Plato goes on to propose a method of ensuring good judgment in music. Such an important matter cannot be left to chance, says Plato, and yet, with one exception, every state has done so. Only Egypt has recognized the importance of regulating by law, not leaving to chance, the matter of musical judgment:

> So they drew up the inventory of all the standard types, and consecrated specimens of them in their temples. Painters and practitioners of [all] other arts of design were forbidden to innovate on these models or entertain any but the traditional standards, and the prohibition still persists, both for these arts and for music in all its branches. If you inspect their paintings and reliefs on the spot, you will find that the work of ten thousand years ago—I mean the expression not loosely but in all precision—is neither better nor worse than that of today; both exhibit an identical artistry.[113]

The notion of fixed and permanent *standard types*, the canonization of types permanently by law, appears more than once in the book. If we are prepared to treat Plato's discussion of music as metaphorical as well as literal—which would be quite in keeping with his outlook and customary mode of procedure—we may feel compelled to recall that it was not only in the arts that Egypt—at least as Plato and other Greeks apparently understood it—established fixed and permanent 'standard types', not only here that distinctions of quality were not left to chance but regulated by law. The same mode of ordering things applied to social relations. Men themselves were divided into fixed permanent standard types by the caste system.

The impression that Plato has this analogy in mind when he praises the Egyptian philosophy of art is strengthened when he returns to the idea of fixed types in music later in his argument. Significantly, this time he is not talking about Egypt, but about Athens before its decline. Although the Athens he is speaking of here seems more historical than the mythical early Athens of the *Timaeus*, apparently written not long before the *Laws*, it is worth recalling the comparison he draws in the former work between an early uncorrupted Athens and the Egypt of a later day. The fact that he is implicitly drawing a similar comparison in the *Laws* in his discussions of musical types lends further support to the view that these discussions have broader, social implications.

The discussion of musical types in Athens occurs in the context of Plato's account of how the two archetypal states—Persia and Athens, the one excessively devoted to monarchy, the other to liberty—fell into decline. The argument concerning music is offered in explanation of the corruption of Athens, which took the form of a decline in authority and a general lawlessness. The explanation begins thus:

> Next as to the state of Attica; we are similarly to show that unqualified and absolute freedom from all authority is a far worse thing than submission to a magistrate with limited powers. In the old days of the Persian assault on the Greeks—or perhaps I should say on the denizens of Europe at large—my countrymen enjoyed a venerable constitution with magistracies based on a four-fold system of social classes; . . .[114]

At the very outset of his explanation of Athenian corruption, then, Plato remarks on the advantages of a division of society by law into classes. He singles out the division of Athens into four social classes as the institution most worthy of praise, the very first factor—indeed the only specific institution—which he mentions as the basis of social health in Athens before its corruption. Although this class system clearly did not go far enough for Plato, as he demonstrates in his own proposals, it was at least the last vestige of social typology fixed by law in Athens. It can hardly be accidental that the discussion which begins with this explanation of Athens' social well-being in earlier times ends with an account of corruption in music as a 'universal confusion of forms', a lawless mixing of musical types. And here Plato gives us a clear indication of how we are to understand the earlier excursions into musical problems:

> seeing that our fate has, in a way, been the same as that of the Persians—though they reduced the commonalty to utter subjection, whereas we encouraged the multitude towards unqualified liberty—our foregoing conversation has been, in a way, very pertinent to the question what should be said next and how it should be said.[115]

He then proceeds to explain how the problem of music relates to the question of social order: 'Under our old laws, my friends, our commons were not masters; in a sense they were the willing servants of the laws.'[116] And it is the laws of music which serve to illustrate this point and to trace the decline into lawlessness, the 'progress in extravagant liberty of living':

> Our music was then divided into several kinds and patterns.... Now these and other types were definitely fixed, and it was not permissible to misuse one kind of melody for another. The competence to take cognizance of these rules, to pass verdicts in accord with them, and, in case of need, to penalize their infraction was not left, as it is today, to the catcalls and discordant outcries of the crowd, nor yet to the clapping of applauders; the educated made it their rule to hear the performance through in silence, and for the boys, their attendants, and the rabble at large, there was the discipline of the official's rod to enforce order. Thus the bulk of the populace was content to submit to this strict control in such matters without venturing to pronounce judgment by its clamours. Afterwards, in course of time, an unmusical licence set in with the appearance of poets who were men of native genius, but ignorant of what is right and legitimate in the realm of the Muses, possessed by a frantic and unhallowed lust for pleasure. They contaminated laments with hymns and paeans with dithyrambs, actually imitated the strains of the flute on the harp, and created a universal confusion of forms....[117]

This 'universal confusion of forms' led to 'a general conceit of universal knowledge and contempt for law, and liberty has followed in their train'.[118]

Plato is, of course, levelling a familiar criticism at democracy, encountered again and again in the *Republic*, that the standard of popular opinion and majority will has replaced the true and absolute standard of the good, the 'sovereignty of the Audience' having replaced the 'sovereignty of the best'. Still, there is more to this passage than the familiar argument. Plato stresses the point about the fixing of types, and he chooses to distinguish between a healthy condition and a corrupt one on the basis of the degree to which types are kept distinct and are not 'misused' for one another. A corrupt condition is characterized by a 'universal confusion of forms'. Lawlessness seems to be identified with this confusion of forms, the rule of law with a clear and fixed determination and separation of types. The clear separation of types is certainly essential to the concept of social order in the *Republic*, where justice is defined as the clear distinction and separation of social functions and the different types of men who fulfill them, and where right and wrong have a good deal to do with adherence to type. If the *Laws* is intended to replace the *Republic*'s 'rule by philosophers' with the 'rule of law', it is important to consider the implications of Plato's concept of 'lawfulness' in music for the concept of *law* and the *rule of law* as such. That Plato intends to apply this concept of law in music to the social order in general is strongly suggested not only by the context in which the discussion of music appears, including its juxtaposition with his remarks on the class-system of Athens, but by the direction of his subsequent arguments and the nature of the specific proposals he makes for the regulation of social relations. As we have seen, the groundwork for Plato's transformation of the concept of law has been laid in the *Statesman*.

Plato appears to be saying that the object of law, in fact the essence of law itself, is the clear and fixed separation of human types, the 'canonization' of social classes or *castes*. Seen from this perspective, Plato's comment on 'the men of native genius but ignorant of what is right and legitimate in the realm of the Muses . . . [who] contaminated laments with hymns and paeans with dithyrambs . . . and created a universal confusion of forms' can not too fancifully be understood as a comment on the reformers, perhaps Solon and especially Cleisthenes, who created a confusion of social types, allowing the special functions of one class—notably the political function—to be usurped by others, and leaving such matters to chance in a climate of social mobility, or *lawlessness*. In his own Magnesian city, of course, Plato's object is to reverse this development, not simply by reviving in a new form the old 'four-fold system of social classes', but much more essentially by permanently fixing the distinction and separation between the two principal social categories, especially by means of his land tenure system. The other specific measures he proposes in the remainder of the *Laws* serve to enhance the maintenance of this social typology enforced by law: the various measures intended to curtail and control commercial activity and the rise of a 'bourgeois' class; the close supervision of all 'banausic' activities; the educational system in which subjects like music, theology, mathematics, and astronomy all contribute to the perception of 'harmony'; and not least, perhaps, the surprisingly strong emphasis on military training for the ruling class, which seems excessive in view of Plato's opening attack on states organized for military purposes and for external warfare, until one realizes that military force concentrated in the hands of the exclusive ruling class has a necessary role to play in solving the problem of 'internal warfare' that is the polis' chief concern, according to Plato.

It is worth stressing that, despite Plato's criticisms of Sparta for its excessive concern with external warfare, his own city is hardly less a garrison state, in which military preparedness and training play an exceedingly important role. For that matter, Sparta's own concern in maintaining its military character was undoubtedly less external than internal. The subject helots represented a constant danger that demanded constant military preparedness, if the Spartiate population was to maintain its dominance and its power to exploit the subject population. Plato's concern with internal strife as the central 'political' problem was perhaps not so very different from that of Sparta.

One might ask why Plato's city should have a more serious military problem in exploiting its productive classes than Athens had in controlling its large slave population, why Athens never required a permanent military establishment for the purpose of maintaining slavery, indeed had a police force composed of slaves. One crucial factor, of course, is that Athenian slaves, unlike helots, did not constitute a community that could easily unite in rebellion; but this would be true of Plato's workers too. Perhaps Plato has another consideration in mind: the fact, stressed in Chapter II, that there was no clear division of labour between slaves and citizens in Athens, and that the relations of exploitation cannot have been as salient in a city where slaves and free labourers worked side-by-side at the same tasks as in a city like Plato's where the social structure is based on a clear and rigid division between labourers and exploiters, 'conditions' and 'parts'. Plato himself, in the *Republic*, remarks on the social equality between masters and slaves which he regards as characteristic of the democratic polis as it degenerates into complete lawlessness: 'The full measure of popular liberty is reached when the slaves of both sexes are quite as free as the owners who paid for them.'[119] The 'lawfulness' of his Magnesian city, of course, lies in its clear distinction between the labouring and free classes; but the cost of that 'lawfulness' must be constant vigilance on the part of the free.

To return, then, to our original proposition that Plato's argument on music provides the key to order and the regulation of civil strife, the orchestration of class relations, we can perhaps conclude that, for Plato, the permanent fixing of social grades and categories by law (enforced by military power in the hands of the ruling class) to prevent confusion and chaotic movement among classes is the best way to avoid civil strife, as well as to avoid the necessity of accommodation and reform arising out of class conflict. The civil unrest of Solon's day was clearly the result of social and economic change and the increasing social power of the middle and lower classes. The 'corruption' of Plato's day resulted from the rise of the vulgar masses. The object, then, is to ensure that the relative positions of the classes are not left to chance, but fixed explicitly and rigidly by law. The Egyptians have demonstrated how effective is the practice of 'drawing up an inventory of all the standard types' and fixing them once and for all with no possibility of innovation. They have demonstrated it in their unchanging music, as well as in their unchanging social structure embodied in the caste system.

If in the *Laws* the rule of law replaces the *Republic*'s utopian rule of philosophy, it must be understood that the rule of law has a special meaning here: above all, it implies the rigid structuring of social behaviour by means of legally fixed social position or class. If the essential function of the rule of law is to reduce the arbitrariness of human authority, that function, too, has a special meaning for Plato. For him, the rule of law means that, just as judgment of the good and bad in music need not be left to chance or to opinion if musical types are standardized by law, we may also eliminate the chaos and arbitrariness of social relations by standardizing social types. Even the *Republic* leaves too much to chance by depending too much on the judgment of men, albeit philosophers, to distinguish the good from the bad and to determine who shall belong to the ruling class. The *Laws* removes that decision as much as possible from the realm of human choice and error. Having apparently concluded that the essential factor that separates good men from bad is the difference in their social circumstances, Plato predetermines the distinction between good and bad men by carefully separating and permanently fixing the social conditions that respectively produce virtue and vice, and binding men by law to their hereditary social conditions. The result of his attempt to eliminate chance as much as possible from the judgment of good and bad in society is necessarily a polis ruled by a hereditary landed aristocracy, not only because the separation between the noble and the 'banausic' must be clear and permanent if virtue is to remain uncontaminated, but also because, as we have seen, inherited wealth—rather than a livelihood derived from labour or trade—is a necessary condition for virtue.

10. *The Role of Philosophy*

What, then, *is* the role of philosophy in this city governed by the rule of law? An answer to this question would make a fitting conclusion to this discussion, telling us a great deal about Plato's whole enterprise and his conception of philosophy and philosophers in general. The role of philosophy in the *Laws* should be particularly revealing, because this work, unlike the *Republic*, assigns to the philosopher his proper function in the more or less real world of an earthly city. Moreover, an answer should not be difficult to find, since the role of philosophy is embodied in a particular institution, the Nocturnal Council, whose duties are carefully prescribed. The similarity of this body to Plato's own Academy has been noted by others.[120] The principal difference between the two institutions is that the Nocturnal Council has a central and recognized role in the politics of the 'Magnesian' city, while the Academy's political role in democratic Athens was the private and self-appointed role of educating statesmen, usually would-be advisers to foreign politicians who were more open to Plato's aristocratic ideals than were the democratic politicians of Athens.

The discussions of the Council, like those in the Academy, range far and wide, covering all aspects of science, theology, and philosophy; but the ultimate object of these studies is always the same:

> The matter of the discourse held at their conferences shall always be the laws of their own community, with such relevant suggestions of moment as they may learn from other quarters, and, in especial, all branches of study they may judge to advance their inquiries by shedding light on points of law that would be left unduly dark and perplexed if these studies were neglected.[121]

The participants in the discussions will not be ivory-tower philosophers, but active participants in the political life of their city, its past, present, and future political leaders, meeting at the hour—from daybreak to sunrise—which gives the Council its name because they are too much engaged in the affairs of the city to meet during the day; and their studies are obviously to be applied to those affairs. Whether the objectives of the Academy were ever stated so clearly cannot be known with any certainty; but there can be no question that a primary function of that body was to prepare political leaders, advisers, and framers of constitutions for states that showed greater promise of fulfilling Plato's ideals than did hopeless Athens. Syracuse, Tarentum, and briefly Macedon, are examples of states which had the benefit of advisers from the Academy, in the case of Syracuse, of course, Plato himself. Whatever other purposes the Academy may have had, it cannot be doubted that one of the foremost was purely political. The Academy offered one of the few remaining opportunities for political action left to the aristocratic-oligarchic party, which, having been defeated in Athens, could only hope for and assist the establishment of alternative polities elsewhere.

In the city of *Laws*, where 'philosophers' have been granted their rightful place, the objectives of philosophy are even more explicitly political: the Nocturnal Council is the general overseer of the laws—a supreme court to interpret the laws, an ongoing constitutional convention to revise them when necessary, a school for public officials, a moral censor, all in one. In short, the Nocturnal Council is the guardian of the rule of law; and as such, in the final analysis, it must be the guardian of the class system which for Plato is the essence of lawfulness. Its philosophical studies, too—emphasizing mathematics, astronomy, and theology—are admirably suited to that function, since the common principle of all the Council's studies, the single underlying principle of things which it is the object of all philosophical study to reveal is, again, *harmony*, the proper ordering of unequal parts in a complex whole.

Considering Plato's philosophical enterprise as at least an adjunct to, if not a function of, his social theory and political ideology, an arresting thought suggests itself as we look back on our discussion of his social doctrine. For the grand old man of philosophical *idealism*, Plato has proved to be remarkably materialistic in his outlook, firmly grounding the quality of the soul in its material social conditions. There is, however, no contradiction in Plato's position. In this case, idealism is not an alternative to materialism as an explanation of the relationship between mind and matter. Indeed, Plato's idealism is, in a sense, a function of his materialism, his conviction that the nature of the mind is related to its social conditions. Idealism, which finds truth beyond the world of appearances and particulars, is the expression of a particular kind of social condition. It represents for Plato a state of mind and knowledge that reflects a certain liberation from the material world and the realm of necessity, a liberation that comes with freedom from labour and the necessarily material and particular concerns of earning a livelihood. It is therefore the highest expression of the aristocratic condition. The true aristocrat's relation to the material world takes the form of a very earthly kind of freedom from it. In this sense, Plato's philosophical idealism is an idealization of the material conditions of aristocracy; and idealism is, as it were, the materialism of the aristocracy.

Notes to Chapter IV

1. Victor Ehrenberg, *The People of Aristophanes: A Sociology of Old Attic Comedy* (2nd ed.; New York: Schocken Books, 1962), p. 111.
2. *Ibid.*
3. See W. Robert Connor, *The New Politicians of Fifth-Century Athens* (Princeton: Princeton University Press, 1971), pp. 175–98, for a useful discussion of the withdrawal from politics.

4. Ehrenberg, *op. cit.*, p. 109.

5. *Seventh Epistle*, 325d–e (Glenn R. Morrow translation, Library of Liberal Arts). Although doubts have existed about the authenticity of the *Epistles*, the most recent scholarship seems agreed on the genuineness of at least the *Seventh* and *Eighth Epistles*.

6. Huntington Cairns, Introduction, in *The Collected Dialogues of Plato Including the Letters*, ed. Edith Hamilton and Huntington Cairns (Princeton: Princeton University Press, 1961), [Bollingen Series LXXI], p. xvi.

7. Francis M. Cornford, Introduction, in *The Republic of Plato*, trans. and ed. Francis M. Cornford (New York and London: Oxford University Press, 1945), p. xxiv.

8. On the whole, it seems more likely than not that Plato is giving a reasonably accurate account of Protagoras' views—if only because the views Plato puts in Protagoras' mouth are so different from his own and yet are surprisingly persuasive, in contrast to the ideas of Sophists in Plato's later works. After the *Protagoras*, Plato tends to make his Sophistic opponents less effective, blustering, inconsistent, ill-tempered, or completely amoral. The *Protagoras*, on the other hand, has a refreshing quality of youthful honesty about it, so that even Socrates comes off not altogether well and Protagoras is more of a match for him than are the interlocutors supplied later by a more disingenuous Plato.

9. *Protagoras* 319b–d (W. K. C. Guthrie translation, Penguin Books). Hereafter referred to as *P*.

10. *P*. 324d.

11. Havelock, *op. cit.*, pp. 93–4.

12. *Ibid.*, p. 93.

13. J. B. Skemp, Introduction in *Plato's Statesman* (London: Routledge and Kegan Paul, 1961), pp. 27–8.

14. *Ibid.*, p. 30.

15. *Ibid.*, p. 28.

16. *P*. 322d.

17. *Laws*, 716c.

18. *Gorgias*, 481d.

19. We have already argued that the teachings of the Sophists must have done a great deal to determine the form that the new moral code would take.

20. Werner Jaeger, *Paideia: The Ideals of Greek Culture* (2nd ed.; New York: Oxford University Press, 1945), I, p. 34.

21. See above, pp. 92–3, for a consideration of the misleading suggestion that Thrasymachus' argument is a democratic one or at least symptomatic of the Athenian moral climate.

22. A. D. Winspear, *The Genesis of Plato's Thought*, (3rd ed.; Montreal: Harvest House, 1974), p. 210.

23. Ehrenberg, *The Greek State* (2nd ed.; London: Methuen, 1974), p. 51.

24. *Laws*, 739–40.

25. See Jaeger, *op. cit.*, I, pp. 5ff., on the association of *areté* and nobility (as a class attribute).

26. *Republic*, 495e. Hereafter referred to as *R*. The Cornford translation will be used throughout.

27. Francis M. Cornford, *The Unwritten Philosophy* (Cambridge: Cambridge University Press, 1967), pp. 129–30.

28. In one sense, Plato's views on the consequences of the social division of labour are quite compatible with the view that inequality and hierarchy are 'natural', since the hierarchical division of labour with its profound consequences is assumed to be so necessary and inexorable, so *natural* itself that the hierarchy of souls it produces is as necessary, inevitable, and 'natural' as if that hierarchy were the product of innate differences among men. Plato's views on this question are not unique in the history of social thought. Indeed, they are probably the rule rather than the exception throughout most of that history.

29. *R*, 401e.

30. *R*, 410d–411a.

31. *R*, 395b–c. The word *eleutheria*, translated as 'freedom' by Cornford, is in fact ambiguous, denoting also the qualities to be found in the life of an aristocrat, or 'gentlemanliness'.

32. It is often difficult to determine whether 'philosophic' refers only to souls of 'gold' or also to souls of 'silver'. Plato always appears to have difficulty keeping the latter distinct. In any case, gold and silver are always paired in opposition to iron and brass.

33. Needless to say, Plato's strictures against farmers do not apply to the kind of landed proprietors who constitute the citizen-class of the *Laws*. He would certainly draw a distinction between labouring peasant-farmers, and landed proprietors who command the labour of others and whose duties are rather of a managerial, supervisory nature.

34. Again, this kind of wealth, the movable, alienable wealth of a commercial class, must be distinguished from the inalienable property in land that is characteristic of aristocracy—a kind of property that for Plato is, as we have seen, at least an approximation of the 'propertylessness' of the *Republic*'s ruling class.

35. *R*, 547d.

36. *R*, 553c.

37. Cf. for example, Cornford, *The Republic of Plato*, p. 264.

38. *R*, 491c.

39. *R*, 491e.
40. *R*, 491a.
41. *R*, 495d–e.
42. *R*, 492a–b.
43. *R*, 496b–e.
44. Cf. Jaeger, *op. cit.*, I, p. 11.
45. Finley, *op. cit.*, p. 125.
46. As we shall see, *style* is absolutely central to Plato's ethic, as it was to his aristocratic contemporaries and as it has been to all aristocratic codes since. Perhaps the best, and most strikingly Platonic, statement of the 'gentleman's' creed of style, of 'grace' and 'decorum' is Castiglione's *Book of the Courtier*. It may also be true that, while style and 'good form' have no doubt always been part of the aristocratic ethic, it is particularly characteristic of declining or threatened aristocracies to place an exaggerated emphasis on style and form (and on the lower classes' 'vulgarity', 'insolence' and 'presumption'), to stress *social* distinctions when their economic and political exclusiveness and superiority are being challenged.
47. Ehrenberg, *The People of Aristophanes*, p. 97.
48. *Ibid.*, p. 102.
49. Aristotle, *Constitution of Athens*, trans. and ed. Kurt von Fritz and Ernst Kapp (New York: Hafner, 1950), p. 28.
50. *R*, 396c. Plato is here referring specifically to forms of expression —gestures, tones of voice, and so on—which characterize different modes of dramatic recitation, but it is clear from the context that style reveals the man in all things.
51. Ehrenberg, *The People of Aristophanes*, p. 350.
52. See, for example, *R*, 489e–490a, where the *kalos kagathos* and the philosophic nature are clearly synonymous. Ehrenberg, *The People of Aristophanes*, p. 107, incidentally, points out that, although the characterization *kalos kagathos* was later extended to non-aristocratic 'gentlemen', it was always confined to the upper classes. In other words, the term was never simply a characterization of certain moral qualities irrespective of class. Plato's use of the term to describe his philosopher cannot be insignificant.
53. Cf. Winspear, *op. cit.*, pp. 236–9.
54. Xenophon, *Oeconomicus*, IV 2–3 (E. C. Marchant translation, Loeb Library).
55. Aristophanes, *Frogs*, 717–732.
56. *R*, 389d–e.
57. Cornford, *Unwritten Philosophy*, p. 19.
58. Winspear, *op. cit.*, p. 88. Needless to say, Aristoxenus is here explaining the significance of the famous 'Pythagorean theorem'.

59. Cf. *ibid.*, pp. 75ff.

60. Cornford, *Unwritten Philosophy*, p. 20.

61. Aristotle, *Politics*, 125a. (Barker translation).

62. Ehrenberg, *The Greek State*, p. 51. Ehrenberg discusses the opposition of *isonomia* and *eunomia*. It is sometimes suggested that *isonomia* implies *no* rule.

63. Francis M. Cornford, 'Psychology and Social Structure in the *Republic* of Plato', *Classical Quarterly*, VI (1912), pp. 246–65.

64. Herodotus, II, 124.

65. Martin Ostwald, *Nomos and the Beginnings of Athenian Democracy* (Oxford: Clarendon Press, 1969), p. 73.

66. See Isocrates, *Busiris*, 15–23, for an account of Egyptian institutions by a contemporary of Plato. Isocrates makes them look remarkably like Plato's *Republic* and, in what appears to be an oblique reference to Plato, refers to philosophers who admire Egypt.

67. Aristotle, *Politics*, 1329b.

68. Herodotus, II, 164–8, for example refers to a division between the warrior class and the classes involved in trade and 'mechanic' occupations, claiming that the warriors were debarred from such activities. He even suggests that those Greeks who had contempt for 'banausics', regarding as noble those who remained aloof from crafts and especially those who engaged only in military pursuits, may have borrowed their attitude from Egypt (167). He then goes on to mention the special privileges and especially the land-rights which belonged exclusively to the warrior and priestly classes (168). Thus, Herodotus suggests a kind of division in Egypt between a privileged ruling class of warriors and priests, together with the king, and a separate class of producers. Although Herodotus' testimony is not as accurate as could be wished, there is some truth in the picture he draws.

69. *Laws*, 707a–b.

70. See, for example, A. E. Taylor, *Plato: The Man and His Work* (New York: Meridian, 1956), p. 120n.1.

71. *Statesman*, 271e–272b (J. B. Skemp translation, Routledge and Kegan Paul). Hereafter referred to as *S*.

72. *S*, 274b–d.

73. Cf. Eric Havelock, *The Liberal Temper in Greek Politics* (New Haven and London: Yale University Press, 1957), pp. 42–3.

74. *S*, 275d.

75. *S*, 267e.

76. *S*, 309e.

77. *S*, 308e.

78. *S*, 308e–309a.

79. *S*, 311b–c.

80. *S*, 287c–d.
81. *S*, 289c.
82. *S*, 289c.
83. *S*, 290a.
84. Ostwald, *op. cit.*, p. 55. Among the earlier meanings of *nomos*, which continued in use after its application specifically to statutory law, are 'pasture' and 'usage, custom, convention'.
85. *Ibid.*, p. 160.
86. *S*, 300e.
87. *S*, 301d–e.
88. *Laws*, 770e. Hereafter referred to as *L*. The A. E. Taylor translation is used throughout. (London: J. M. Dent, 1960, Everyman's Library).
89. *L*, 806d.
90. *L*, 846d.
91. *L*, 919c–d.
92. *L*, 919d.
93. *L*, 920a–b.
94. *L*, 739e.
95. *L*, 741e.
96. The latter provision, apart from reducing the possibility of commercialization, has the further advantage that reliance on naval power can be avoided. It is a well-known fact that the concentration of Athenian military power in its navy was an essential factor in giving that polis its democratic character. As Plato himself points out: '... states which owe their power to a navy also bestow the reward for their security on an inferior element of their forces. As they owe the security to the arts of the sea captain, the lieutenant, the oarsman, and to a miscellaneous and not overreputable crowd, there is no possibility of awarding honours aright to the various individuals.' (*L*, 707a–b).
97. *R*, 552a.
98. *L*, 744c.
99. For example, speaking of the selection of commissioners for the market and the city, Plato requires that they be '... men at once of capacity and of leisure for public affairs', and that they must therefore come from the highest property-class. (*L*, 763d).
100. It is *almost* certain that it was Solon who first admitted *thetes* to the assembly. At any rate, Plato and his contemporaries clearly believed that Solon was responsible for giving the *thetes* political power, as is suggested, for example, by the testimony of Aristotle in the *Constitution of Athens*, 7–9.
101. It should be noted that not only thetes, who usually comprised

the majority of the population, but also many hoplites were engaged in 'banausic' occupations.

102. Aristotle, in distinguishing between the *parts* and the *conditions* of the polis is formulating explicitly the position that Plato adopts in the *Laws*. The productive classes in Aristotle's ideal polis, as in Plato's Magnesian city, are merely the *conditions* for the civic life of the leisured citizen class, who are the integral *parts* of the polis, just as slaves in the *oikos* are simply animate instruments or conditions for the life of the household.

103. We have relied on Glenn R. Morrow, *Plato's Cretan City* (Princeton: Princeton University Press, 1960), pp. 78–9, for these remarks on the dispute concerning the ancestral constitution, though, of course, our conclusions about Plato's position are our own.

104. *Ibid.*, pp. 123–4.

105. Demetrius of Phalerum, puppet of Macedon and admirer of Aristotle, as ruler of Athens in 317–307, acting on Aristotelian principles and introducing reforms often remarkably reminiscent of Plato's *Laws*, actually did reduce the political importance of the Cleistheneian tribes and demes as part of his attempt to 'oligarchize' Athenian democracy.

106. Cf. Morrow, *op. cit.*, p. 534.

107. *L*, 627e–628a.

108. *L*, 671e–672a.

109. *L*, 689a–c.

110. *L*, 653b.

111. *L*, 653e–654a.

112. *L*, 654d–e.

113. *L*, 656d–657a.

114. *L*, 698b.

115. *L*, 699e.

116. *L*, 700a.

117. *L*, 700a–d.

118. *L*, 136a, 701a.

119. *R*, 563b.

120. Cf. Morrow, *op. cit.*, pp. 509–10.

121. *L*, 951e–952a.

V

Aristotle: Tactician of Conservatism

While Aristotle's doctrines seem to reflect an aristocratic and oligarchic bias as clearly as do the teachings of Socrates and Plato, his anti-democratic outlook strangely has received less attention than their own. Certainly his strictures against the lower classes and his defence of slavery tend to be no less extreme than their views, even if his pragmaticism, his practical turn of mind with its common sense, flexibility, and empirical temper, and his occasional display of sympathy for democracy, have evidently spared him much of the criticism directed against Plato. Largely because he has seldom been closely examined as an historical figure in a specific social context, Aristotle is frequently and mistakenly taken to be an ivory-tower philosopher, remote from the political actualities of his day, whose thought possesses a 'timeless impersonality and absolute philosophic sovereignty....'[1]* Contrary to this interpretation, the underlying theme of the following pages is that Aristotle's social and political ideas are fundamentally ideological, forged as weapons to be used in the political struggles of his age. The portrait of Aristotle and his political thought presented here is far from being a complete one. Our treatment will obviously have to be highly selective. Stress will be placed upon certain aspects of Aristotle's life rarely discussed in popular treatments or related to his social and political ideas, and although mentioned, seldom probed in the literature

*Notes for this chapter begin on p. 253.

for specialists. Once Aristotle has been fixed in a precise socio-historical context and shown to be a consummate 'political animal' acting within that context, his basic social values and attitudes will be evaluated in an effort to show how they apparently reflect his own status in Greek society; how they seem to have influenced his ideal of the morally good life; how they shaped his conception of the household and its relation to the polis; and finally how they affected some of his central and intimately connected political ideas: justice, *stasis*, 'polity', and utopia. By way of conclusion, brief consideration will be given to his social and political ideas in practice by depicting the reforms of his disciple, the enlightened despot Demetrius of Phalerum, who ruled Athens from 317 to 307 BC. From the analysis of Aristotle's political thought it should be apparent that, despite certain differences, he is a worthy political successor of Socrates and Plato, sharing their fundamental anti-democratic and authoritarian perspective.

1. *Biographical Speculations*

Although the bare facts of Aristotle's life are familiar, their outline is necessary for a clearer understanding of the subsequent biographical emphases and speculations. He was born in 384 BC. in Stagira (Stavro), a small member polis of the Chalcidic confederation that had come under the aegis of Macedonia. His father, Nicomachus, who claimed descent from Asclepius, the legendary Homeric healer, was physician to Amyntas III, King of Macedonia (393–370) and father of the renowned Philip II (382–336), conqueror of Greece. Asclepius was also reportedly the ancestor of Aristotle's mother, Phaestis of Chalcis on the island of Euboea. Both parents died before their son was seventeen, so that he was perhaps raised by a guardian, Proxenos, the second husband of his sister, Arimneste. Because his father was a member of the hereditary medical guild of the Asclepiadae, the young Aristotle, according to custom, was probably taught something of the physician's art, especially the elements of dissection, and seems to have received an excellent basic education. In 367 he was sent to Athens where he entered the Academy, remaining there first as a student, and then as a member of the 'faculty' until 348, or evidently just before Plato's death. It was during the latter part of this period that Aristotle probably wrote his dialogues, only fragments of which survive. While intellectual differences seem to have arisen between Plato and the young Stagirite, as they did between the master and several of his leading disciples, Aristotle evidently deeply admired the elder philosopher and in turn was an esteemed friend and valued colleague.

The last half of Aristotle's life is a tale of travels, intellectual maturity and productivity, and a second sojourn in Athens. On leaving the Academy he perhaps spent a short time in Macedonia, and then visited Hermias, tyrant of Altarneus in the Troad, the mountainous north-western region of Asia Minor on the Aegean Sea. Here he spent about three years in close association with Hermias, marrying Pythias, his niece and adopted daughter. Then, withdrawing to Mytilene on the isle of Lesbos, he returned after a time to Macedonia in 343–342, where according to the traditional account—the evidence is far from positive—he tutored Alexander, the son of Philip, for several years, until 340 when he retired to study and write in Stagira. In 335, after the assassination of Philip the year before, and after the succession of Alexander and the final capitulation of Athens to Macedonia, Aristotle returned to the city where he resided and taught for a dozen years. It is technically incorrect to call Aristotle the founder and the first head of the famous Lyceum, an honour which must go to his friend and student, Theophrastus. Without special dispensation, Aristotle as a metic could own no real property in Athens and consequently could not acquire land and buildings for a school. After his master's death Theophrastus, also a metic, did receive a dispensation from Demetrius, ruler of Athens, for just such a purpose. Apparently living in a rented house, Aristotle accumulated a large collection of books, later to become the library of the school, lectured to students in the public gymnasium called the Lyceum, an establishment frequented by foreign Sophists and rhetors, and wrote works like the *Nicomachean Ethics* and the *Politics*. During the stay in Athens, his wife Pythias died after bearing a daughter named after herself. Subsequently, Herpyllis, a woman probably of humble origin, perhaps a maid or housekeeper while Pythias was still alive, became his mistress, by whom he had one son, Nicomachus. With the death of Alexander the Great in 323, Aristotle was forced to leave Athens, dying of a stomach disorder the following year in Chalcis.

If general agreement exists about most of these facts, some significant details relevant to an appreciation of the outlook of Aristotle tend to be neglected. To begin with, it is worth remembering that his birthplace and the polis of his father, Stagira, was oligarchical, as were the other member cities of the Chalcidic confederation. Furthermore, Macedonia with which Aristotle was associated throughout his life was not a polis but a large feudal kingdom with an army dependent upon tribal chieftains and their followers, of some ten thousand square miles with a population of about eight-hundred thousand. Approximately half the size of Nova Scotia, the kingdom of Macedonia far exceeded the area and population of any of the poleis in the Greek world.

Hence, Aristotle was born into and closely connected during his life with a political environment that in its aristocratic, oligarchic, and authoritarian features was far different from democratic Athens.

In addition, commentators customarily fail to point out or to emphasize that the Stagirite was of the highest socio-economic status. Father and mother were of excellent Greek aristocratic stock, and the family was undoubtedly refined, cultured, and wealthy. As physician to Amyntas III, Nicomachus evidently was not simply a servant, but a loyal friend and trusted adviser of the sovereign, amply rewarded for his endeavours. He seems to have resided at court at least from the time Aristotle was born until the king's death in 370. The son was probably brought up in the royal household, having as his playmate the crown prince Philip, two years his junior. Apparently, then, here in the Macedonian court began a life-time friendship with one of history's great political figures. Also during his first years in the court of Amyntas, Aristotle could well have become acquainted with Antipater, thirteen years his senior, who became Philip's right-hand man, Alexander's regent in Europe, and confidant and protector of the Stagirite during his second stay in Athens. Evidence exists that the royal family of Macedonia was most lavish in its financial support of Aristotle's scientific and scholarly endeavours, also corroborated by his last will and testament indicating that he died a wealthy man. His estate comprised two properties with houses—his father's in Stagira and his mother's in Chalcis—and the means to furnish them; apparently fifteen or more slaves; ample provision for his mistress Herpyllis and the two children, Pythias and Nicomachus; additional cash legacies totaling more than a talent; and seven pieces of sculpture, some still to be commissioned and executed. Aristotle seems to have left a far larger estate than did Plato, who was not a poor man. Indeed, in the Athens of 322 Aristotle would have been a wealthy individual, worth perhaps as much as six talents, placing him on a level (he was a metic) with the elite of some three-hundred citizens out of a total citizen population of about 21,000. So it is understandable that the Stagirite, blessed by nobility and riches, the consort of princes and their lieutenants, could be sceptical about the virtues of democracy and the capabilities of the common man.

The well-worn image of Aristotle, the detached philosopher, aloof from the political conflict of his age will probably have to be discarded. He seems to have lived a life in large part determined by politics and to have played a role as an active partisan for the aims and interests of Macedonia. It is not improbable that Aristotle went to Athens in 367 not solely to study but also as a political refugee from the bloody dynastic dispute following the death of Amyntas III of which his parents may have been victims. The Academy, a nursery of political intrigue, was an incomparable school in which the young Aristotle could learn the art of practical politics. He seems to have left the Academy not after Plato's death and not because he was passed over in the selection of a new head in favour of the master's nephew, Speusippus, but probably as a result of the increasing anti-Macedonian hostility in Athens stirred up by Demosthenes against Philip, whose imperialistic expansionism in northern Greece threatened vital Athenian interests. As a metic with close Macedonian ties, Aristotle was compelled by prudence to flee, and after returning to Macedonia, to journey to Atarneus. The Stagirite's guardian, Proxenus, possibly originated from Atarneus, and Aristotle may have already been acquainted with Hermias who reportedly had been a student at the Academy, and undoubtedly knew two former students, Erastus and Coriscus, now the tyrant's close associates in the Troad. Because of the threat of Persia, Philip had an interest in Atarneus and forged an alliance with Hermias. Aristotle seems to have become a cherished friend and adviser of Hermias who made a profound and lasting impression upon him. Aristotle's relationship with Philip may have cooled temporarily when in 341 the King apparently 'sold out' Hermias to the Persians in order to prevent the possibility of their alliance with Athens against Macedonia. Nevertheless, the philosopher may have conducted negotiations for Philip with various poleis in the period before the decisive battle of Chaeronea in 338 by means of which Macedonian hegemony over Greece was made complete.

Aristotle returned to Athens in 335 after the assassination of Philip and Alexander's suppression of the revolt of Thebes, Athens, and other recalcitrant poleis. Unlike Thebes, Athens was spared destruction and treated most generously by the young conqueror, due perhaps to the pleas of Aristotle. According to one account, the Athenians in appreciation of the many outstanding services performed by the Stagirite for their city—which may have included just such a personal intercession with Alexander—erected an honorific column with an inscription to the philosopher. Whatever the truth of the story and the speculations surrounding it, Aristotle was obviously a member of the alien Macedonian establishment controlling Athens through the presence of a military garrison and the support of friends among the aristocratic-oligarchic classes. His grand-nephew, Callisthenes, was an official historian on Alexander's staff (until he was executed in 327 for supposedly being involved in the pages' plot upon the ruler's life); and another nephew, Nicanor, was one of the king's leading generals. More importantly, Alexander's efficient and autocratic vice-roy in Europe, Antipater, had become the philosopher's good friend and patron, and was the executor of his last will and testament. While none of

Aristotle's correspondence with Philip is extant and little has survived of four books of letters to Alexander, one account refers to nine books of letters written from Athens by the Stagirite to Antipater in Macedonia which Chroust speculates were in fact 'regular official accounts or intelligence reports' on affairs in the city.[2] It is even possible that Aristotle constructed his model in the *Politics* of the 'polity', or best practicable constitution, as a solution to the problem of political instability in Macedonian dominated Greece, broaching the idea with Antipater, who did actually introduce such a scheme in Athens in 321, the year after the philosopher's death.[3]

From the standpoint of many Athenians and their democratic anti-Macedonian leaders like Demosthenes, Lycurgus, Hyperides, and Himeraeus, the Stagirite must have been disliked as a symbol of the Macedonian yoke and the subversive aristocratic-oligarchic forces in the city. When Alexander died in 423 and Antipater was abroad, Aristotle found himself without friends or protection in a hostile Athens that declared war against Macedonia and became the foremost spokesman of Greek freedom. Fearful for his life in such dangerous circumstances and haunted by the fate of Socrates, Aristotle expressed his concern: 'I will not let the Athenians offend twice against philosophy,' and 'To continue to stay in Athens would only have been to court trouble. . . .'[4] After his departure for Chalcis where he spent his last year, he was indicted by the angry Athenians for impiety and charged with having composed a memorial hymn honouring Philip's former tyrannical ally, Hermias of Atarneus, and an inscription for a statue in his honour at Delphi, and with failing to worship and respect the traditional gods of their city.

2. *Social Values and Attitudes*

Aristotle's conservative, anti-democratic social values and attitudes deserve more attention than they have been allotted by some commentators. Insufficient emphasis is usually given to his rather pessimistic view of man and human conduct, an outlook that typifies what has come to be known as 'realism' and that in his case may have been a consequence of long years of activity in an age of intense political struggle. Nor has this realism commonly been related to his veneration for tradition, admiration for the 'collective wisdom' of the species, and acceptance of the status-quo. Although apologetic reference is normally made to his conception of the natural slave, little effort is generally made to highlight his idea of the natural superiority and inferiority among men, an extreme formulation even for his own time and status; his gentlemanly contempt for the lower classes and their labour; the significance he gave to good birth and wealth as the conditions of true happiness; and the aristocratic nature of his moral ideas. The total picture, in fact, that emerges is of an aristocratic conservatism diametrically opposed to Athenian democratic values, one going somewhat beyond the commonly held opinions of educated men of his own class, on some points even exceeding the positions of Socrates and Plato. Only when these values and attitudes of Aristotle have been grasped can the full import of his political recommendations be appreciated. Perhaps the reason he has been spared the rough treatment of Plato at the hands of liberal commentators in recent years has been his shrewd sense of the practical, of what can be accomplished with the imperfect human material at the disposal of the statesman, and his willingness to compromise his ideals for the sake of social and political necessity.

For Aristotle man is fundamentally wicked, and this evil nature is responsible for the troubles and disorders occurring under existing systems of government.[5] Human misanthropy is reflected by the fact that men may commit criminal acts not simply from material deprivation but because they delight in the iniquitous, and plot and execute new crimes of the most heinous nature solely to satisfy their desire to do evil.[6] Indeed, the most infamous crimes, such as the tyrannical seizure and abuse of power, are committed not out of economic necessity, but for the sake of superfluity, for the purpose of satisfying what Plato would have called the 'lawless' appetites that develop only after the basic or necessary desires have been satisfied. Men are never content; their desire is insatiable.[7] In practice their zeal for the acquisition of wealth, property, power, and reputation knows no bounds.[8] Such gloom about man's nature is expressed most clearly in the *Politics*, apparently because Aristotle believes that the full consequences of human egoism, man's limitless ambition and avarice and restless pursuit of power are most clearly observed and felt in the political arena. This explains his strong advocacy in general of the importance of checks upon government, of the rule of law, and of the accountability of office-holders, for: 'The power of acting at will leaves men with no defence against the evil impulses present in all of us.'[9] Nor is the lawless pursuit of power unique to his own times, but a universal characteristic of political life that with some exceptions has always existed and will continually exist. Yet in contemporary Greece he seems to believe that these human tendencies have been accentuated because most poleis are either democracies or oligarchies, forms of rule conducive to the unleashing of the appetites rather than their control. Politics, then as it actually exists in his world of strife and turmoil, he suggests, is little more than a perpetual conflict between the rich and the poor, each class out of hubris or envy seeking what it considers a rightful share in the distribution of goods.[10] Most men, as he put it earlier in the *Eudemian Ethics*, enter politics for the sake of money and greed.[11] As a political thinker Aristotle would have had little to learn from the bleak analyses of the human condition found in Augustine, Machiavelli, Hobbes, and Locke. In fact, they may have learned from him.

Man conceived by Aristotle is a frail reed. Statesmen and political reformers must keep this characteristic in mind to prevent their actions and projects from ending in disaster. Good conduct among men is a rare occurrence.[12] Unless the politician and moralist recognize and accept this basic feature of the human condition, all their efforts will be to no avail and may simply worsen the situation. In their prescriptions for the betterment of human society they should not make greater demands of the raw human material than it can bear, remembering that it can easily be overtaxed.[13] Aristotle criticizes Plato, who recommended perfection, for overlooking that 'perfection in everything is perhaps a difficult thing'.[14] Morally virtuous action for most men is an impossibility, hence we must be content to 'sail in the second best way and take the lesser evil. . . .'[15] Men in general are not philosophers, nor should they be expected to be so. Not for them is the philosophic wisdom necessary for the highest life. The sooner the philosopher acknowledges this primary characteristic of human nature the wiser he is. As Aristotle comments in one of his earliest works, the *Protrepticus*, an exhortation to the tyrant Themon of Cyprus to lead a contemplative life, most men should be 'excused and justified' for being content with the kind of knowledge that will enable them to live a 'plain ordinary life', a 'normal, average' one.[16] Aristotle, then, fully aware of what he believes to be the genetic selfishness of man, his inherent weakness and incapacity of rising above that condition, warns his readers that they must learn to live with these realities, make the best of them, never attempting the hopeless and dangerous task of turning a sow's ear into a silk purse. With few exceptions politics, therefore, is the art of the possible always involving the choice of lesser evils.

In view of these convictions it is not surprising that Aristotle thinks that philosophic enquiry, if it is to be of any relevance to human life, must adhere closely to the realities of life, taking into consideration how men have actually lived, what they have done, and in general how they have perceived themselves. If the shoe is to fit and be serviceable, it must be designed for the wearer. From the standpoint of modernity, we might say that Aristotle believed that social ethics and political philosophy must be rooted in history and permeated by a profound understanding of historical man. Far from dismissing received opinion as a false guide in practical affairs, something Plato had done,

Aristotle was keenly sensitive to the truth that it might contain, a truth generated out of the problems of life that had to be met and solved throughout the ages. In the *Metaphysics* he refers appreciatively to the fact that ancient opinions about heavenly bodies as gods and the divinity of nature 'have been preserved until the present like relics of the ancient treasure'.[17] And in his last years he implies that myth is one of the primary repositories of these ancient truths.[18] Although in any philosophic enquiry commonly held opinion can never be accepted at its face value, it is always a useful point of departure for such investigations, and after careful examination should he supplemented and corrected.[19] The wisdom and truth embedded in the traditions, opinions, and institutions of the past can only be ignored at the philosopher's peril. For example, in determining the nature of happiness the commonly expressed views on the subject cannot be neglected.[20] Some of these ideas may have been held by many men in the past, others by only a few men of great repute. It would be foolhardy to assume that all are wrong, hence the 'presumption is rather that they are right in at least one or even in most respects'.[21] When we discover something in the field of human conduct universally held to be true, we should indeed accept it as the truth.[22] Even in 'inferior things' there is some natural good that aims at the truth which is properly theirs despite themselves. Almost everything, Aristotle repeats, has been discovered or invented in the past—and this is certainly true of political arrangements—independently at different times and places, although some have not been put into practice or utilized scientifically.[23] Therefore, on the basis of learning from the past we should employ and adapt what has already been devised and devote our energies to discovering and inventing what little has not already been accomplished, or more likely, to filling in the detail of what has been done as in the arts, for 'time is a good inventor or collaborator in such an effort'.[24] The trouble with many of Plato's innovations such as community of property, Aristotle insists, is that if they were really good, they would have been recognized as such in the past and incorporated into our traditional way of life.[25] Unless led astray like Plato, 'We are bound to pay some regard to the long past and the passage of the years....'[26] Aristotle's words in the *Rhetoric* convey his attitude: 'what is long established seems akin to what exists by nature'[27] and, of course, nature can be nothing but good.

Aristotle also wrote in the *Rhetoric* 'that men have a sufficient natural instinct for what is true, and usually do arrive at the truth'.[28] But man as an individual, frail reed that he is, cannot by himself attain the truth. The wisdom of past and present is a collective wisdom. Man alone is weak and ignorant; man in union with his fellows, whether as the citizen of a polis or a member of a group of scientific collaborators, becomes strong and wise, a view clearly expressed in the *Metaphysics*:

> The investigation of the truth is in one way hard, in another easy. An indication of this is found in the fact that no one is able to attain the truth adquately, while, on the other hand, we do not collectively fail, but every one says something true about the nature of things, and while individually we contribute little or nothing to the truth, by the union of all a considerable amount is amassed. Therefore, since the truth seems to be like the proverbial door, which no one can fail to hit, in this respect it must be easy, but the fact that we can have a whole truth and not the particular part we aim at shows the difficulty of it.[29]

The social counterpart of this revealing statement is the well-known section of the *Politics* in which he pays one of his few compliments to democracy and the democratic principle of the 'sovereignty' of the people.[30] Individual citizens by themselves, he argues, may be inferior in respect to wisdom and moral virtue, nevertheless, when they come together as in a democratic assembly, their collective quality like that of a new person may surpass even the few best. Hence, he concedes that they are perceptive enough to elect magistrates and to hold them accountable upon the expiration of their tenure of office, although acting as individuals they are not sufficiently qualified to hold office. This last qualification is significant, for as we shall see, it enables Aristotle to recommend membership in the assembly for all freemen without a property requirement or a minimal one, while at the same time reserving the actual offices of government for the well-born and wealthy, thereby assuring their political domination. Admittedly, the great value he places upon opinion evidently leads him to express more sympathy for democracy than does Plato. But his limited admiration for it is outweighed by his veneration for the wisdom of tradition, a wisdom that in his opinion cannot be invalidated by majority vote. Consequently, his realism and traditionalism seem to be essential components of his social conservatism.

Aristotle's aristocratic approach to life is further expressed by his fundamental belief in the existence of natural distinctions of quality and value among men, differences existing by birth rather than environment. His idea of the natural superiority of some men and the natural inferiority of others may be rather extreme in the ancient world, since even Plato suggests that human superiority and inferiority to a great extent result from the beneficial or degrading effects of one's social position and calling, one's role in the social division of labour.[31] By referring to a 'naturally finer being' in the *Rhetoric*, Aristotle obviously implies that some humans are naturally superior to others.[32] An appreciation of this basic assumption of the Stagirite requires some acquaintance with his theory of the natural hierarchy of being. Nature, he thinks, consists of a hierarchy from inanimate objects through plants, animals, and men to the gods. The position in the hierarchy depends upon the naturally ordained *telos* or purpose or essence of the object or being; some ends or purposes are superior to and include the ends of those objects or beings below them in the scale. Each level of being is served by the levels below it and in turn serves the levels above it. This hierarchy of purpose or function in terms of the cosmos as a whole is one of qualitative distinctions, of natural differences, of moral value. In each case the superior being is morally entitled to rule the inferior who in turn is morally obligated to obey the superior. Within the cosmic hierarchy all being that forms a single whole composed of different parts arranged organically according to a specific end or purpose embodies the principle of hierarchy and subordination, one element or part being superior to the others. An animal, a man, a polis are such compounds or wholes as Aristotle calls them. The hierarchy of the cosmos and the hierarchies of the compounds within the cosmos are fixed, immutable, and continuous. All natural motion or change within the cosmos is toward a fixed, preordained position of rest, i.e., the fulfillment of the natural purpose or function of the object, or as it is termed: the actualization of potential. In this sense rest is the natural and good state of the cosmos and all objects within it. Motion, not rest has to be explained. Is motion in any given case natural or unnatural? Natural motion, which is good, is always movement toward the fulfillment of essence. Motion is unnatural and consequently an evil if it is not in accord with pre-ordained essence, if it represents a deviation from essence that hinders or prevents its realization, that thwarts the achievement of final rest. All of this applies to the motion of both non-animate and animate objects, and includes human activity.

Obviously, to the modern mind, from the social standpoint the most startling aspect of Aristotle's theory of a natural cosmic hierarchical structure is the idea of the natural and moral superiority of some human beings as against the natural and moral inferiority of others. Some by virtue of their natures are entitled to rule, others are obligated to obey. The most explicit formulation of this notion is found in Aristotle's conception of the natural slave which is too well-known to be laboured.[33] Suffice it to say that for him some men are sufficiently inferior in respect to their rational powers (or physical powers or both) to be 'animate article[s] of property'[34] of naturally superior men, their 'servant[s] in the sphere of action'.[35] Aristotle has in mind household slaves who are non-Greeks or 'barbarians', and therefore by his definition rationally inferior to Greek freemen. Although such a person is superior to the animals that act only by instinct, his reason is capable only of apprehending reason in others and of obeying their commands, but not sufficient for acting rationally in an independent fashion. Non-Greeks or barbarians, both male and female, are little better than slaves and inferior to Greek males and females. As the soul must naturally and rightfully rule the body, or as the tool must serve the artist, so the Greek freeman is justified in ruling the non-Greek as a natural slave. Occasionally the barbarian may be fully rational, but his rationality is never combined with a completely developed physique, a combination that characterizes the true human being, the Greek. Yet even among Greeks the adult male is superior to the adult female whose reason can never equal his own, and both are superior to the child—male or female—whose rational faculties have yet to mature. And among Greek male adults, as we shall see, gradations of the naturally superior and inferior exist.

If Aristotle believes in a natural social hierarchy among Greek adult males, are the ranks and orders composing it genetically determined, the result of birth, or are they conventional, the consequence of custom and law or a function of the environment, of one's position in the social division of labour? While he is usually rather vague and imprecise about the nature of the source, he does suggest that at least one fundamental distinction between the superior and the inferior is genetic, dependent upon good birth or its lack. When he discusses the constituents of true happiness—and only the fully developed and morally superior individual can be truly happy—good birth usually appears to be a vital ingredient, along with wealth.[36] One of his earliest works, probably written while he was a member of the Academy, is entitled, 'On Good Birth', in which he argues that good birth, far from being trivial, is precious and good, and that a genuine difference exists between the well-born and the low-born.[37] Those 'born of a long line of rich or good ancestors' are 'better born than those whose possession of these advantages is recent'.[38] His later definition of good birth in the *Rhetoric* is as follows:

> The good birth of an individual, which may come either from the male or female side, implies that both parents are free citizens, and that, as in the case of the state, the founders of the line have been notable for virtue or wealth or something else which is highly prized, and that many distinguished persons belong to the family, men and women, young and old.[39]

As in the earlier work he is still contemptuous of the newly rich, who tend to be insolent and arrogant, ostentatious and vulgar.[40] However, despite his faith in the superiority of the man of good birth over all others including the parvenu, Aristotle is quite realistic, admitting that the well-born are not necessarily identical with the noble. The well-born person may rapidly deteriorate, failing to live up to his fine stock, whereas the noble is the well-born who is true to his stock.[41] Hence, good birth is the condition of nobility, even if all well-born are not noble, or as Aristotle asserts in the *Politics*: 'the descendents of better men are likely to be intrinsically better; . . .'[42] But men of good birth and virtue—the naturally superior—are rare, for as Aristotle again says in the *Politics*: 'In no state would you find as many as a hundred men of good birth and merit: . . .'[43] The additional advantage of good birth is that it also usually means inherited wealth, far to be preferred to newly acquired riches, and along with good birth, Aristotle is quite clear that wealth, if not identical with natural superiority, is certainly a necessary condition for it. From this evidence Aristotle's position would seem to be as follows. In any polis out of the total number of men who are both well-born and wealthy, there is a handful of the truly superior.

If then Aristotle believes that natural and moral superiority among Greeks is genetically transmitted, dependent upon good birth and inherited wealth, what is his attitude toward the overwhelming majority of freemen, the ill-born? Here the distinctions of natural superiority and inferiority seem to be environmentally and occupationally determined rather than genetic as in the case of the well-born and wealthy at the top of the human hierarchy and the natural slaves at the bottom. The newly rich, defective as they may be as a class and inferior to the well-born with inherited wealth, are clearly superior to the poor, because, as we shall see, riches in addition to good birth are a necessary condition for the truly virtuous and happy life. But what of the masses who are not wealthy? Aristotle states quite unequivocally in the *Rhetoric* that the noble and the just—those who can fully realize their potentiality as human beings and attain true happiness—do not practice 'sordid crafts', those that make them dependent for their livelihood on others in the sense that they work for wages or must sell their products for a profit in order to survive.[44] In the *Eudemian Ethics* he classifies certain kinds of occupations connected with the necessary as preventing those who pursue them from achieving true happiness and well-being.[45] These are the 'vulgar arts', concerned with a reputation; 'servile occupations' that are sedentary and wage-earning; and 'commercial' vocations that entail buying and selling in markets and shops. And in the *Politics* he exclaims that 'none of the occupations followed by a populace which consists of mechanics, shop-keepers, and day labourers, leaves any room for excellence'.[46] Later in the same work in his incomplete description of the ideally best polis—reminiscent of Plato's Magnesia of the *Laws*—Aristotle proposes the exclusion of artisans, shop-keepers, farm labourers, and all wage-earners from citizenship on the grounds that such occupations are 'ignoble and inimical to goodness'.[47] As in the *Laws*, the citizens consist of a class of landed proprietors with the necessary leisure to devote to the military, deliberative, judicial, and religious functions of the polis. In this connection, a rather sophistic distinction is made between the conditions necessary for the existence of the polis as a whole and the fundamental organic or integral 'parts' of the system that are served by the conditions.[48] To the former he assigns the non-citizen class of artisans, shop-keepers, and labourers; and to the latter, the propertied citizens. Perhaps Aristotle's outlook in regard to lesser occupations in the polis can best be summarized by his view that we can discount the opinions of the multitude about happiness, comparing them to children, sick people, and the insane with whose opinions no normal person would trouble.[49] Just as these persons cannot be transformed by argument and persuasion but need years to change, or medical treatment or political correction, so years of remedial subjection are necessary for the multitude before they can have any perception of the nature of true happiness.

But if Aristotle sees the multitude as definitely inferior to the well-born and the wealthy, only a cut above natural slaves, degraded physically and mentally by their sordid callings, dependent for their survival upon wages or the sale of their products at profit, and without the leisure to participate in civic life, he does commend an intermediate class. This group consists of self-sufficient landed proprietors who evidently work their land with the help of a few slaves or part-time labourers, and are the backbone of what Aristotle calls the best form of democracy and the 'middle-class' of his 'polity', the best practicable polis.[50] They are followed by a class of independent herdsmen, leading a pastoral life and tending their own flocks.[51] Although inferior to great landed proprietors, both 'yeoman' and herdsman are decidely superior to the urban multitude of artisans, shop-keepers, and labourers. So while Aristotle's aristocratic background and perspective are reflected in his idealization of the landed gentry, his disdain for the parvenu, and his contempt for the working classes, he does put in a good word, as one might expect, for the ancient yeoman. The independence and self-sufficiency provided by farming, its symbolic connection with 'mother earth', and its contribution to manliness and the military virtues must all have had an enormous appeal for Aristotle and provided him with an important justification for his position.[52]

Aristotle's aristocratic conservatism, therefore, is characterized by a 'pessimistic realism' in regard to the human condition, a veneration for tradition, the collective wisdom of the species, and the status-quo; a belief in a natural hierarchy of human beings dominated by the well-born and wealthy; and a bias for rural life and values as against the urban. Of particular significance is his ranking of all male adults according to degrees of natural superiority and inferiority into what may be summarized as a seven-tiered hierarchy:

1. Well-born and wealthy who are virtuous
2. Well-born and wealthy not distinguished by virtue
3. *Nouveau riche*
4. Small independent farmers or peasants
5. Independent nomadic herdsmen
6. Urban multitude: artisans, merchants, shop-keepers, labourers
7. Natural slaves and barbarians

The well-born who are also wealthy are naturally and morally superior to all other groups, a superiority that is inherited and that entitles them to rule. Although not identical with true virtue and happiness, good birth and inherited wealth are their necessary condition. The well-born and wealthy who are virtuous are the only true human beings; the others, in varying degrees, have failed to actualize their potential. The most inferior class of natural slaves and barbarians is genetically inferior. Between these two extremes, the superiority and inferiority of the other classes seem to depend on environment and occupation more than on genetic transmission and inheritance. In addition to the clear preference for good birth and inherited wealth, weight in the scale is also given to landownership (the source of the wealth) and agriculture as opposed to commerce; to freedom from dependent labour, self-sufficiency, and rural life and values. The total perspective is both conservative and aristocratic, as might be expected from one of Aristotle's birth and connections.

3. *The Aristocratic Ideal*

Aristotle's aristocratic conservatism is even more apparent in his discussion of the principal moral virtues in Books III and IV of the *Nicomachean Ethics*. He examines in some detail eleven virtues which, in the order treated are: courage, self-control, generosity, magnificence, great souledness or high-mindedness, a nameless virtue between ambition and its lack, gentleness, friendliness, truthfulness, wittiness, and shame. Together they constitute a model of gentlemanly or aristocratic conduct —*kalokagathia*. Each virtue represents a mean—the famous 'golden mean'—between excess and deficiency, hence a life in accord with them is a life of moderation. Each to one degree or another is concerned with honour, that highest of aristocratic values, for as Aristotle says, 'Virtuous actions are noble and are performed because they are noble',[53] and the award of nobility is honour. He has in the main adapted for his own use the virtues commonly accepted in his gentlemanly world as the moral standards to be followed. He neither subjects them to critical philosophical analysis nor does he question their validity. To him they are the time-hallowed hallmarks of a traditional way of life which he accepts, respects, and wishes to strengthen. A life of true happiness will depend upon acquiring these virtues by committing oneself to them through upbringing and habituation, and then learning through experience and the emulation of the already virtuous how one should act in accordance with them in the variety of concrete situations with which one is confronted.

In following Aristotle's description of the virtues that are the fundamental conditions for true happiness and the realization of our full humanity, the reader is struck by the fact that as a whole they would be impossible of attainment by the great masses of Greek freemen. From Aristotle's perspective, indeed, only members of the upper strata of Greek society could ever adhere to this moral code and consequently be truly virtuous and happy. Seven of the virtues—courage, self-control, gentleness, friendliness, truthfulness, wittiness, and shame—anyone, regardless of his social rank or station, apparently might have some hope of acquiring. But the other four to which Aristotle pays more attention—generosity, magnificence, great souledness, and the nameless mean between ambition and its opposite—would clearly be beyond the powers of all except a few of the well-born and wealthy. And for Aristotle these four virtues are the very foundation of the genuinely ethical life. If by some improbable occurrence an ordinary freeman, or more likely one who had entered the *nouveau riche*, were to attempt to acquire such virtues his conduct would most certainly fall short of the mean and be characterized by one of the extremes in each case, for example, by extravagance, vulgarity, vanity, and ambition. More importantly, the very attempt to rise above his station could be considered presumptuous and wrong. And when one notes the qualities of conduct falling short of the eleven virtues either as excesses or deficiences one discovers a typical aristocratic caricature of the 'multitude' as being 'ignoble' and 'uncultured' and in general characterized by crudeness, lack of decorum, lack of propriety, boorishness, buffoonery, boastfulness, obsequiousness, lack of dignity, small-mindedness, vulgarity, ostentation, insolence, and shamelessness. Hence, it is obvious, from Aristotle's analysis, that the truly virtuous and happy can only come from the well-born and the wealthy. They are the natural rulers. In contrast, the ordinary Greek freeman, although superior to the natural slave, is born to be a minion of his natural betters, a necessary condition of their existence, but never an active participant in the morally good life. He is destined to live his years in drudgery and discipline, years that can never be truly happy or satisfying, years of constant subordination to the privileged few.

The four most significant virtues—generosity, magnificence, great-souledness, and the nameless mean between ambition and its absence—for the morally good life as defined by Aristotle seem to fall exclusively within the gentlemanly prerogative and are incapable of attainment by the great majority of people. Only the well-born and wealthy, and by no means all of them, can ever hope to guide their lives by such standards, thereby becoming truly virtuous and happy. Of these four virtues the most important is great-souledness (*megalopsychia*)—the mean between vanity and pettiness—sometimes called high mindedness or magnanimity. Greatness of soul is a typical aristocratic quality quite foreign to the modern perspective, entailing a feeling of superiority, haughtiness, pride, self-confidence, and an over-weening self-respect. To us the individual of greatness of soul is not likely to prove a very congenial creature, yet to Aristotle the quality is 'the crown, as it were, of the virtues',[54] both the condition for and the consequence of their possession. In short, greatness of soul includes and in a way transcends all other moral virtues; the great-souled man is the truly virtuous man. By his very nature he is self-controlled, courageous, generous, magnificent, etc. He is the natural aristocrat, the superior being who dazzles all, dominates all by his grandeur. The great-souled man, devoting himself to 'great and lofty matters'[55] and not preoccupied with power and wealth precisely because they come to him naturally, is primarily concerned with acquiring honour and avoiding dishonour; but even honour is not of the greatest concern. He is one who expects great things and actually deserves them. No one can possess greatness of soul without being truly good and noble, without *kalokagathia*. Nobility of birth, wealth, and power help to liberate the spirit from petty and vulgar concerns, and hence contribute immeasurably to greatness of soul. But let Aristotle speak for himself about the other characteristics of greatness of soul or high-mindedness:

> A high-minded person is justified in looking down upon others for he has the right opinion of them, but the common run of people do so without rhyme or reason.... It is, further, typical of a high-minded man not to ask for any favours, or only reluctantly, but to offer aid readily. He will show his stature in his relations with men

> of eminence and fortune, but will be unassuming toward those of moderate means. For to be superior to the former is difficult and dignified, but superiority over the latter is easy. Furthermore, there is nothing ignoble in asserting one's dignity among the great, but to do so among the lower classes is just as crude as to assert one's strength against an invalid. He will not go in for pursuits that the common people value, nor for those in which the first place belongs to others.... He cannot adjust his life to another, except a friend, for to do so is slavish. That is, [by the way,] why all flatterers are servile and people from the lower classes are flatterers. He is not given to admiration, for nothing is great to him.... When he encounters misfortunes that are unavoidable or insignificant, he will not lament and ask for help. That kind of attitude belongs to someone who takes such matters seriously. He is a person who will rather possess beautiful and priceless objects than objects which are profitable and useful, for they mark him more as self-sufficient.
>
> Further, we think of a slow gait as characteristic of a high-minded man, a deep voice, and a deliberate way of speaking. For a man who takes few things seriously is unlikely to be in a hurry, and a person who regards nothing as great is not to be excitable. But a shrill voice and a swift gait are due to hurry and excitement.[56]

So much of this passage and especially the last paragraph graphically illustrate how difficult it is to distinguish between moral virtue and aristocratic *style* in Aristotle's ethical code.

Such is Aristotle's ideal of the gentleman which, of course, must be rounded off by reference to justice and to the intellectual virtues, an ideal incapable of being realized except by the well-born and the wealthy. Thus members of the lower social orders are destined to remain 'sub-human' servants of their natural masters. Aristotle's distinction between the gentleman of good taste and propriety and the crude and vulgar parvenue who lacks a sense of proportion and discrimination, for example Cleon, is clearly reflected in the *Constitution of Athens*, usually but not always attributed to him. A number of passages in the work reflect a decided aristocratic bias and a conviction that Athenian democracy has become a lawless tyranny of the majority under the guidance of unscrupulous, self-seeking, and vulgar demagogues.[57] Aristotle appears quite prepared to see this rule of the crude and ungentlemanly *demos* replaced by an oligarchy of gentlemen. His aristocratic prejudices are summarized in a sentence from the *Politics*: 'It may be remarked that while oligarchy is characterized by good birth, wealth, and culture, the attributes of democracy would appear to be the very opposite—low birth, poverty, and vulgarity.'[58]

4. *Oikos and Polis*

Aristotle's aristocratic perspective also informs his idea of the family or household (*oikos*) and the related concepts of household management (*oikonomia*) and acquisition (*chrematistic*). Scholars usually do not stress that for Aristotle man fundamentally is not only a *zoön politikon*, a polis animal or being, but also a *zoön oikonomikon*, a family or household animal or being, and a *zoön koinonikon*, a community or association animal or being.[59] Of these three related aspects of man's nature, the last is in a way the most basic. All three depend upon man's rational nature, the possession of reason and language that sets him above all other animals. However, that man is by nature both a household and a polis being presupposes that by virtue of reason he creates and lives in communities or associations. *Koinonia*—variously translated as community, association, society, partnership, fraternity—is any group whose members have something in common, from mankind in general to a business arrangement.[60] Such communities include the household and polis, villages, religious cults, symposia, clubs, commercial combinations, and schools such as the Academy. Each form of *koinonia* is characterized by a particular kind of friendship or good will (*philia*), the bond that holds together its members. The *philia* binding the members of the household is a species of innate affection, while the friendship uniting the citizens of the polis is *homonoia*, or concord, more in the nature of agreement as to ends and values, a kind of contractual understanding. Obviously, from Aristotle's standpoint the two most important types of *koinonia* are the household or *oikos* and the polis. Although man begins his life in the household, he can only actualize his potential as a full human being in the polis.[61] Without the household there could be no polis, but without the polis man in the complete sense of rational self-fulfillment cannot exist. The household is the realm of necessity—man is born into it involuntarily—whereas the polis is a realm of freedom because it is a voluntary association created by man. The one, existing by virtue of blood ties, is the essential condition of an individual's very biological existence and economic survival; the other, to which a person may or may not belong, provides the necessary and sufficient conditions for truly becoming a man. Gods and beasts, but not men in terms of self-fulfillment, can live apart from the polis. Therefore, according to Aristotle's theory of the hierarchy of social being, the *telos* of the household is inferior to and serves the higher purpose of the polis. Despite similarities between household and polis, Aristotle thinks that a small polis is not comparable to a large family. In other words, the difference between household and polis is qualitative instead of simply quantitative.

Nevertheless, most of this fails to suggest any basic opposition in Aristotle's thinking between *oikos* and polis.[62] In the *Eudemian Ethics* he explicitly states that the household is the 'source and spring' of friendship, justice and the polis,[63] a view he maintains in the *Politics* in his discussion of the relationship of household and polis. The initial impetus for the creation of the household is sexual: men unite with women for reproductive purposes.[64] This is a natural inclination shared by humans with non-rational animals, and in this sense the cohabitation of men and women in the household is more natural than their union in the polis. If non-rational animals of the opposite sex naturally unite for the sake of procreation, rationally endowed men and women create the household not only to reproduce their kind but also for a further 'biological' reason. Unlike the beasts they are mutually dependent in satisfying basic needs necessary for life itself. Out of the natural inclination for procreation, which they share with non-rational animals, men create a more lasting union than theirs because they are not by nature self-sufficient. Since man is a rational being who can deliberate as to what is advantageous and disadvantageous he recognizes the benefit arising from the permanent association of the household. In order to satisfy their needs for survival a basic division of labour takes place between male and female and continues to develop with the addition of children, slaves, and servants to the household. A hierarchical system of functions and relationships springs up naturally that is directed toward the utility of the whole. Another reason given by Aristotle for the household is man's natural affection, his inclination to be gregarious and sociable, that goes beyond utility in cementing relations within the family circle and is in turn enhanced by mutual advantage. Since human beings, because of their reason, can deliberate as to what is just and unjust, and good and evil, in addition to the beneficial and disadvantageous, the hierarchical division of labour in the household soon gives rise to questions of morality, fairness, equity and justice. The household, therefore, is the nursery for the idea and practice of justice in both the broad sense of righteousness or moral virtue itself and in the more limited connotation of the proper distribution of honours and awards for services rendered to the well-being of the whole. Justice in the family is guaranteed by the bond of natural affection which is the beginning of the friendship that becomes so important to the wider spheres of human relations. For where there is justice, Aristotle claims, there is always the need of friendship, but where friendship exists so does justice.

In isolation, however, the household can never fully satisfy the biological, social, and rational or moral needs unique to man. A larger and more comprehensive self-sufficient form of social organization becomes imperative. For the purposes of mutual defence, the economic exchange of goods and services, and a richer and more complete social and moral life, men unite historically first into villages and then into poleis, each the natural out-growth of the household, natural in that they serve to satisfy human needs arising in the family and out of man's nature. However, the polis alone, is self-sufficient because solely through it does man become a full human being in that it provides all the conditions necessary for the satisfaction of his biological, social, and moral needs. Hence, Aristotle can proclaim paradoxically that while the individual is *historically* prior to the polis, the polis is *logically* prior to the individual. In other words, the polis is the necessary and sufficient condition for the fruition of the human being. So if in the natural hierarchy of communities, in which each end includes and is superior to the ends below it, the chief end of the family is 'biological' or economic life; and of the village and other associations such as cults and clubs, social life; then the ultimate end, superior to and including the other ends, beyond which there can be no other ends, is that of the polis, the morally good life. Of course, communities below the polis in the scale like the household still have indispensable contributions to make to the moral life of man, for, as we have seen, the beginnings of moral life take place in the household; but only the polis can complete those beginnings. In his typical fusion of fact and value Aristotle offers in the guise of a definition an ideal of the polis that may or may not be realized in practice. In so far as an actual polis falls short of providing the self-sufficient conditions necessary for the morally good life, and consequently the actualization of man's rational and moral potential, it is not a true polis as Aristotle defines the term. Most existing poleis fall far short of this ideal, their laws being 'only a promiscuous heap of legislation; ...'[65] Moreover, since the morally good life can only be attained by the well-born and wealthy living in a secure and congenial environment, an authentic polis is one so arranged as to guarantee their domination and the permanence of their way of life. Aristotle has defined the polis in general not in socially discriptive language but in aristocratic terms.

By no stretch of the imagination, then, are *oikos* and polis opposed concepts in Aristotle's realm of ideas. Both are concerned with the good life, even if the polis is to a greater extent than the *oikos*. If the polis is higher in the hierarchy of value, it cannot exist without the 'biological', social, and moral foundation of the household. In sum, household and polis are mutually sustaining and complementary rather than antithetical institutions. Such a conclusion, however, does not do full justice to the importance accorded the *oikos* by Aristotle. The household is the absolutely essential condition for an aristocracy—a class of the well-born and wealthy—and of an aristocratic way of life. For the notables, the household because of the blood ties of the family is the fundamental condition of everything they hold dear, the *sine qua non* of their criterion of superiority—good birth and inherited riches. The very essence of aristocracy is the transmission of property from generation to generation through blood relationships centering in the household. The problems of marriage, of maintaining and strengthening the proper connections of good birth and wealth, are crucial considerations for the continuation of an aristocratic line and way of life. Noble birth and inherited wealth cannot be diluted and dissipated by imprudent marriages, by the improper mixture of golden natures with brazen souls. And in a non-aristocratic society such as Athens the preservation of the aristocratic household is vital for the survival of the correct values and a noble way of life. For these reasons one can perhaps appreciate why Aristotle, himself an aristocrat who had lived many years in a democracy, placed such emphasis upon the household.

Aristotle's definition of the household emerging from his discussion of the subject in Book I of the *Politics* is as ideal as his conception of the polis. He is not describing the household of the numerous Athenian city-dwellers—the artisans, tradesmen, and labourers—nor the menage of the landed majority of the small peasant proprietors of Attica. His household is no more an average or typical Greek establishment than his polis in the most general terms is identical with any existing one.[66] To begin with, he stipulates that: 'A complete household consists of slaves and freemen'.[67] The point is that not only should the proper household include one slave, but also apparently several slaves. Quite a few Athenian households had no slaves, something recognized by Aristotle when he wrote 'oxen serve the poor in lieu of household slaves';[68] and many households possessed only one slave. Aristotle's household, then, is far from being the standard domicile. Furthermore, for Aristotle the head of the household because of the slaves is evidently relieved of any need for work. How different this is from the situation in many humble Athenian households in which, for example, the slave laboured alongside the master in his workshop, while on small peasant holdings the single slave might in addition to his domestic obligations help the farmer in the fields. In all fairness to Aristotle, however, he did not seem to be averse to the children of the household occasionally performing menial functions appropriate only to slaves as an educational and correctional measure. The regular assistance of the slave (or slaves) in poorer homes by the sons and daughters was customary practice. Preferably, the master portrayed by Aristotle will not himself have to command the slaves, for such supervision is essentially demeaning since it 'has no great or majestic character....'[69] So one slave will serve as steward in order to free the master for politics and study, an arrangement which only well-to-do Greeks could manage. The master's primary task in regard to slaves is not so much to see that they perform their allotted functions efficiently as it is to provide them with moral guidance through 'admonition' and instruction,[70] a duty that could not have been typical of very many Greek households of any class. Aristotle's household, therefore, is an idealized upper-class household—most definitely not the household of everyman, a conclusion that is further substantiated by his recommendation that parents should basically train their sons in what is good in itself, in the liberal arts, not in what is necessary or useful,[71] something, of course, that most Greeks could simply not afford to do. His lengthy condemnation of a purely utilitarian upbringing for children and his warning against over-specialization even in the liberal arts is clear evidence that his household bears little resemblance to that of the vast majority of Greeks. The aristocrat 'will not go in for pursuits that the common people value, nor for those in which the first place belongs to others'.[72] He is essentially an amateur.[73]

Aristotle's household, consequently, is an aristocratic ideal that should not be mistaken for a description of the normal Greek institution. Although Aristotle insists that it differs in kind from the polis, he resorts to political language and metaphor to characterize its basic nature. It is a highly structured system of authority with a strict division of function among its members, ruled by a patriarchal head who plays the multiple roles of husband, father, and master. Aristotle explicitly rejects democracy as a way of life for the household. The members should not be on an equal footing, nor should they be allowed to act as they please, something that results from the weakness of the head. His rule should depend upon his natural superiority and not upon the possession of great wealth. He should never encroach upon the proper tasks of the other members, but should confine his rule to his own proper functions. A special relationship and brand of authority exists between him and each of the other members. The first distinction in the household is between the head's domination founded upon natural superiority and the others' subordination due to natural inferiority. The second distinction is between freemen and slaves. The head's domination differs basically in regard to the kind of authority he exercises over each of these last two groups, corresponding to Aristotle's classification of constitutions into those that are good and those that are perverted or despotic.[74] Toward his wife the head is like a true statesman in relation to his fellow-citizens. Their association is basically aristocratic, depending upon his merit and his confining himself to what is proper for a man. When he infringes upon her role, his rule degenerates from an aristocracy into an oligarchy. In respect to his children he is a monarch.[75] His rule over wife and children is essentially for their interest and benefit as in the case of the good forms of constitution. However, toward the most inferior members of the household, the labouring non-propertied slaves, aristocratic husband and monarchic father assume the role of the master, or *despotēs*, a despot who rules them for his own advantage rather than their good. In essence, then, the household of Aristotle is an authoritarian structure in which more likely than not a majority of its members in the form of non-propertied labouring slaves are subjected and exploited by a minority of freemen for the sake of the good life.

The importance of Aristotle's ideal aristocratic household in his intellectual outlook is suggested by the fact that it seems to serve as a model for the ideal polis he begins to portray in Books VII and VIII of the *Politics*. At least the parallels between the two appear to be significant. Like the household, the ideal polis is divided between a majority of non-propertied labouring members—slaves, serfs, and metics—upon whose efforts depend the physical well-being and leisure of the minority of propertied non-labouring members. In both cases the former class is dominated by the latter and has no part in the direction of the common enterprise. As we have seen, Aristotle in describing the ideal polis differentiates between 'parts' and 'conditions'.[76] 'Parts' refer to the non-labouring propertied citizens who like husband, wife, and children of the household share in the good life. 'Conditions' denote the labouring non-propertied farmers, artisans, tradesmen, and household slaves, who provide and maintain the material basis for the good life. The ultimate end of both household and ideal polis is not economic advantage or profit, but the morally good life, although by itself the household is not a sufficient means for the attainment of this goal. In this ideal polis the integral parts who are privileged to share in the pursuit of the good life, while constituting a 'society of equals', are divided into those who rule and those who are ruled according to a natural principle of superiority and inferiority, age, the elders and the youth.[77] Hence, the elders perform the deliberative, judicial, and religious functions, while under their direction the youth have the major responsibility for defence. Here again in general is the kind of natural division that should prevail in the household between husband and father on the one hand and wife, mother, and children on the other. Aristotle hastens to add that the government of the ideal polis is one of freemen, consequently the elder rulers act in the interest of the younger citizens, not as despot over slaves.[78] A final similarity between Aristotle's treatments of the ideal polis and the household is the common emphasis upon leisure. The 'conditions' of the ideal polis are necessary for the leisure of the 'parts', although without leisure themselves, or as Aristotle says quoting a proverb: 'There's no leisure for slaves....'[79] Only by being liberated from having to pursue a demeaning occupation for the sake of earning a living, can the freemen have the leisure for study and civic participation as well as the spiritual freedom so necessary for the morally good life, a life that is clearly the prerogative of a fortunate, cultured few. So the household apparently is the ideal polis in embryo conceived out of Aristotle's aristocratic predilections. The similarities between Aristotle's *oikos* and ideal polis are often overlooked perhaps because of several of his emphases. First, he always stresses that the polis, unlike the household, is a 'community of equals', forgetting that only citizens—the 'parts' rather than the 'conditions'—are members of that 'community'. Second, he underscores the single ruler of the household as against the 'many' in the polis, since all citizens alternate between ruling and being ruled, again neglecting to indicate clearly that only the 'parts' and not the 'conditions' are the 'many' in this case. By dismissing the 'conditions' Aristotle points up the difference between household and polis; but once 'conditions' as well as 'parts' are included in the picture, the parallels are obvious, and in a sense the differences tend to be more quantitative than qualitative. Nor should it be forgotten that while Aristotle's ideal polis, broadly speaking, duplicates the hierarchy of the household, democracy rejected the hierarchical distinction between 'conditions' and 'parts'—with the exception of slaves—as being applicable to the polis.

Just as *oikos* and polis are intimately linked ideas instead of opposites for Aristotle, so economics or *oikonomia*, the art of household management, and politics, the art of the polis, are closely related. While economics in this special sense is subordinate to the supreme or master art of politics, both are ultimately concerned with the ordering of human relationships for the achievement of the morally good life, the one in the household and the other in the polis.[80] Aristotle may even have conceived of politics in the image of economics just as he seems to have modelled his ideal polis upon the household. At any rate, economics and politics should supplement and complement each other. In Book I of the *Politics* Aristotle separates *chrematistic* or the art of acquisition from *oikonomia*, the art of household management. As an 'ancillary art' the former should function to provide a supply of objects capable of being stored, necessary for life and useful for the maintenance of household and polis.[81] In its ancillary role to the art of politics *chrematistic* is what we today might call economics, having to do with resources, property, exchange, trade, commerce, money, accumulation, taxation, revenue, etc. That 'political-economy' in the sense of 'political-chrematistic' would not necessarily for Aristotle in particular or the Greeks in general be a contradiction in terms, and that *chrematistic* is also an important concern for household management or *oikonomia* is testified to by the Stagirite's comment in the *Politics*: '... states—like households, but to an even greater extent—are often in want of financial resources and in need of more ways of gaining them. This is the reason why some of those who adopt a political career confine their political activity to matters of finance.'[82] The objects supplied by *chrematistic* should be limited by the end for which they are acquired and accumulated, whether in household or polis. The purpose that should determine and govern the accumulation of wealth in each case is the morally good life. Economic goods are necessary for the morally good life in household and polis. However, they should be sufficient as to kind and number, not too many and not too few, a golden mean between excess and deficiency. When the optimum wealth for the good life has been reached, further acquisition is both unnecessary and immoral. So Aristotle is adamantly opposed to economic accumulation for its own sake. Acquisition can only properly be an instrument for man's efforts to realize his true being. This is the natural art of acquisition or *chrematistic*. Any attempt to go beyond what is necessary for human self-fulfilment debases man, and is consequently the unnatural art of acquisition.

Although, as we have just seen, Aristotle recognizes a legitimate or natural *chrematistic*, his more frequent references are to the unnatural form which he severely criticizes. His argument against the unnatural art of acquisition centers on the crucial distinction between production for use and production for exchange, between use value and exchange value, a momentous discovery for economic theory that seems to have been generated by the Stagirite's aristocratic prejudices.[83] Every commodity, he believes, can either be used or exchanged. Shoes, for example, can be worn or exchanged for a more needed commodity. Exchange, which is unnecessary in the household, becomes necessary in the village where each member sharing things in common with the other members contributes his surplus to a common fund to be used by those who lack a particular commodity.[84] In this way a farmer without vineyards may exchange his surplus wheat for the surplus wine produced by a fellow villager. Such exchange is a natural form of acquisition because its object simply is 'to satisfy the natural requirements of sufficiency'.[85] From these innocent origins, however, develops the unnatural exchange for profit because of the necessity of transactions over a great distance. When man's needs can no longer be satisfied by local production, surpluses are exchanged for foreign imports, and to facilitate the exchange money is invented. Even then trade is natural as long as its purpose is self-sufficiency. But as trade for profit becomes a possibility, men begin to devote themselves to profit 'at the expense of other men'[86] rather than to the legitimate goal of self-sufficiency, and study how they can make the greatest profit. Once *chrematistic* becomes the art of producing monetary wealth instead of the objects necessary for self-sufficiency, it is unnatural. The goal of the tradesman is now solely the accumulation of money without any restriction by the ends that it should properly serve. Aristotle rejects the scarcity factor so fundamental to modern economics; human needs are not limitless, but have very definite bounds. The culmination of this process of the transformation of natural into unnatural acquisition occurs when all tasks in society begin to be performed for the sake of the single tyrannical end of unlimited accumulation. Men even borrow money in order to make money, and the lending of money itself becomes an important mode of profit. Some of Aristotle's harshest words are for what he calls the 'most unnatural' kind of acquisition,[87] usury, that makes a profit from money itself instead of from the exchange process money was designed to serve. From the economic standpoint, therefore, Aristotle believes that the well-ordered polis should resemble the well-ordered *oikos* writ large. Both should be based upon the principles of natural acquisition for use rather than for exchange, limited by the objective of the morally good life, and not given over to profit making or accumulation for its own sake. Far from being in opposition, politics and economics in the senses both of household management and *chrematistic* are intimately related in Aristotle's aristocratic outlook.

Although certain of these views of Aristotle will no doubt win the sympathy of some modern readers, there can be no doubt as to their fundamental aristocratic, agrarian, and anti-commercial inspiration. Perhaps this is one of the better examples of how the logic of a system of ideas, irrespective of its source, produces perceptive ideas of the greatest significance, innovative notions that transcend the historicity of their origins and are of immense value in other contexts at other times.[88] Aristotle's devastating critique of unnatural acquisition or exchange for profit is at once an attack upon democracy and a warning to his fellow aristocrats to mend their ways. He seems to identify accumulation and trade for profit with the rise of democracy and the decline of a dominant agrarian, aristocratic class. Commercialism and democracy are two sides of the single coin of vulgarity, insolence, brazeness, and the lack of taste and decorum, in a word all that is at odds with the truly aristocratic. Of course, the tremendous expansion of what Aristotle called unnatural acquisition had taken place with the flowering of democracy in Athens. By the time of the establishment of democracy after the reforms of Cleisthenes and the victory over Persia, the food market in the Athenian agora had been firmly instituted, and in general the market as an institution was possibly much more popular and widely accepted there than it was in the Ionian countryside and elsewhere in Greece.[89] When Aristotle was writing the *Politics*, the Athenian commercial agora had already acquired an international reputation. The appearance of deposit banks that made loans to merchants helped Athens to become the major money market of Greece.[90] One worry for Aristotle may have been that the greatly increased commercial activity meant the much freer disposal of possessions, thus undermining the hereditary principle of entailed, inalienable property at the heart of aristocratic power. Another worry was undoubtedly that many aristocrats had succumbed to the temptation of commercial aggrandizement in order to shore up their rapidly diminishing capital. The thirst for profit, he feared, was inexorably obliterating the distinctions of status and the values appropriate to rank, upon which the true government of merit should be grounded.[91] The 'levelling' of democracy was reducing all vocations and endeavours to the same acquisitive impulse. Every ability, every capacity began to be determined by the voracious appetite for money.[92] But another aspect of the situation perhaps caused him as much concern for it was at the root of the problem as he saw it. A way of life devoted to profit is the result of the emancipation of the masses from subjection to their natural superiors, and a novel condition of equality. Having cast aside the security of the control and guidance of the well-born and wealthy, a new 'state of mind' arose among the ordinary people now struggling alone for survival; one aimed solely at money making.[93] With the advent of popular participation in government those with the most servile occupations, skilled artisans and labourers who offer their services for hire, not only promote and proliferate the life of profit but also introduce it into the world of politics. The real danger is that the tyranny of the majority extends the tyranny of profit to the whole of life, nothing being sacred.

Hence, despite their different ends, Aristotle did not completely oppose household to polis; rather he thought of them as mutually sustaining and cooperative institutions. If the two forms of association are distinct with respect to their essential aims—the purpose of the *oikos* is to deal with 'daily recurrent needs' while that of the polis is the morally good life—the way in which Aristotle elaborates the distinction only emphasizes their fundamental connection. The mode of providing for daily recurrent needs, that is the nature of the 'economy', must be such that it contributes to the attainment of the morally good life. It must be a fundamentally agrarian, aristocratic domestic economy based on the aristocratic *oikos*. And the opposition of 'political' activities to those concerned with the 'economic' provision for daily recurrent needs serves to exclude the 'animate' conditions of society, the productive classes that supply material necessities, from political life. Thereby Aristotle emphasizes the hierarchical nature of the polis and its similarity to the *oikos* relationship of master and slave. His definitions of household and polis, far from being descriptive of historical reality, are in fact aristocratic ideals, since the good life itself is an end attainable only by the well-born and the wealthy through the instruments of the properly ordered household and polis. So basic is the household to Aristotle that he apparently conceptualized the ideal polis as an *oikos* writ large. The connection of *oikonomia*, or household management, and politics reflects the mutual interdependence of household and polis. In a sense, 'political-economy' as a marriage of the arts of politics and household management, far from being a contradiction in terms for Aristotle, might represent to him the true art of politics of the ideal polis that would be based upon some of the central precepts of the *oikos* such as hierarchy and a particular kind of division of labour together with the principle of natural acquisition that in one form at least is characteristic of the *oikos*. *Chrematistic* or the art of acquisition, something comparable to economics in the modern sense, is closely linked with both household management and politics. Since the essence of household and polis has to do with the quest for the morally good life, acquisition for the support of each should properly be subordinated to that aim, just as the appetites should be governed by reason. Democracy and unnatural acquisition are the political and economic dimensions of a single malady afflicting all of Greece, and particularly Athens: the replacement of the agarian, aristocratic way of life by the base conduct and values of urban *hoi polloi*.

5. *Justice, Stasis, 'Polity', and Utopia*

Aristotle's aristocratic conservatism is also reflected in his idea of justice, the nature of its relationship to his conception of *stasis* (factionalism and civic disorder), and in his recommendations for its prevention, in particular his notion of the 'polity' and his fragmentary sketch of an ideal polis or utopia. A discussion of the Stagirite's ethical ideal is not complete without reference to a final moral virtue, justice.[94] However, justice as a moral virtue in one important sense differs from the other moral virtues previously described in that it includes them. It is complete excellence in relation to our fellow man, moral virtue in general. As Barker suggests, a more appropriate translation might be 'righteousness'.[95] Aristotle also distinguishes this 'universal' justice from 'particular' justice, which in turn he divides into 'distributive' and 'rectificatory' justice. Distributive justice concerns the allocation of anything that is to be shared by members of the polis, for instance, the distribution of honours and awards. Rectificatory justice deals with righting a wrong that has occurred in a commercial transaction, with awarding damages to the plaintiff in a civil court. Aristotle also differentiates among other varieties of justice, but our interest is only in his idea of distributive justice so expressive of his aristocratic values and so basic to an understanding of his political thought in general.

Justice had been concerned traditionally with the question of each person receiving no more and no less than he deserves, 'To each his due', particularly as it related to judicial decisions. Ideally, according to Aristotle, distributive justice is based on the distinctly aristocratic principle of 'proportionate equality'. From this standpoint, 'To each his due' means equal things to equal persons and unequal things to unequal persons, but definitely not equal things to unequal persons. In other words the principle of proportionate equality assumes the distinction between superiority and inferiority among human beings. The allotment of honours and awards in the polis to the superior should be greater than that to the inferior, if the standard 'To each his due', is to be maintained. But if this is the case what criterion will be used for differentiating the superior from the inferior? For Aristotle the only correct criterion to be employed in making the distinction is the contribution that one makes to the highest end of the polis, the morally good life. Those who contribute most to this end by their conduct are the superior, thereby entitled to the greater share in the honours and awards to be distributed; while those who contribute less are the inferior to whom a proportionately smaller share of the honours and awards is rightfully due. Hence, Aristotle believes that a major share of the honours and awards to be divided among the members of a polis should go to the *aristoi*, the best in the sense of the truly meritorious and morally virtuous.

However, since aristocracies in the authentic sense of the rule of the best are practically non-existent, distributive justice in practice falls short of the ideal. So most of what Aristotle says about distributive justice concerns its defective forms as they are found in the two most common types of polis in the Greek world, oligarchies and democracies. Both oligarchs and democrats have only a partial and imperfect notion of distributive justice. In respect to the allocation of honours and awards in a polis, oligarchs believe that those who are wealthy or of noble birth should be given a greater share than those who are poor and of humble origins. Democrats hold that all freemen, whether rich or poor, noble or humble, should share equally in the distribution of honours and awards. If men are superior in one respect, so the oligarchs assume, such as wealth or birth, they are superior in all respects; while the democrats argue that equality in one attribute such as free birth signifies equality in every way. Aristotle admits that both oligarchs and democrats appear to have a good case for their respective positions.[96] The rich possess most of the land and are more reliable in regard to contracts; and those of good birth, always bringing prestige to their polis, are more active in civic affairs and are likely to be 'intrinsically' better than the ill-born. On the other hand, the people as a whole are likely to possess more of these attributes than any single group or individual. If the end of the polis were simply economic life then the case of the oligarchs—emphasizing the standard of wealth—would be very strong indeed, and the position of the democrats could not be neglected. But since the highest purpose of the polis is the morally virtuous life both the oligarchic and democratic ideas of distributive justice are defective.

Although Aristotle finds both conceptions imperfect, falling short of the ideal of distributive justice in a genuine aristocracy, they do not appear to be equally defective, a point that is seldom made in this connection. Clearly, he means that the oligarchic position while imperfect is less so than that of the democrats. The oligarchs' flaw is their identification of superiority with wealth and good birth, and inferiority with poverty and lowly birth. Of course from Aristotle's perspective this criticism is rather weak since he believes that the truly meritorious and morally virtuous will always be found among the wealthy and noble, although it must be acknowledged that he also thinks they would always be a bare handful, while in an oligarchy this minority would be treated as equals to the vast majority of their class who lacked their excellence. But, at least in relation to the masses the oligarchs retain the principle of proportionate equality. On the other hand the democrats have rejected proportionate equality and replaced it by the principle of 'numerical' or 'arithmetical' equality. In the distribution of honours and awards in the polis democrats make no distinction between the superior and inferior, reducing all to the lowest common denominator: equal things to unequals. This levelling assumption of the democrats renders their conception of distributive justice more defective and imperfect than that of the oligarchs. Therefore, Aristotle offers a scale of four types of distributive justice from the most perfect to the least perfect. At the top is the ideally best in a true aristocracy. It is followed, as we shall see, by the best practicable, a mixture of the principles of proportionate and numerical equality to be found in the 'polity'. Next is the form in an oligarchy based upon proportionate equality; and finally the most imperfect type in a democracy founded upon numerical equality.

Aristotle's interest in the defective forms of distributive justice found in oligarchies and democracies is much more practical and hard-headed than merely academic. Since oligarchies and democracies are the most widespread kinds of constitutions among the Greeks,[97] and since the type of distributive justice in each is imperfect, the consequence is wide-spread factionalism and civic disorder, even revolutionary action—in a word what was called *stasis*.[98] In oligarchies the poor who are in a majority may feel that the proportionate division of honours and awards is unequal and unfair in a numerical sense. On the other hand, in democracies the wealthy and well-born may think they are entitled to more than an equal share of honours and awards, that because of their superiority the distribution is unequal and unfair in proportionate terms. The discontented individuals and groups in both forms of polis may mobilize their forces, combine, and through legal or illegal means, resorting ultimately to revolutionary acts and civil war, attempt to change the situation in their favour. Consequently, what first seems to have been a somewhat theoretical problem proves to have a direct practical bearing on the urgent concrete question of political instability and change so plaguing the Greeks at least since the Peloponnesian War. Aristotle is convinced that the 'cause' of *stasis* is to be found in inequality, that a passion for equality—either numerical or proportionate—is at the root of *stasis*. From the very beginning of Book V it is clear that his motivation is to offer recommendations for the maintenance of the status-quo, to indicate how oligarchies and democracies can best preserve themselves. In a word this can be done by the rulers of each polis making certain concessions to the opposing principle of equality. Oligarchies should in some measure institutionalize the principle of numerical equality and democracies should move toward incorporating something of proportionate equality. As we shall see, however, the solution to *stasis* is somewhat less straightforward than this suggests.

What, then, in more detail are Aristotle's views about *stasis* and the nature of his recommendations to deal with the problem? In general *stasis* may entail two kinds of change: a basic constitutional change, for example, the replacement of an oligarchy by a democracy; and an alteration of a particular constitution such as an oligarchic modification of a democracy. Oligarchies tend to be less stable and more troubled with *stasis* than democracies because divisions and conflicts can take place not only between the oligarchic ruling class and the people, but also within the ranks of the oligarchs themselves. In democracies, however, disturbances usually only break out between the rich and well-born on one side and the people on the other. If a passion for equality is the general cause of *stasis*, the 'occasions' for an eruption of disorder and conflict may be various and have relatively small beginnings. Those in authority may take undue advantage of their positions to make profits and to act with high-handedness and insolence toward other citizens. Individuals of outstanding eminence may emerge to endanger the liberties of their fellows. The sudden increase in size and strength of one class or social group and the corresponding decline of another may lead to the beginning of a new power structure not represented by the existing system of government. Different ethnic origins may eventually be a source of friction, tension, and turmoil.

Aristotle discusses separately and at some length the nature of stasis in democracies and oligarchies. His analysis of democracies reflects his bias toward the well-born and wealthy—or 'notables'—and his hostility to the people. Conflict between notables and people is blamed chiefly upon the demagogues who whip up their followers against the well-born and wealthy.[99] They are 'discreditable', their conduct is one of 'wanton license', and their treatment of the notables 'unjust'. While Athens is not mentioned he probably is thinking of the new breed of politicians, beginning with Cleon, who, as we have seen, are denounced so scathingly in the *Constitution of Athens*, and ending with those who in his own times headed the popular anti-Macedonian 'party'. He admits in his discussion of *stasis* in oligarchies that the unjust treatment of the people by the notables is one of the principle causes of trouble, but then quickly turns to a lengthy consideration of conflicts within the ruling class.[100]

As to precautions to be taken against *stasis*,[101] Aristotle emphasizes that in oligarchies and democracies the rich and the poor will always exist. Once this permanent fact of political life is recognized every effort should be made to create the conditions for harmonious coexistence and to prevent the ferment of class-warfare. Among other things Aristotle recommends the rule of law and cultivation of a respect for law, encouragement of a 'middle-class', the restriction of office to the meritorious, the prevention of venality and corruption, security of the propertied and wealthy in democracies and attention to the poor in oligarchies, and moderation in policy, laws, and leadership. Above all the key to stability and order is education of the citizens in the appropriate spirit of their constitution—whether it is oligarchic or democratic. They should be taught to act so as to cherish and safeguard their particular way of life.

An interesting aspect of Aristotle's theory of distributive justice and *stasis* is his conviction that the oligarchic and democratic classes will always have to co-exist.[102] Both oligarchies and democracies are and cannot be other than mixtures of the two classes. But, and this is the crucial point in his calculations, of the total free-born population in *both* oligarchies and democracies, the notables are always a minority; and the people, always a majority. Neither class, however, in Aristotle's mind at least, can do without the other. Obviously the notables in both forms of polis absolutely depend upon the vital economic services performed by the majority. Without their labour, degrading as it is, the minority of notables could not survive under either governmental system. As Aristotle himself admits in the incomplete exposition of the ideally best constitution in Books VII and VIII of the *Politics*, artisans, merchants, shopkeepers, and wage-earners are necessary conditions of the polis, although they are not 'parts' of it, i.e., citizens, as are the land-owning notables. Is it, however, true that the notables are as necessary for the poor, as they are for the notables? Aristotle's answer would be a definite 'yes', adding that the notables are even more necessary. Because the notables are by nature superior to the people; because they possess leisure (admittedly dependent upon the labour of the inferior poor) so crucial for the performance of the critical functions of leadership, deliberation, military defence, and religion; and finally because the polis itself has for its highest naturally ordained end (as he defines it) their self-realization, the people are fundamentally dependent upon them if the polis itself is to continue as the only way of life compatible with being fully human. It is clear that Aristotle has so defined the polis and the notables (among whom are a few of the best and truly human) in relation to it that their security and welfare becomes essential for its lasting existence. Hence, in a democracy any effort to eliminate the notables, to confiscate their property, and to divide their wealth on the principle of numerical equality would be disastrous for all concerned.

The orientation of Aristotle's remedies for *stasis*, then, is toward securing the lives and the role of the well-born and wealthy minority in both oligarchies and democracies. Obviously, in a democracy the role of the notables cannot be as great as it is in an oligarchy, but they still have significant functions to perform, Aristotle argues, that must be safe-guarded and if possible strengthened without antagonizing and arousing the people. Given the fact that oligarchies and democracies are the prevailing forms of constitution in Greece—although both fall short of true distributive justice—and that both are constantly endangered by *stasis* in which the minority of notables is ultimately always at a disadvantage, the ever practical Aristotle is primarily concerned with what is possible in the circumstances, not with theoretical efforts to impose ideal solutions. So he focuses his attention upon the problem of the maintenance of harmonious class relations in both oligarchies and democracies, usually with an eye to the preservation of the interests and influence of the minority of notables. The pressing problem from his standpoint is not so much in oligarchies where by the adoption of a moderate, prudent, and enlightened policy, the notables should have no great difficulty in maintaining themselves. Instead, the urgent question is the plight of the notables in a democracy, for example, the tenuous position of the aristocratic-oligarchic friends of Macedonia among the hostile Athenian people. Only against this background of theoretical and practical considerations can the *raison d'être* of the *Politics* he adequately understood. Aristotle's fundamental prescription for the disease of *stasis* can be reduced to the idea of combining in a polity the oligarchic principle of proportionate equality in such a way with the democratic principle of numerical equality as to oligarchize democracy. This may fall far short of the ideal of distributive justice in an aristocracy; but given the situation, it will save the polis and along with it the notables, remove the deadly sting of the levelling principle of numerical equality, providing a bastion against the omnipresent danger of the tyranny of the masses.

That Aristotle concentrated his efforts upon the problem of oligarchizing democracy is suggested by the nature of his prescriptions in Book IV of the *Politics* for a 'polity' or best practicable polis, and his remarks on the best forms of democracy and oligarchy in Book VI.[103] He probably worked out the idea of the polity as a remedy for *stasis* in Greece, and possibly was even able to persuade his friend and protector, Antipater, to reform Athens along similar lines. A polity, Aristotle explains, is politically a mixture of oligarchical and democratic elements and is socially based upon a large middle-class—landed proprietors who are neither rich nor poor, possessing, however, 'moderate and adequate property'.[104] He states that polities inclined toward democracy are usually called polities while those with more oligarchic than democratic traits are generally termed aristocracies. However, 'A properly mixed "polity",' he writes:

> should look as if it contained both democratic and oligarchical elements—and as if it contained neither. It should owe its stability to its own intrinsic strength, and not to external support; and its intrinsic strength should be derived from the fact, not that a majority are in favour of its continuance (that might well be the case even with a poor constitution), but rather that there is no single section in all the state which would favour a change to a different constitution.[105]

In its political structure and arrangements a polity may mix oligarchical and democratic elements in a number of ways. For instance, the rich may be fined for failing to sit in courts as in oligarchies; and the poor, following the rule in democracies, will receive payment for such service.

Again, the oligarchic principle of election by voting instead of the democratic use of the lot for choosing magistrates may be combined with the democratic elimination of property qualifications for office. Or finally, a mean might be selected between the high property qualification for membership in oligarchic assemblies and the absence of such a requirement or a very low one which characterizes democracies.

From this all too brief description it is evident that for Aristotle the preferable kind of polity would incorporate two of the dominant principles of oligarchy that would tend to outweigh the democratic elements. First, the social base would be landed proprietorship, although of moderate limits. Second, membership in the assembly, i.e., full citizenship rights and a determining voice in government, would require a moderate property qualification. This means that the effective body of citizens ruling would consist almost entirely of the 'middle-class' of independent farmers, who would probably be excluded in an oligarchy, the notables, and perhaps a few comfortably off artisans and merchants. They would be the only ones entitled to stand for office and to elect office-holders by a show of hands, and those toward the bottom of the property scale would be remunerated for court service. The rest is simply insignificant democratic window-dressing, because the locus of power will be the propertied classes, and the masses of shopkeepers, artisans, and wage-labourers will not qualify for active meaningful citizenship.

Perhaps even more illuminating in regard to the weight Aristotle gives to 'oligarchic' elements in his practical political recommendations is his discussion of the best forms of democracy and oligarchy. His comments about each are in fact continuations of his treatment of the polity because he suggests that both are in effect kinds of polity.[106] He contrasts the best form of democracy with the worst type of democracy which consists of mechanics, merchants, shop-keepers and day labourers whose lives revolve around the market-place. In other words he is insistent that Athens is democracy at its worst. The best democracy seems to be little different from the polity, for it is agrarian, consisting of farmers, the 'first and best kind of populace', who 'not having any great amount of property, are busily occupied; and ... have thus no time for attending the assembly'.[107] Evidently they are independent landed proprietors of the middling-sort, peasants or yeomen, who work the land themselves aided by slaves and wage-labourers. Presumably all citizens will have the rights of electing magistrates, calling them to account after their term of office, and sitting in court, although a very low property qualification may be necessary for the exercise of these rights. However, all office-holders must meet property qualifications, and the highest offices should perhaps be restricted to those with the most property. As with the polity proper, the best democracy is obviously not a popular regime but an agrarian polis dominated by the larger propertied interests. No wonder that Aristotle takes great pains to point out that the notables should have no reason to complain about such a system.[108] Aristotle also mentions the possibility of laws placing limits on the amount of land acquired, forbidding the disposal of land originally allotted to one's family, and prohibiting mortgaging a certain proportion of one's estate. Such measures would strengthen and encourage the preservation of the 'middle-class' of landed proprietors, with beneficial consequences for all.[109] Except for this stress on the maintenance of a large agrarian, middle-class, Aristotle's few stipulations for the best oligarchy would seem to be similar. He proposes a relatively low property assessment for full citizenship and the lower offices, and a higher property qualification for the more important offices.

Therefore, Aristotle seems more interested in securing the position of the notables in a democratic system than in opening up the crucial offices to popular participation. Whether he is writing of polity or what amounts to the same thing, the best democracy and the best oligarchy, his recommendations ensure that power is effectively concentrated in the hands of the wealthy and well-born. In each case he would give the labouring masses at best only a token role. The 'rule of law' means for him primarily the rule of the notables to be strictly accountable at the end of their terms of office to the more modest property holders, but with the virtual dormancy of the assembly, and elimination of any interference in decision-making by the day-to-day control of the people. Aristotle took a jaundiced view of any form of popular participation—even in the assembly of lesser property holders. Throughout all of this his socially conservative aristocratic and agrarian values, attitudes, and interests come to the fore.

A fundamental problem in the analysis of Aristotle's political theory is that one must rely almost entirely upon the *Politics*. In the case of *Plato* there are at least half a dozen dialogues of extraordinary literary quality, some like the *Republic* and *Laws* of great length, that deal with politics and government. Unfortunately all Aristotle's dialogues have been lost and much of what remains of his vast output could hardly have been intended by him for publication in their extant form. The *Politics* seems to be little more than an incomplete series of rather full notes by Aristotle, possibly compiled and edited at a later date by another hand. Consequently, we have no detailed presentation of Aristotle's ideal polis, as we do with Plato in the *Republic*, since all that survives of such a project is a bare beginning in Books VII and VIII. Nevertheless, even on the basis of these last unfinished pages of the *Politics*, some tentative conclusions can be drawn about the nature of Aristotle's 'utopia'. Its most obvious characteristic would seem to be a striking similarity, not as one might expect to Plato's own ideally best polis of the *Republic*, but rather to his 'best practicable' Cretan city of Magnesia in the *Laws*. Even though Aristotle rather pedantically and sometimes unfairly criticizes the *Laws* in Book II of the *Politics*, the minor nature of the criticisms together with his description of Magnesia as a polity, albeit excessively balanced in favour of oligarchy, tend to confirm his reliance upon the Cretan city for his own utopia.

Like Plato's design for Magnesia, Aristotle's ideal is an attempt to apply expert knowledge to the construction of a well-ordered, yet practicable polis. Each thinker sets about to rationalize human society in accordance with a number of basic moral and social principles that are taken to be beyond dispute. Many parallels exist between the two poleis, probably because of the agreement of their philosophic founders over the essential principles upon which they would be established, among the most important being:

1. Men are of fundamentally unequal ability and moral value.
2. They can be molded by education, example, and law.
3. Callings that entail labour for a livelihood, that are banausic, commercial or agricultural, corrupt the soul.
4. The true moral life is essentially aristocratic.
5. The primary purpose of the polis is to facilitate the realization of the true moral life.
6. The economic foundation of the polis is private landed property in the hands of a minority.
7. This minority of noble, propertied, and leisured have the exclusive right to rule.
8. The majority of low-born, propertyless, and labouring have the absolute duty to serve.
9. Agrarian life is superior to urban commercial life.
10. The polis should be economically self-sufficient and politically autonomous.
11. Social order and unity are preferable to change and conflict.

Now for the details of the poleis that embody these principles. Both poleis are small in area and population, economic autarkies relatively isolated from other societies and agrarian in nature, dependent upon large forces of slave and non-citizen labour. Somewhat less worried than Plato by the problems posed by convenient access to the sea and the threat of commerce, Aristotle with the spectre of democratic Athens in mind nevertheless would exclude oarsmen and sailors from citizenship. The poleis are virtually garrison states, planned as havens of security in a hostile world. Moreover, military strength and constant vigilance are needed for internal security. Aristotle is more explicit than Plato about the necessity of an armed citizenry to meet any outbreak of civil disobedience in maintaining the domination of the propertied masters over the subjected labouring population. Every measure is to be taken to prevent change and to create conditions of harmony and solidarity, so that in effect both poleis are envisioned as immortal social orders. Neither is democratic, even in respect to the citizen body, and each is dominated by an elite of landed property-holders. Characteristic of both is a major social division between the majority of labouring propertyless and the governing minority of non-labouring propertied. Aristotle looks explicitly to Egypt, as Plato seems implicitly to do, for the model of what he takes to be the absolutely necessary division in a well-ordered polis between the class of agricultural labourers and the class of warriors. As we have already noted, the former class composed of slaves and the free artisans and merchants, together providing the requisite economic goods and services, are called 'conditions' of the polis by Aristotle. He terms the latter class, which comprises integral components of citizens, 'parts' of the polis. The 'conditions' labour in order to satisfy the needs of the 'parts', are barred from owning property and prohibited from having any voice or role in government. Citizens, propertied and free from manual labour, are members of the assembly, which by the scheme of Plato and probably that of Aristotle, will be a relatively powerless voting body that does little in the way of deliberating or governing. Popular political participation even for such a select citizenry is not a desideratum for either thinker. Although Aristotle believes that citizens should have leisure for civic affairs, this means primarily ample opportunity for the majority of citizens to perform their military duties. Citizens of Magnesia and Aristotle's utopia are divided into two age groups: the elders and the youth. For Aristotle the former are more fit to rule, whereas the latter are more fit to being ruled, a sentiment shared by Plato. To the elders belong the deliberative, judicial, and religious functions that should be performed, certainly for Plato and probably for Aristotle, by means of various councils and institutions distinct from the assembly. Defence is the responsibility of younger citizens, and religious functions are to be conducted by the eldest. So in the *Laws* and the *Politics*, as well as in the *Republic*, the ideal social system is basically bi-partite, consisting of the citizens—elderly rulers (and priests) and young warriors —and the non-citizens—a mass of inferior 'disenfranchised' slaves, workers, artisans, and merchants. Unlike the plan of the *Republic*, however, the property arrangements of the other two are reversed by depriving the economic producers of property and introducing it among the citizen elite of youth and elders. The Cretan city is divided into four propertied classes (and twelve tribes) with the more affluent elders dominating the whole. While there does not seem to be any common agricultural land to provide for the extensive system of common tables, citizens evidently are required to allot a portion of their produce for this purpose. Aristotle does not have an opportunity in Book VII and the incomplete Book VIII to deal with the details of land distribution or of governmental institutions. However, he does stipulate that there should be public land for the common tables, and like Plato recommends two allotments of land for each citizen: one on the frontier and one near the central city. It also seems safe to assume that for him as for Plato, the wealthiest elders will be in firm control. And he would also seem to agree with Plato in prescribing the rule of law, strict accountability of office-holders, and minute direction of the lives of the citizens. A comprehensive system of education directed by the polis with emphasis on the 'socializing' function of common tables and strict supervision of children and family life by public officials is a feature of both poleis. Perhaps the major difference between the blueprint for Magnesia and the fragmentary utopia of Aristotle is that Plato prescribes a more liberated role for women in respect to eligibility for membership in the assembly and for public office, and generally in his attempts to free them to some extent from their traditionally sequestered life. Apart from this and minor differences which have not been emphasized here, our sketchy comparison has revealed the common aristocratic, authoritarian, and anti-democratic pattern of the political thought of the two philosophers.

Aristotle's ideally best polis, therefore, with some variation and in much more detail, would seem to be a kind of idealized version of his best practicable 'polity', including the best types of democracy and oligarchy. The basic principles are apparently the same in both cases, at least in so far as we can understand the nature of the polity from the Stagirite's abbreviated description. At the risk of repetition, a brief summary of what we have already discovered about the polity will help to indicate and underscore its resemblance to the utopia. An agrarian base is an essential of the polity, and in order to strengthen it restrictions may possibly be placed upon the freedom of acquiring and disposing of landed holdings. The citizen-body is composed largely of midling landed proprietors: 'middle-class' or 'yeoman' farmers. Their domination is assured by the introduction of a moderate property qualification for membership in the assembly, thereby excluding those whose lives centre upon the agora: artisans, shopkeepers, and labourers. Since the assembly will be in the hands of midling farmers, many of whom can ill-afford to attend regularly, its business will tend to be directed by the more affluent. The power of the well-to-do is also furthered by the oligarchical device of popular election for public office and perhaps by property qualifications for them, graduated according to their importance. Popular participation, hence, in vital political deliberation and decision-making will be kept at a minimum.

By his recommendation of the polity—in fact little more than the oligarchizing of the democracy so as to create government of the people by the notables for the people—Aristotle had devised a shrewdly ingenious scheme worthy of the wily Philip himself. If implemented in Greece, and particularly in Athens, the result would be the best of all possible worlds by eliminating the ever-present threat of *stasis* through pacifying the people and preserving and strengthening the notables and their values, and productive of a general condition of domestic peace in which Macedonian hegemony might be more securely and easily maintained. And it should not be forgotten that the reform of the Greek poleis along the lines of the polity and Macedonian hegemony were mutually sustaining means for the preservation of peace and the domination of the notables. Macedonia could intervene at any time in order to maintain the balance of power in each polis in favour of the notables and to suppress civic disturbances wherever they might appear.

6. *Principles in Practice: The Despotism of Demetrius of Phalerum*

Some substantial evidence of what Aristotle's political principles and particularly his basic formula of the polity would have been like in practice exists in the form of the Athenian dictatorship of Demetrius of Phalerum from 317 to 307. Indeed, generally speaking, his regime might be considered the supreme example of a Socratic laboratory in social and political experimentation, for the influence of Plato through the ideas of Aristotle and Theophrastus is readily perceived.[110] More specifically, the role of this despot affords an unparalleled opportunity to observe and appraise the Stagirite's theory in action. Demetrius was the first actual governing 'philosopher-king' in the Socratic tradition, or as Dow and Travis write: 'In all antiquity he was the most accomplished philosopher actually to rule a state.'[111] However high a regard one may have for the basic Socratic political ideas in abstraction, one may begin to have doubts about them when confronted with their concrete implications for practice as exemplified by the actual policies of such an inspired philosopher-king.

Born about 350 in Phalerum, the ancient harbour of Athens, Demetrius was the son of Phanostratus. Whether the family was noble or not is unclear, but the often unreliable Diogenes Laertius insists that Demetrius was originally a household servant.[112] While he himself threw in his lot with the pro-Macedonian aristocratic-oligarchic group, his brother, Himeraeus, became a member of the democratic 'party' and a dedicated anti-Macedonian leader. A friend and pupil of Aristotle's successor, Theophrastus, and possibly of Aristotle himself, Demetrius is said by Plutarch to have lectured at the Lyceum.[113] His voluminous writings, unfortunately all lost, included works on politics and law, and a defence of Socrates.[114] He entered Athenian politics in 325–24, acquiring a reputation for his oratory,[115] and became one of the active allies of Macedonia for the next seven years. With the death of Antipater in 317, Athens once more revolted, only to be suppressed by his son Cassander who assumed his father's position in Greece and appointed Demetrius regent of Athens supported by a Macedonian garrison. The new regent was given the title of *prostates*, 'one who stands before', a common title of Athenian leaders since the last part of the fifth-century. As soon as he assumed power he began the task of drafting a new law code or constitution for the city, which evidently was completed and went into effect in 315–14. According to tradition he was known as the third great law-giver of Athens—the others being Solon and perhaps Draco—and some three hundred and sixty bronze statues are said to have been erected in his honour.[116] His rule came to an end in 307 when he was overthrown by Demetrius son of Antigonus, and a democratic regime was established. One story relates how the statues in his honour were immediately destroyed by the angry populace.[117] Forced to flee to Thebes, Demetrius later journeyed to Egypt, possibly serving Ptolemy and assisting in the foundation of the famous Alexandrian library.

Demetrius governed Athens as an enlightened, philosophic despot for a decade. Highly intelligent, cultured and urbane, he was a shrewd and capable politician who relished the good life despite the puritanical flavour of his regime. His court soon became the social and cultural as well as the political centre of the polis. Although his friend Theophrastus was a metic like Aristotle and therefore could not own property, through a special dispensation contrived by Demetrius he was able to acquire land and buildings for a school, and become the first legal head of the Lyceum. Under the patronage of the philosopher-king the new establishment of Theophrastus flourished, over-shadowing the Academy, and soon became an important centre of aristocratic-oligarchic influence. Another student of Theophrastus, the founder of the New Comedy, Menander, was also an intimate of Demetrius.

The Peripatetics were well-entrenched and constituted a formidable political power as well as being the major intellectual force of the period. The fascinating aspect of the law code of Demetrius is that it was a conscious, concerted effort by a brilliant intellectual and eminent politician to apply Aristotelian precepts to the reform of the city. There seems to be little doubt that the design of the constitution relied heavily upon the scholarly investigations and studies of Theophrastus who was also probably an important collaborator in its drafting. His *Nomoi*, a renowned work in the ancient world of which only thirty fragments have survived, apparently exercised a profound influence upon the efforts of Demetrius.[118] The book was a comprehensive and systematic comparative study of Greek legislation and legal institutions. It was perhaps begun by Aristotle and completed by Theophrastus, dependent on the rich constitutional material collected by their students as were the *Constitution of Athens* and the *Politics*. So the constitution of Demetrius was not a hasty and ill-considered effort, but a thoroughly researched and thoughtfully conceived instrument, meticulously fashioned and grounded in philosophic principles by some of the best minds of antiquity. As such it is one of the world's significant and too little known experiments in constitution-making.

Demetrius and his associates quite clearly knew what they were about. A prime illustration of their rational approach to politics was their institution of the first population census in antiquity. The new constitution was the conscious embodiment of the main features of Aristotle's polity for the Aristotelian purpose of ensuring the domination of the propertied classes and preventing the 'tyranny of the majority' by excluding the masses from any important role in government. According to Plutarch the new regime, while oligarchic in name, was monarchic in practice.[119] As in the case of the reforms of Antipater of 321–319, also evidently an attempt to follow the model of the polity, the code of Demetrius was probably presented as a revival of the ancient constitution of Solon, some indication of its conservative nature. Antipater had restricted full Athenian citizenship to those with a property qualification of 2,000 drachmae or more, which meant that only 9,000 of the 21,000 citizens were entitled to sit in the assembly.[120] In other words, all the *thetes* had been deprived of full political rights. He also reduced the role of the popular courts, possibly abolishing choice by lot, and ended the subsidies for assembly and theater attendance. Demetrius, by lowering the property qualification for membership in the assembly from 2,000 to 1,000 drachmae, somewhat widened his base of support from 9,000 to 12,000 out of 21,000 to include the upper levels of the *thetes*, and could thus cleverly claim to be something of a democrat.[121] However, his other reforms belied such a claim, for a definite attempt was made to reduce the role of popular participation in a variety of ways. The democratic features of choice by lot and rotation of offices were replaced by election. In addition to the abolition of the assembly and theater attendance subsidies, many of the traditional tribal activities which involved popular participation were curtailed. Moreover, the increase in size of certain of the juries meant their domination by the upper classes, and the assembly while larger than that decreed by Antipater remained relatively inactive during the ten years of the regime. Important provisions of the new constitution also aimed at securing and strengthening the propertied classes. To prevent the wasteful extravagance of the rich and the dissipation of their fortunes, sumptuary laws were introduced, the liturgies demanded by the democracy were abolished, and an effort was made to reduce uncertainties in regard to titles and liabilities of property.[122] Finally, the drafters seem to have taken to heart Aristotle's warnings against lawlessness and the use of office for private gain.[123] The rule of law was established in the form of the code itself that would be immune to change by the assembly and in the principle of the vigorous execution of the law and the accountability of all office-holders. A committee of seven Guardians of the Law or *nomophylakes* was established to control magistrates and the assembly;[124] a Board for the Regulation of Women—*gynaekonomoi*—had among its functions the enforcement of the sumptuary laws and general supervision of the private lives of citizens;[125] and some of the censorial duties of the all but defunct Areopagus were revived.

Hence, the constitution of Demetrius is evidence that Aristotle's essentially aristocratic social and political ideas have dangerous practical implications for democracy. Under the despotism of Demetrius based on Macedonian power, the Athenian economy flourished—annual revenue was estimated at 1,200 talents—with peace, security, and prosperity for the well-to-do.[126] But good times for the propertied were accompanied by an extreme rise in the cost of living that created great hardships for the populace, forcing many of them to emigrate. The anti-democratic and oppressive nature of the reforms is attested to by the fact that the Athenian people during the restored democratic regime of 307 abolished, with a few exceptions, all the new laws and institutions of Demetrius. His reforms do indicate something very fundamental about the nature of the Stagirite's conception of polity. It seems to have been some kind of compromise between the ideal polis of Books VII and VIII of the *Politics* and what in his mind was required by the political realities of Athenian democracy. Moreover, it should be apparent that Aristotle's political position did not exist in an intellectual vacuum, but was rooted in a philosophy that provided the ultimate theoretical justification for the conservative measures of Demetrius. His autocratic regime symbolized in rather mild form the dangerous practical implications of a school of thought founded almost a century before by Socrates.

Notes to Chapter V

1. Anton-Hermann Chroust, *Aristotle: New Light on His Life and on Some of His Lost Works* (London: Routledge and Kegan Paul, 1973), I, p. ix. Chroust is extremely critical of this common view.
2. Chroust, *op. cit.*, I, p. 171.
3. A suggestion put forward by Sir Ernest Barker in his standard translation of *The Politics of Aristotle* (2nd ed.; Oxford: Clarendon Press, 1948), pp. xx, xxiv, 183, 184n.MM.
4. Quotations given in *ibid.*, Appendix V, pp. 388–9.
5. Aristotle, *Politics*, 1263b (50–1), hereafter cited as *P*. The translation used is that of Barker, *op. cit.*; for convenience his pagination is placed in parentheses following the standard citation to Bekker.
6. *P*, 1267a (65–6).
7. *P*, 1267b (67).
8. *P*, 1323a (280). Cf. *Rhetoric*, 1382b5: 'And since most men tend to be bad—slaves to greed, and cowards in danger. . . .' W. Rhys Roberts translation.
9. *P*, 1318b–1319a (264). Cf. *P*, 1253a (7): 'Man, when perfected, is the best of animals; but if he is isolated from law and justice he is the worst of all.'
10. *P*, 1296a (182–3).
11. *Eudemian Ethics*, 1216a25.
12. *Nicomachean Ethics*, 1109a29, hereafter cited as *NE*. The translation is that of Martin Ostwald in The Library of Liberal Arts edition.
13. *NE*, 1110a24–6.
14. *P*, 1265a (57).
15. *NE*, 1109a35.
16. Quoted in Chroust, *op. cit.*, I, p. 233.
17. *Metaphysics*, 1074b1–15. W. D. Ross translation.
18. He wrote to Antipater: 'The more I am by myself, and alone, the fonder I have become of myths.' Quoted and commented upon by Barker, *op. cit.*, p. 389.
19. *P*, 1282b (129).
20. *NE* 1098b9–11.
21. *NE*, 1098b27–9.
22. *NE*, 1173a1–5.
23. *P*, 1264a (52), 1329b (304).

24. *NE*, 1098a23–5.
25. *P*, 1264a (52).
26. *Loc. cit.*
27. *Rhetoric*, 1287a15.
28. *Rhetoric*, 1255a15–16.
29. *Metaphysics*, 993a30–993b6.
30. *P*, 1281b (123–5).
31. For a brief discussion of the two views see M. I. Finley, *The Ancient Economy* (Berkeley and Los Angeles: University of California Press, 1973), pp. 81–2.
32. *Rhetoric*, 1367a16.
33. Aristotle's most complete discussion of natural slavery is found in Book I of the *Politics*.
34. *P*, 1253b (9–10).
35. *P*, 1254a (10).
36. For instance *NE*, 1099a30–1099b5; *Rhetoric*, 1360b19–30.
37. *On Good Birth*, D. W. Ross translation. XII.
38. *Ibid*., p. 61.
39. *Rhetoric*, 1360b34–8.
40. *Rhetoric*, 1387a16–30, 1390b16–1391a20.
41. *Rhetoric*, 1390b16–30.
42. *P*, 1283a (132).
43. *P*, 1301b–1302a (206).
44. *Rhetoric*, 1367a30, 1373a6–10, 1381a20–5.
45. *Eudemian Ethics*, 1215a20–5.
46. *P*, 1319a (265).
47. *P*, 1328b (301). Cf. *P*, 1278a (108): 'The best form of state ... will not make the mechanic a citizen.'
48. *P*, 1328a–1329a (298–303).
49. *Eudemian Ethics*, 1214b30–1215a5.
50. *P*, 1318b–1319a (263–4), 1295b (180–2).
51. *P*, 1319a (265).
52. *Oeconomica*, 1343a25–1343b6. G. Cyril Armstrong translation. Referring to this passage, M. I. Finley, *op. cit*., p. 122, describes it as a 'painfully naive restatement of good Aristotelian doctrine....', and adds: 'It is, in short, one of many formulations of the landowning ideology of the ancient upper classes.'
53. *NE*, 1120a23.
54. *NE*, 1124a1.
55. *NE*, 1123a35.
56. *NE*, 1124b5–1125a16.
57. *Constitution of Athens*, 22.4, 25.1, 26.1, 28.1–5, 32.2–3, 41.2.
58. *P*, 1317b (259). Newman and other editors bracket this sentence.

59. One exception is M. I. Finley, *op. cit.*, p. 152.

60. Aristotle's idea of *koinonia* and the related concept of *philia* are found in *P*, 1252a–1253a (1–7), 1260b (39), 1267b (99); and esp. *NE*, Books VIII–IX.

61. On the relationship of household and polis and their respective ends see *P*, 1252a–1253a (1–7); 1280a–1281a (118–20).

62. Our position on *oikos* and polis is at odds with the views of Hannah Arendt in *The Human Condition* (Garden City: Doubleday, Anchor, 1959), pp. 27–34.

63. *Eudemian Ethics*, 1242b1. J. Solomon translation.

64. For this and the following see *P*, 1252a–1253a (3–7), 1278b (111); *NE*, 1155a15–20, 1162a16–30.

65. *P*, 1324b (285).

66. On the household, *P*, 1253b–1260b (8–38).

67. *P*, 1253b (8).

68. *P*, 1252b (4).

69. *P*, 1255b (18).

70. *P*, 1260b (37).

71. *P*, 1338a (337).

72. *NE*, 1124b23–4.

73. *P*, 1337b (334).

74. *NE*, 1160b23–1161a9; Aristotle's tri-partite typology of constitutions is in *P*, 1279a–1279b (112–15).

75. Cf. *P*, 1255b (17), where Aristotle says that the authority of the head of the household is monarchical.

76. *P*, 1328a–1329a (298–303).

77. *P*, 1329a (301–2), 1332b–1333a (315–16).

78. *P*, 1333a (316).

79. *P*, 1334a (312).

80. *P*, 1259b (33–4): 'It is clear from the previous argument that the business of household management is concerned more with human beings than it is with inanimate property; that it is concerned more with the good condition of human beings than with a good condition of property (which is what we call wealth); and, finally, that it is concerned more with the goodness of the free members of the household than with that of slaves.'

81. For the discussion of *chrematistic*, *P*, 1256a–1259a (18–31).

82. *P*, 1259a (31). That to the Greek 'political-economy' would have been a contradiction in terms was maintained by Sir Ernest Barker in 1906, in *The Political Thought of Plato and Aristotle* (New York: Dover, 1959), p. 357. Hannah Arendt, *op. cit.*, p. 28, repeats the idea, without, however, citing Barker.

83. *P*, 1257a (23).

84. Here the interpretation of the text is that of Karl Polanyi, 'Aristotle Discovers the Economy', in *Primitive, Archaic, and Modern Economies: Essays of Karl Polanyi*, ed. George Dalton (Boston: Beacon Press, 1971), pp. 109–10, 113–14.

85. *P*, 1257a (24).

86. *P*, 1258b (28).

87. *P*, 1258b (29).

88. See István Mészáros, 'Ideology and Social Science', *The Socialist Register 1972*, pp. 57–66.

89. Polanyi, *op. cit.*, pp. 101–2. W. Kendrick Pritchett, *The Greek State at War* (Berkeley, Los Angeles, London: University of California Press, 1974), Pt. I, p. 42 and n.60, however, believes that a marketing system had developed throughout Greece much earlier than the fourth century, as Polanyi contends in *Trade and Market in the Early Empire* (Glencoe, Ill.: The Free Press, 1957), pp. 84–5.

90. Barker's comment in *P*, p. 29n.2.

91. Of course, for Aristotle gentlemanly wealth should not be for utility or profit; it should be non-productive, only for enjoyment. See *Rhetoric*, 1360b, 1367a.

92. *P*, 1258a (26–7).

93. *P*, 1257b–1258a (26).

94. Aristotle's main considerations on justice are found in *NE*, Book V; *P*, 1280a–1284b (117–37), 1301a–1302a (203–7), 1317b (258).

95. Barker's introduction in *P*, pp. lxix–lxxi.

96. *P*, 1280a (117–18).

97. A point made by Aristotle in *P*, 1296a (183), 1301b (206).

98. Book V of the *Politics* is devoted to an analysis of *stasis*.

99. *P*, 1304b–1305a (215–16).

100. *P*, 1305a–1306b (217–20).

101. *P*, 1307b–1310a (224–34).

102. *P*, 1309b (232).

103. *P*, 1293a–1296b (173–84), 1318b–1319a (263–5), 1320b (270).

104. *P*, 1295b (182).

105. *P*, 1294b (178).

106. *P*, 1320b (270).

107. *P*, 1218b (263).

108. *P*, 1318b–1319a (264).

109. *P*, 1292b (171).

110. For reference to specific Platonic elements such as the *nomophylakes* or Guardians of the Law, the training and equipping of choruses as public expense, and the curtailment of funeral expenses, see Glenn R. Morrow, *Plato's Cretan City: A Historical Interpretation*

of the 'Laws' (Princeton: Princeton University Press, 1960), pp. 195n.99 199n.107, 215n.146, 379–80, 463n.215.

111. Sterling Dow and Albert H. Travis, 'Demetrius of Phaleron and his Lawgiving', *Hesperia*, XII (1943), p. 144.

112. Diogenes Laertius, *Lives of Eminent Philosophers*, V, 75.

113. Plutarch, *Moralia*, 850.

114. See list of works in Diogenes Laertius, *op. cit.*, V, 80–1. Among them is a book, *Of Megalopsychia*. Diogenes also refers to the work on Socrates in IX, 15, 37, 57. In addition, see Plutarch, *Life of Aristides*, XXVII.

115. Diogenes Laertius, V, 75; Cicero, *De Officiis*, I, i, 3.

116. On the statues see Diogenes Laertius, V, 75. Cicero in *De Re Publica*, II, i, 2, says that Demetrius revived the state when it was 'bloodless and prostrate' [Loeb Library trans.] just as other heroes had done in the past, such as Minos, Lycurgus, Theseus, Draco, Solon, and Cleisthenes.

117. Plutarch, *Moralia*, 820.

118. Herbert Block, 'Studies in Historical Literature of the Fourth Century B.C.', pt. III, 'Theophrastus' *Nomoi* and Aristotle', in *Athenian Studies Presented to William Scott Ferguson*, Harvard Studies in Classical Philology, Supplementary Vol. I (Cambridge, Mass.: Harvard University Press, 1940), pp. 355–76.

119. Plutarch, *Life of Demetrius*, X. This is a life of Demetrius son of Antigonus.

120. On Antipater's reforms see Barker's Introduction, *P*, pp. xxiv–xxv.

121. According to Plutarch, *Life of Demetrius*, X, Athens had ceased to be a democracy under Antipater. Strabo, *Geography*, 9, 1, 20, states that Demetrius in his own *Memoirs* of the regime said that he had improved, not destroyed Athenian democracy.

122. Aristotle may have been the inspiration of some of these reforms. *P*, 1308b (227), 1309a (229). Also see, Cicero's reference to them, *De Legibus*, II, xxvi, 66.

123. *P*, 1307b (225), 1308b–1309a (228–9).

124. *P*, 1287a (146), 1298b (192), 1322a (275), 1322b (277), 1323a (278).

125. *P*, 1299a (195), 1322b–1323a (277–8).

126. W. W. Tarn, ch. XV, 'The Heritage of Alexander', in *Cambridge Ancient History*, ed., J. B. Bury, S. A. Cook, and F. E. Adcock (Cambridge: Cambridge University Press, 1933), VI, p. 496, writes that Demetrius 'acted entirely in the interests of the wealthy....'

VI

Conclusion: The Socratics Against Athens

The Socratic legacy has been a peculiar and often parodoxical one. In spite—or perhaps because—of their antipathy to Athenian democracy, Plato and Aristotle have often been treated both as disinterested witnesses of Athenian reality and, not always with logical consistency, as spokesmen for Greek ideals. Their testimony has been accepted with particularly uncritical eagerness in the modern world by those whose fear of democracy in their own time has driven them to seek allies in antiquity. Historians of ancient Greece and classical scholars whose hearts and minds have been engaged in the social turmoil of their own age have not always been scrupulous in employing evidence supplied by the Socratics and have allowed it to speak in contradictory, if ideologically serviceable, ways. The Socratic philosophers have been accepted as witnesses and as representatives, as scathing critics and as spokesmen, roles that have not always been compatible. Modern historians frequently write of 'the Greeks' and 'Greek values' when they actually mean 'Plato and Aristotle' and their ideals. At the same time, however, such scholars tend to accept uncritically the bitter and contemptuous judgments on their contemporaries which show these philosophers to be completely at odds with the vast majority of their fellows.

It may be relevant, therefore, to sum up what we have already said or implied throughout the book about the general usefulness of the Socratics as a source of knowledge about democratic Athens. Some consideration of their social ideals in the light of Athenian popular values may help to place in perspective not only the claims made for the philosophy of the Socratics as the epitome of Greek norms, but also their reliability as witnesses. A witness need not, of course, share the values of those he observes. Indeed, to be a discerning critic he must to some extent set himself apart. Nevertheless, the truthfulness of the observer cannot withstand a fundamental antipathy to the object of his examination, and scorn is not a very trustworthy guide. We should not be too ready to accept the contempt of the Socratics as evidence of the moral bankruptcy of their contemporaries. Nor should we be willing, as is too often done, to think of Socratic opposition to the Athenian demos as a confrontation between lofty ethical standards on the one hand; and on the other, the rule of expediency, selfishness, greed, and power. Quite simply, the Socratics cannot be valid witnesses of historical reality if they are treated as the embodiment of moral ideals which were violated by their amoral fellows. Their testimony can be significant only if we recognize that it reflects a confrontation between two sets of irreconcilable social values and moral principles.

Socrates, friend and associate of the aristocracy, founded a philosophical school with a pronounced aristocratic moral and social bias at a time when the traditional Athenian nobility was in the process of decay. His most important successors, the patricians Plato and Aristotle, developed, modified, and systematized his ideas, and maintained agrarian aristocratic ideals in a period of Athenian history marked on the one hand by the steady decline of the old landed gentry and peasantry and their agrarian economic base, and on the other by the growth of democracy more firmly grounded in the urban classes of craftsmen, shopkeepers, and labourers. All three philosophers were vitally concerned with the moral, social, and political questions of their time and place. Despite theoretical differences among them, they shared certain basic values and attitudes rooted in a similar partisan approach to the practical events of the day. Upholding their agrarian, aristocratic values against prevailing trends, they steadfastly opposed democracy and democratic institutions. Their moral and political philosophies to a significant degree reflect the aristocratic belief in the moral superiority of the well-born, cultivated, and wealthy over the low-born working classes of artisans, tradesmen, and peasants. From the aristocratic perspective of the Socratics, the common people, the producing classes, were largely instruments or 'conditions' for the well-being, the freedom, and moral development of the leisured classes. The Socratic social and political ideal was a functional hierarchy governed by an elite of the meritorious, which in practice meant rule by the noble and wealthy. At the core of the shared outlook of the Socratics was an ethical ideal incapable of being realized by the common man, presupposing a freedom from the world of material necessity in a practical as well as a philosophical sense. This practical and philosophical 'idealism' was reflected in an authoritarian political design. The three philosophers, then, far from giving ideal expression to Greek cultural values were joined together by a common antagonism to many of the prevailing norms of democratic Athens.

At best, perhaps, we can credit Aristotle alone with a degree of sympathy for 'ordinary' Greeks, or at least a certain pragmatism and flexibility that led him to concede more to them than did his rigid predecessors. Just as Aristotle rejected the excessively abstract and ethereal aspects of Plato's doctrine of ideal forms, so he also modified Platonic ethical principles by trying to bring them down to earth, by subscribing to the more conventional standards of the Greek gentleman that in Plato had assumed an impossibly idealized and unattainable shape. Moreover, unlike Plato, the Stagirite emphasized the crucial roles of moral character and of practical experience as distinct from philosophic wisdom, and acknowledged received opinion and the collective wisdom of mankind as generally reliable guides to action. His appreciation of conventional values found a political parallel in his recognition of the need to make some concessions to democratic claims, in the interests of civic peace. He, therefore, softened the harsh Platonic ideal with his proposal for a middle course, a mixed polity that would assure the political supremacy of the well-born and wealthy by making concessions to the people, a solution that he thought might guarantee stability and unity under the rule of law and prevent what he saw as the lawless, irresponsible, and ignorant tyranny of the majority. Underlying these pragmatic proposals, however, were always the agrarian aristocratic postulates of his predecessors. These principles in their more extreme Platonic character are still visible in Aristotle's own ideal constitution from which the practical compromises of the 'polity' have disappeared.

But if Aristotle's concessions to 'ordinary' Greeks made him a somewhat more reliable witness for them, his less rigid approach also has rendered him a more effective and influential spokesman for Greek aristocratic ideals. It is largely through his more human formulation that the values of the Greek gentleman as well as the principles of Socratic virtue and Platonic wisdom have survived to influence later political thinkers who had similar interests and ideals at heart, figures such as Thomas Aquinas, Marsilio of Padua, Jean Bodin, Richard Hooker, Burke, Montesquieu, and Tocqueville. More recently the imprint of the Socratics through Aristotle can be found in varying ways in the social and political ideas of Burckhardt, Ortega, Maritain, Hannah Arendt, and Bertrand de Jouvenel. If Socrates was the 'saintly' founder of the philosophic school in which Greek aristocratic ideals achieved their apotheosis, and Plato was its grant strategist, then Aristotle was the brilliant tactician who ensured its survival and lasting influence.

Without understanding clearly the quality of the common ideology and partisanship that animates their political thought and the degree to which they opposed the shared values of the Athenian community, it is absurd to look to the Socratics as witnesses and spokesmen. Socratic philosophy was directly and intimately connected to the concrete social world in which they lived and acted. If we fail to appreciate the nature of the connection, we relegate the doctrine to the graveyard of abstractions, making it useless either as a philosophic comment on the human condition or as a historical document. Moreover, if we are to come to grips with the Socratics, we must also understand their contemporaries and their intolerance of Socratic teachings. The Athenians fully appreciated whose side the ideas of the Socratics supported and justified in the real world of politics. The trial and execution of Socrates and the indictment against Aristotle cannot be excused, but they can be understood. And if we are to treat their lives and teachings as witness for the Greeks, or even to comprehend their philosophic meaning, we must not fail to recognize what their enemies felt. We must understand, for example, what Demochares, nephew of the great democrat Demosthenes, meant when he defended Sophocles' proposal in 306 for a law prohibiting all philosophic schools that did not have the express consent of the Athenian people, contending that: 'The Academy stands condemned by its fruits; so that even if the law of Sophocles disturbs Plato's brood while seeking to destroy the Peripatetic nest of traitors, the state will obtain the more benefit.'[1]*

Socratic philosophy, therefore, does not provide a standard for judging Athenian practice. Far from being simply a critique of the failures or excesses of Athenian democracy, it is an attack upon its very principles. Not just the imperfect reality, but even the ideal of that democracy is antagonistic to the Socratic moral code. The Socratic ideal has no place for democratic values and consequently allows no discrimination between good and evil in democratic practice, no real distinction between, on the one hand, democratic freedoms, equality, and self-rule, and on the other hand, licentiousness, mediocrity, and unprincipled, amoral caprice.

There is also a more general sense in which Socratic philosophy is unable to bear witness to Athenian reality. As Professor Dover has pointed out,[2] a dimension that is largely missing from the Socratic moral ideal is any concern for the mundane values of ordinary humane conduct, any stress upon warmth of feeling and simple affection among men, their mutual trust and dependency, and basic decency. Dover has

*Notes for this chapter begin on p. 265.

shown what value the Greeks attached to these qualities as revealed in oratory and drama, which spoke more directly to and for the people than did philosophy. The Greek might sometimes be harsh in holding an adversary to the strict letter of justice, bearing ill-will toward an enemy and exacting revenge for his wrongs; but he also advocated and displayed magnanimity (*epieikeia*) in the form of generosity and kindness toward friend and foe. The generous act of amnesty granted by the victorious Athenian democrats in 403 to the defeated oligarchic supporters of the Thirty Tyrants is a striking case in point. Furthermore, while by our own liberal standards the Athenians are often criticized for their intolerance, they established a measure of toleration unequalled before the modern era, and in some respects unequalled even then. Perhaps nothing testifies more eloquently to Athenian liberality in this respect than Plato's own long and undisturbed career as a teacher of moral values and political principles diametrically opposed to those of the Athenian majority. Athenians could exhibit extraordinary compassion or pity (*eleos*) toward the less fortunate and the suffering. Indeed, Demosthenes called 'pity the weak' an Athenian trait. Kindliness (*philanthrōpia*), not a virtue very prominent in the writings of Plato and Aristotle, played a part in the Greek moral code expressed as good will toward others, gratitude, affection, and a spirit of conciliation. The Socratic code even at its most human gives us no access to this ordinary morality of the common man. In its harshest form, the Socratic ethic, emphasizing as it does unattainably exalted virtues and an apparent disdain for mundane goodness, seems to be divorced not only from Greek popular morality, but even from crucial aspects of conventional aristocratic standards of conduct. To know that Athenians failed to adhere to the Socratic ethic is to know very little about what kind of human beings they actually were.

Socratic social ideals and their antagonism to prevailing values have contributed to one historical distortion that has played a particularly important part in later accounts of Athenian social relations. One of the most common myths about Athenian democracy depicts a citizenry virtually freed from labour, living in leisure on the productivity of slaves and, especially in the case of the poor, on state subsidies for attendance at assemblies, juries, and the theatre, civic functions and entertainments that, according to this view, occupied most of the citizen's time. The myth has undergone a number of permutations and has done service for modern historians with varying degrees of antipathy to democracy.[3] In its more anti-democratic forms, the myth has a great deal to say about the 'idleness' and 'indolence' of the citizenry, by which it means not the leisure of the truly idle rich, but the 'idleness' of the poor citizens for whom public payments were a necessary condition for political participation. The myth has also often been accompanied by a notion of democracy as a scheme for self-enrichment, an instrument with which the 'idle' and 'greedy' poor could plunder and oppress the rich.

To a considerable extent, although not exclusively, this distortion has grown out of the often contradictory Socratic legacy. Plato and Aristotle emphasize the 'corruption' of Athens by a banausic mob, a labouring mass of shoemakers, smiths, and tanners, which, according to them and other critics of the democracy like Xenophon and Aristophanes, dominated the democracy and ruined the polis. At the same time, however, the Socratic philosophers and others of their aristocratic persuasion paint a picture of an undisciplined and apparently idle mob always ready and available to harass their betters in assemblies and juries and to use their political rights to victimize the rich. The portrait has been further complicated by modern writers who have universalized the Socratic contempt for labour, treating it as representative and thus reinforcing the image of the idle mob.

The utter falsity of this idea of the idle mob has been amply demonstrated in our earlier discussion, in which it was stressed that the majority of Athenian citizens laboured industriously for a livelihood. They showed pride in their work and may even be credited with first articulating the ethic of craftsmanship in the concept of *technē*, which Plato adapted to very different values. Moreover, even if Athenians sought to avoid *dependent* labour, the status accorded by them to the labourer—including those citizens reduced to the dependence of wage-labour—was unprecedented in their time and has in many respects been largely unequalled since. It is perhaps no accident that Athena, the chief deity of Athens, was patron of the arts and crafts. In addition Hephaestus, Olympian God of the forge for whom the largest temple in his honour in the Greek world was built overlooking the Athenian agora in the mid-fifth century, and Prometheus, the bearer of fire and the technical skills to man, were widely worshipped in Athens. Certainly, the average Athenian cannot have shared the basic Socratic belief in the moral incapacity of those who laboured or Plato's opinion that the democratic polis, with its increasingly urban character and its development of the arts and crafts, represented the lowest point in a cyclical decline from a golden age. Protagoras' conviction that the arts and crafts were the basis of civilization and human progress, a view that also appears in the *Prometheus* of Aeschylus and Sophocles' *Antigone*, is more in keeping with the reality and the culture of Athenian democracy and the role played in it by labouring artisans and craftsmen.

It is ironic that thinkers whose passionate hatred of Athenian democracy rests above all on their objections to the dominance of the labouring classes in that civic order should also serve as the chief sources for the myth of the idle mob. It is equally ironic that modern historians who have perpetuated the myth, those whose attacks on the idleness of the mob have been most violent, have often been those whose contempt for labour and labourers has been most profound and who have exhibited the strongest faith in the idle rich as the natural ruling class. The myth has perhaps been perpetuated in the spirit of the all-too familiar complaints perennially repeated by the privileged about the 'idleness' and 'indolence' of those who labour for them. In any case, there is a mentality according to which idleness is an attribute of the working poor and not the leisured rich. Precisely this kind of mentality has little difficulty in accepting the Socratic legacy as a reliable historical document. Some historians, Burckhardt to name one, are quite capable of expressing their own contempt for those who must labour, their admiration for the anti-banausic values of the aristocracy, and their conviction that the increasing dominance of the banausic corrupted the polis; while at the same time they castigate the Athenian masses for their idleness and for allegedly sharing without right the anti-banausic values of their betters. This position is not as contradictory as it may seem, providing one understands the idiom. In the rhetoric of the Socratics and their heirs, it seems that a labouring class that is too independent of masters, not sufficiently subordinate to a leisured ruling class, is by definition idle. In other words, such labourers are idle not because they do not work, but because they work and do not serve.

Modern historians who have perpetuated the myth have not, of course, relied solely on Plato and Aristotle for their picture of Athens. But it is these philosophers whose indictment of Greek democracy has attained the highest status as the testament of honourable, almost saintly, wise men who stood far above their fellows, judging them and their moral failures with the anguish of the truly good. It is the Socratics, too, who perfected, systematized, and gave lofty intellectual standing to the idiom in which so many attacks upon democracy have been cast since classical antiquity. Although the history of ancient Greece has been rewritten in the last decades, to some extent the anti-democratic myth lingers on in one form or another, despite its increasingly obvious violation of the historical evidence. Insofar as one can speak of a popular or laymen's conception of Athenian democracy, the myth of the idle mob appears to survive in it virtually unchanged. While the factual distortions have mainly disappeared from the specialist literature, judgments once associated with the myth have sometimes persisted, as it were, disembodied, as for example in the remarks with which Victor Ehrenberg concludes *The People of Aristophanes*, quoted in chapter II,[4] remarks that are the more incongrous since he himself has done so much to correct the historical picture. Even to the extent that the picture has been corrected, moreover, much useful work still needs to be done. In addition to the constant rewriting that history requires, making it alive in the present, the wider implications of the revised picture have to be drawn in theories about the origin and nature of the state, about class and class-consciousness, about pre-capitalist social formations, in short, about man in society. It is difficult to imagine a time when ancient Greece, where men first began to reflect systematically on social and political life, will cease to be a rich mine of insights for students of civilization. While the Socratics themselves will certainly continue to be a precious vein of knowledge, their spell must be broken if the wealth Greek history has to offer is to be fully exploited.

Notes to Chapter VI

1. Athenaeus, XI, 509, quoted in W. S. Ferguson, *Hellenistic Athens* (London: Macmillan, 1911), pp. 106–7.

2. This paragraph relies upon the valuable analysis of K. J. Dover, *Greek Popular Morality In the Time of Plato and Aristotle* (Oxford: Blackwell, 1974), esp. pp. 40, 97–8, 106–8, 110–11, 116, 172–5, 190–205, 285, 291. Professor Dover comments (pp. 1–2): 'If we imagined that either Plato's work or Aristotle's represented an intellectual systematization of the principles which were manifested in the moral choices and judgments of the very ordinary unphilosophical Greek, it is possible that we might go badly astray.'

3. What is suggested here about modern historians of ancient Greece is based on an unpublished book by E. M. Wood, tentatively entitled, *The Use and Abuse of Ancient History*, in which certain important nineteenth-century historians are discussed at length: e.g., William Mitford, August Boeckh, Jacob Burckhardt, and Fustel de Coulanges.

4. Victor Ehrenberg, *The People of Aristophanes: A Sociology of Old Attic Comedy* (2nd ed.; New York: Schocken, 1962), p. 373.

Index

Because the book as a whole concerns the question of class, entries such as 'class', 'class conflict', 'class-consciousness' have been omitted from the index. The same is true of 'Athens', 'aristocracy', and 'democracy', since Athens is generally the focus of the book and the opposition of aristocracy to democracy is a central theme. Only discussions of certain specific problems—the 'decline' of Athens, the class structure of Athens, and the usefulness of the concept of class in dealing with ancient Greece—have been cited.